Verlag | ID: 128-50040-1010-1082

Dieses Buch wurde klimaneutral hergestellt. CO_2-Emissionen vermeiden,
reduzieren, kompensieren – nach diesem Grundsatz handelt der oekom verlag.
Unvermeidbare Emissionen kompensiert der Verlag durch Investitionen in ein
Gold-Standard-Projekt. Mehr Informationen finden Sie unter www.oekom.de.

Bibliografische Information der Deutschen Nationalbibliothek:
Die Deutsche Nationalbibliothek verzeichnet diese Publikation in der
Deutschen Nationalbibliografie; detaillierte bibliografische Daten sind
im Internet unter http://dnb.d-nb.de abrufbar.

© 2014 oekom, München
oekom verlag, Gesellschaft für ökologische Kommunikation mbH,
Waltherstraße 29, 80337 München

Layout und Satz: Reihs Satzstudio, Lohmar
Umschlagentwurf: Elisabeth Fürnstein, oekom verlag
Umschlagabbildung: © Vera Kuttelvaserova
Korrektur: Dave Morris, Berlin
Druck: Bosch-Druck GmbH, Ergolding

Dieses Buch wurde auf 100%igem Recyclingpapier gedruckt.

Falk Schmidt, Nick Nuttall (Eds.)

Contributions
Towards
a Sustainable World

In Dialogue
with Klaus Töpfer

Contents

Initiating Transitions

Addressing Diversity

Ernst Th. Rietschel

Chair of the IASS General Assembly

Foreword

When the IASS was founded in February 2009 on the recommendation of the Alliance of German Science Organisations, it was clear that extraordinary leadership was required to create an Institute for Advanced Sustainability Studies (IASS)—an institute that should both address scientific excellence and build bridges for science–society interactions.

The roots of this institute go back to the Symposium "Global Sustainability: A Nobel Cause" held in Potsdam in 2007, and its *Potsdam Memorandum*, which calls for a "new contract between science and society" to tackle the challenges of a world entering into the Anthropocene.

There are only a few personalities globally who could give life to such a contract, which requires competences in both science and societal issues combined with a passion for sustainability. In my role as chair of the IASS, I am most happy that Klaus Töpfer accepted the invitation to join us for this journey towards sustainability and became founding Executive Director of the Institute in Potsdam, Germany.

Due to his outstanding career, Klaus Töpfer is known to a broad public as "Mister Environment," first and foremost within Germany, where he held the position of Minister for the Environment, Nature Conservation, and Nuclear Safety from 1987 to 1994. However, already at that time—for example through his role at the 'Earth Summit' in Rio 1992, and certainly as Executive Director of UNEP from 1998 to 2006—Klaus Töpfer made it very clear that sustainability is global in nature. Addressing large-scale global challenges calls for responsibility—both individually and institutionally—ranging from the global to the local level; and, at the same time, building on contributions from culturally diverse backgrounds.

With Klaus Töpfer I share the conviction that excellent scientific work is often available but needs to be connected to real-world processes; and also the view that, in addition to better science-to-society communication (a necessary but as yet insufficient ingredient), we require a co-evolution of knowledge by researchers and practitioners. Hence, in addition to the key thematic themes already developed at the IASS, equally important is its transdisciplinary approach to sustainability challenges, i.e., an approach wherein societal concerns are not 'after-thoughts' but are integrated within the research process. To constantly reflect on such an approach itself presents a most suitable line of thinking for an Institute for Advanced Studies.

Under Klaus Töpfer's leadership, and in collaboration with its Scientific Directors Carlo Rubbia and Mark Lawrence, the IASS provides key thematic building blocks for a new contract between science and society—such as its work on energy, which also features in this anniversary volume. Throughout his career, Klaus Töpfer has sought ways and means of respecting the 'limits to growth' presented by natural but also social systems. At the same time, he has always shown sufficient vision to investigate the 'growth of the limits,' being fully aware from the outset that this represented politically realistic terrain.

For this, Klaus Töpfer's work rests on a firm ethical foundation. At its core, it recalls Hans Jonas' claim that our "knowledge must be commensurate with the causal scale of our action." Thus, while a world heading towards 9 billion people in the year 2050 may inevitably exceed current limits, we have to consider the conditions for legitimately doing so, especially in a sustainable, resource-conserving way. Consequently, Klaus Töpfer asks, "What is sustainability in the Anthropocene?" bringing together the challenges of the 21st century for the role of knowledge in general and our ethical position in this world in particular.

Last but not least: accompanying Klaus Töpfer on his way does not allow for shortcuts. Challenges may be daunting; the very concept of ourselves may be in flux; but any potential sustainability solutions must also pass another test: Are they compatible with the form of societal coordination which we call 'democratic'? Some may call this optimistic. For Klaus Töpfer this is the most realistic framework for initiating transformation processes towards sustainability.

I am looking forward to Klaus Töpfer's responses to this challenging agenda, and watching out for new questions emerging from it. As a colleague and friend, I am keen to see transdisciplinarity applied at the IASS as an invitation to society to form a contract with the scientific community.

Berlin, December 2013

Ernst Th. Rietschel

Achim Steiner

UN Under-Secretary General; Executive Director, UN Environment Programme

---

Foreword

Throughout a remarkable career stretching over half a century, Klaus Töpfer has stood as an intellectual and practical force both of and for 'nature' in his native Germany, Europe, and internationally—not least though his tenure as Executive Director of UNEP from 1998 to 2006.

His steadfast support for fresh thinking and determination with respect to linking the environment to social and economic issues crystalized during the early 2000s with the motto "Environment for Development": it became the theme for the United Nations Environment Programme (UNEP) during his tenure and remains a leitmotif for the organization's work today.

Klaus Töpfer famously remarked, "Everyone seems to be against something; UNEP needs to be for something—and it is development."

For the uninitiated or contemporary observers these three words—Environment for Development—may seem rather matter of fact in a world now shaping the post-2015 development agenda and a suite of Sustainable Development Goals. But more than a decade ago, specifically linking UNEP's activities to this overarching theme was a bold and courageous move.

No longer was environment to be siloed as an attractive, luxury good to be cherished once all of society's ills had been addressed: the phrase makes it explicit that without the environment there is no development; and certainly no chance for sustainable development in a world of now seven billion, rising to well over nine billion by 2050.

Klaus joined UNEP at a difficult time, with funding from traditional donors ebbing and the relevance of the institution under fierce scrutiny. With energy, persistence, and unflagging determination he managed to win back confidence and support for the Kenya-headquartered body and effectively set the stage for a new and more flourishing era in its history.

Courage allied to integrity and sound political judgment has been one of Klaus's hallmarks. He has not been afraid to pursue issues and to back initiatives which at the time seemed controversial or at odds with mainstream opinion.

In 2001 Klaus nurtured the scientific investigation into the phenomenon of 'brown clouds,' which some visionary researchers (including Prof. Ramanathan, who has contributed to this anniversary book) were linking to aggravated climate change, human health impacts, and agricultural damage. At that time, it was not a popular move among all member states of the UN, and some sections of the climate change fraternity regarded the topic as a distraction from the urgency of tackling CO_2 emissions.

Today, as a result of Klaus's support and belief that no one should shut the door on legitimate scientific enquiry—no matter how inconvenient to some that might seem—UNEP has brought the world together via the Climate and Clean Air Coalition.

The Coalition, which is targeting fast action on black carbon or soot among several short-lived climate pollutants, is providing a voluntary and complimentary pathway that supports the legal process within the UN Framework Convention on Climate Change.

Klaus also showed courage when establishing a small unit to carry out postconflict assessments in the wake of the Balkans war in respect to the 1990s. In recent years, it has become a highly respected part of the UNEP portfolio among the international community and in assisting war-damaged communities from Iraq to Liberia to better recover from conflicts—those early, heady days are recalled in the chapter by former Finnish Environment Minister Pekka Haavisto.

Klaus's contribution towards a more balanced and sustainable world continues to this day, through the Institute for Advanced Sustainability Studies (IASS), which he founded in Potsdam. For many years he has been concerned that one crucial ecosystem, central to all life on Earth is all too often ignored by governments, business, and society as a whole—namely soil. Via the Institute's Global Soil Forum, Klaus is addressing this disconnect and bringing the challenge to a new generation.

Meanwhile, he continues to shape domestic environmental policy, not least through his co-chairing of the Ethics Commission that made a compelling case for the early phase-out of nuclear power in Germany.

Internationally, he remains a companion to many countries' aspirations towards a sustainable, Green Economy transition, including as a former vice-chair of the China Council for International Cooperation on Environment and Development.

This book celebrates the life and works of Klaus Töpfer in his 75th year—it is a well-deserved tribute to an individual who has been among the pioneers of contemporary environmental policy.

Ever engaged, provocative, willing to reach out to friends and critics alike, Klaus's contribution to human dignity and the intellectual discourse on sustainability is matched by his humor, friendship, eagerness to assist and support, and his overall love of life.

Nairobi, November 2013

Achim Steiner

Falk Schmidt, Nick Nuttall

Sustainable, Transformative, Democratic: Klaus Töpfer's Contributions for Transitions Towards Sustainability

Sustainability challenges such as eradicating poverty, addressing resource depletion, and combating climate change, and their inescapable links to wider issues such as cultural diversity and designing sustainable economic systems, request and require that humanity embraces complexity if they are to be resolved. Yet we live in a world where we can often neither build on consensus regarding the facts and causality of these challenges nor can we rely on a common understanding of the political interventions needed to resolve them. Identifying the forces driving change remains as challenging as it has always been—indeed perhaps more challenging.

Environmental governance of the mid to late 20th century was a response to the impacts visible daily to citizens of Germany and other industrialized nations—from dead fish in rivers to skies darkened by heavy air-pollution. Progress in addressing what were essentially local or national issues was made in respect to cleaning up rivers or delivering the "blue skies above the Ruhr" of the Willy Brandt era. These accomplishments perhaps gave reassurance that pollution in all its forms could be consigned to the history books and that sustainability was a matter of local or national regulation and legislation.

But today we know better. The ability of humanity to damage and degrade the environment and the Earth's life support systems has gone global, with much of the pollution invisible to the naked eye and the drivers of that change often linked to the ways in which societies produce and consume along diverse and far-reaching supply chains.

The optimism of the early 1990s—when conferences like the Rio Earth Summit, born out of the end of the bipolar world, seemed able to transform our collective development paths—has given way to frustration and concern that our institutions are not up to the task. Meanwhile, other actors have also taken the stage, from corporations to mega-cities: governments no longer exercise hegemony over the paths that societies take or need to take.

In the past, humanity may have dreamt of freeing itself from its dependence on nature: but in a world of seven billion people (climbing to well over nine billion by mid-century), *Homo sapiens* are coming to realize that they are more dependent than ever on a complex interface of humankind and nature, including the provision of services ranging from forests to freshwaters, which make development—and indeed life itself—possible.

Our world is more man-made than ever before, and the ability of technology, to systemically alter nature in ways impossible for previous generations to comprehend, requests and requires of us a new relationship with planet Earth. Such a new relationship may speak, in the end, not just of profit and loss but of a new meaning of wealth; and return to a sense of ethics, stewardship, and responsibility. For the time being, it seems paramount to face these new challenges, striving for new ways of understanding and, subsequently, new modes of responses to it.

It is up to us whether the 'Anthropocene,' as Nobel Laureate Paul Crutzen has termed it, proves to be the final geological period for human beings, or if we meet its challenges, thereby allowing future generations to find their ways of taking responsibility for this coupled socio-ecological system called "planet Earth." This constitutes sustainability challenges a priori as ethical in nature.

This reality of an era in which humans are the dominate force begs the question of whether we have the right kinds of research, analysis, consensus, governance structures, and pathways to harness the constructive power of the human intellect and human spirit to address the complexity of the world as we find it today. Thus, one key question for contemporary research on sustainability is: do we have a reasonable understanding of what sustainability in the Anthropocene means?

One of the great conundrums is that there has perhaps never been a moment in history where society has had so much science and so much knowledge of our impacts, and yet we persistently fail to act—at least fail to act in light of our given ways of analysis.

There is also among citizens—and increasingly well-educated citizens—on the one hand a great interest to better understand the challenges that we face, and a great interest to become part of the possible solutions. On the other hand, we witness also a rejection of the reality and complexity and a seeming lethargy, apathy, and often downright challenging of government policies and scientific recommendations about what to do.

The aim of better understanding these contradictions shaped the first key project of the newly established Institute for Advanced Sustainability Studies (IASS) under the framing of "transgovernance" and "knowledge democracy" (Roel in 't Veld). Instead of holding citizens at arm's length, policy makers and scientists need to find ways to engage, interact, and partner with society in the challenges and opportunities of the day in order to realize sustainability.

The radical idea to emerge is that if the Anthropocene is rooted in human causality in a world of "knowledge democracy," then all people are potential sources of answers and therefore central to the solutions. The second essential reasoning is that neither science nor knowledge stands still—in other words, solutions can be less clear cut than some may wish, and may even run counter-intuitive to the prevailing consensus.

Inconvenient as this may be to some scientists and policy makers, only by embracing the science–society interaction as a whole, including cultural and 'value' differences, will humanity have a chance of moving forward and shaping a world fit for this generation and also future generations to come.

Klaus Töpfer, whose 75th Anniversary in 2013 was the inspiration to assemble this volume, has been at the forefront of such thinking for several decades. This includes a long track record of turning vision into reality, and a firm conviction that knowledge can be a crucial building block for transitions towards sustainability. It has been his determination in challenging the status quo and received wisdom that, for example, led to Klaus Töpfer's co-leadership of the Intergovernmental Panel on Climate Change as Executive Director of the UN Environment Programme or his contribution as head of UNEP to the Millennium Ecosystem Assessment, to mention just two large-scale endeavors during his international career. While these kinds of large-scale, indeed planetary assessments have contributed to greater knowledge and understanding, Klaus Töpfer has also been preoccupied with forging the next steps towards transformational change and the engagement of society as a whole.

The IASS, founded and still run by Klaus Töpfer in Potsdam, Germany, was set up to address this gap with the explicit intention of being a new kind of interface between science and society to better understand and initiate transitions towards sustainability. Building upon rich sources of knowledge available on various sustainability challenges, it conducts research *about*, *for* and as an actor on equal footing *within* transformation processes. These presently include, for example, contributions to the German "Energiewende," (energy transition) including its potential for "Energiewenden" globally, and work within the context of the Global Soil Forum and its Global Soil Week. Once again, Klaus Töpfer is at the forefront in bringing such a *transdisciplinary approach* that involves a range of actors from other fields of expertise into the research process in order to deliver new kinds of real-world solutions.

This volume pays tribute to the pioneering approaches of Klaus Töpfer to the sustainability agenda. It is structured in line with the three current focal areas of the research cluster "Global Contract for Sustainability" of the IASS. We are delighted that so many distinguished individuals have contributed to the volume and provided reflections on Klaus Töpfer's contributions, ranging from Nobel laureates, current and former ministers, to leading scientists, friends, and colleagues, many of whom are still in contact with Klaus Töpfer to this day in pursuit of collective sense of urgency and purpose towards a sustainable 21st century.

The first chapter of this book looks at options for "Sustainability Governance" in the era of the Anthropocene. We are particularly honored that Nobel Laureate Paul Crutzen sets the scene with his agenda-setting ideas about an issue that has catalyzed so many overarching research questions for Klaus Töpfer and his Institute. Other key sustainability challenges are highlighted by John Schellnhuber (Science and Society on Climate Change) and Reinhard Hüttl (Soils), who are the two co-chairs of the IASS Strategic Advisory Board. Additional topics are aired by Joachim von Braun (Land–Urban Interactions), Mario Tobias (ICT), Mark Lawrence, Scientific Director with Klaus Töpfer at the IASS, and Veerabhadran Ramanathan (both on atmospheric research). Ernst U. von Weizsäcker and finally Matthias Kleiner together with Caroline Lodemann reflect on the theoretical and practical implications for science on sustainability governance if it is to become a transformative force in societies.

The second section puts transformations in its center, with a focus on energy transitions. Carlo Rubbia, Nobel Laureate and Scientific Director with Klaus Töpfer at the IASS, reminds us of the massive challenges and great opportunities in finding new low-carbon energy options for a world of 9 billion people. This is one of the thematic red-ribbons running through the IASS since its inception. Laurence Tubiana and colleagues compare the German and French energy situations; Karsten Sach, Manfred Konukiewitz, and Klaus Milke together with Christoph Bals address energy changes in light of international climate and renewable energy negotiations, making the case that renewables have moved from being a 'niche' topic to the game changer. This triad of energy–renewables–climate is then complemented by Uwe Schneidewind together with Mandy Singer-Brodowski on the role and contributions of transdisciplinarity. Meanwhile, Günther Bachmann's contribution takes a historic perspective in reminding us of the societal basis underpinning the successful implementation of ideas, which is particularly true of technological ones. The section is concluded by Volker Hauff, who discusses the opportunities and remaining gaps in achieving governance for transformations.

The third section builds on an underlying and enduring conviction of Klaus Töpfer: sustainable development will remain incomplete if it does not recognize and embrace culturally diversity, fresh—and often challenging—new thinking on the economic and social pillars of sustainable development. The chapter starts with Wan Gang, Chinese Minster for Science and Technology, followed by Fengting Li and colleagues; Ambassador Juan Mayr of Colombia; and Former Vice-President of the Islamic Republic of Iran, Massoumeh Ebtekar, who provide an overview of cultural diversity in practice through the lens of the Dialogue about Sustainability, in which Klaus Töpfer has been a partner for many years. The contributions by James Gustave Speth, Senator Timothy Wirth, and Ralf Fücks provide new perspectives on the unsustainability of current pathways and the need for more sustainable future economic and social systems and processes. Angelika Zahrnt not only describes superbly Klaus Töpfer's strongest ally—his powerful rhetoric and speaking skills—she also highlights his constant struggle to regain our ability to act autonomously and thus responsibly. Claus Leggewie and Ulrich Beck address the transnational and cosmopolitan dimensions of sustainability transformations that are either happening or are urgently needed. Finally, Ulrich Beck succinctly captures the spirit of Klaus Töpfer's work: "The future is open. It depends on decisions we make." This has been the stance and the leitmotif of Klaus Töpfer throughout his professional career as we mark, with this book, his 75th anniversary.

Governing
Sustainability

Paul J. Crutzen

The Anthropocene:
When Humankind Overrides Nature
*Atmospheric Chemistry, Biosphere, Climate
in the Anthropocene*

Supported by great technological and medical advancements and access to plentiful natural resources, the expansion of mankind—both in numbers and per capita exploitation of Earth's resources—and its consequences have been astounding, as shown by the many examples referenced by McNeill (2000) (see Table 1: A partial record of the growths and impacts of human activities during the 20th century).

During the past three centuries, the human population increased tenfold to more than 7000 million. This expansion was accompanied, e.g., by a growth in cattle population to 1400 million (about one cow per average size family). Urbanization has increased more than ten times in the past century (Crutzen 2002). Similarly large were the increases in several other human activities, such as world trade, energy use, and industrial output. More than half of all accessible fresh water is used by mankind. Fisheries have reached their limits of about 90 million tons per year; instead, aquaculture (52 million tons per year) is growing at a staggering rate of about 9% per year (UN 2010, 2556D). Within a few generations mankind is exhausting the fossil fuels that were generated by the biosphere over several hundred million years. The resulting release of sulfur dioxide, which is at least two times greater than the sum of all its natural emissions (Smith et al. 2011), has led to acid rain, causing forest damage and fish death in biologically sensitive regions such as Scandinavia and the northeast of North America. Although the situation in these regions has improved, the problem has worsened in East Asia.

Up to 80% of the world's land surface has been affected by human action (Crutzen 2002); land under cropping has doubled during the past century at the expense of forests. Excessive quantities of fixed nitrogen are applied in agriculture, causing eutrophication of surface waters and groundwater. Human activity has increased rates of species extinction by orders of magnitude (Wilson 2002). As a result of increases in agriculture, deforestation, intensive animal husbandry, and burning of fossil fuels, several climatically important 'greenhouse' gases have substantially increased in the atmosphere over the past two centuries: CO_2 by more than 40% and CH_4 by more than 100% (Vitousek et al. 1997), contributing considerably to the observed global average temperature increase of approximately 0.6°C during the past century. Global average temperatures are projected to rise by 2.0–4.5°C (IPCC 2007) during the current century. Sea level is expected to rise by 9–88 cm (and 0.5–10 m by the end of the current millennium). However, the scale of actual changes may be larger. Glaciers and ice caps are melting at unexpected rates.

Table 1: *A partial record of the growth and impacts of human activities during the 20th century (1890s–1990s).*

Item	Increase Factor
World population	4×
Total world urban population	13×
World economy	14×
Industrial output	40×
Energy use	16×
Coal production	7×
Carbon dioxide emissions	17×
Sulfur dioxide emissions	13×
Lead emissions	≈8×
Water use	9×
Marine fish catch	35×
Cattle population	4×
Pig population	9×
Irrigated area	5×
Cropland	2×
Forest area	20% decrease
Blue whale population (Southern Ocean)	99.75% decrease
Fin whale population	97% decrease
Bird and mammal species	1% decrease

Source: McNeill (2000).

Paul J. Crutzen

Mankind also releases many toxic substances into the environment, and even some (the chlorofluorocarbon gases $CFCl_3$ and CF_2Cl_2) that are not toxic at all but which, nevertheless, have led to the Antarctic springtime 'ozone hole.' Much more ozone would have been destroyed but for the adoption of international regulatory measures to end production of CFCs by 1996. Nevertheless, due to their long residence times in the atmosphere, it will take at least another half century for the ozone layer to largely recover.

Considering these and many other major and still growing impacts of human activities on Earth and atmosphere at all scales, it is more than appropriate to emphasize the growing impact of mankind on the environment by using the term 'Anthropocene Human Age' for the current geological epoch. The results of human activities are projected to be long lasting. According to Loutre and Berger (2000), because of past and future anthropogenic emissions of CO_2, the climate will probably continue to depart significantly from natural behavior over the next 50,000 years.

To assign a more specific date to the onset of the Anthropocene is arbitrary, but I proposed the latter part of the 18th century, when the global effects of human activities became clearly noticeable—for instance in data obtained from glacial ice cores that show the beginning of rapid growth in the atmospheric concentrations of several greenhouse gases: CO_2, CH_4, and N_2O. Such a starting date also coincides with James Watt's invention of the steam engine in 1784.

Mankind will remain a major geological force for many millennia—maybe even millions of years to come. To develop a world-wide accepted strategy to sustain healthy ecosystems against human-induced stresses will be one of the great future tasks of mankind, requiring intensive research efforts and wise application of the knowledge thus acquired.

Hopefully, as we move deeper into the Anthropocene, it will no longer be characterized by the continued human plundering of Earth's resources and excessive dumping of waste products in the environment, but instead by vastly improved technology and population management, and by wise use of available solar energy and of Earth's resources.

Thus, what is the Anthropocene? Current Definition and Status

The International Commission on Stratigraphy oversees the Working Group on the Anthropocene, from which the following discussion is derived. The term Anthropocene has been widely used since its coining by Paul Crutzen and Eugene Stoermer in 2000 to describe the present time interval, in which many geologically significant conditions and processes are profoundly altered by human activities, including changes in:

- Erosion and sediment transport associated with a variety of anthropogenic processes—including colonization, agriculture, urbanization, and global warming;
- The chemical composition of the atmosphere, oceans, and soils—with significant anthropogenic perturbations of the cycles of elements such as carbon, nitrogen, phosphorus, and various metals;
- Environmental conditions generated by these perturbations—including global warming, ocean acidification, and expanding oceanic 'dead zones';
- The biosphere, both on land and in the sea—as a result of habitat loss, predation, species invasions, and the physical and chemical changes noted above.

The Anthropocene is not a formally defined geological unit within the Geological Time Scale. The Anthropocene Working Group is considering a proposal to formalize the Anthropocene as a potential geological epoch (i.e., at the same hierarchical level as the Pleistocene and Holocene epochs), with the implication that it is within the Quaternary Period but that the Holocene has terminated. Alternatively, it might also be considered at a lower hierarchical level (Age), which would imply it is a subdivision of the ongoing Holocene Epoch.

As mentioned above, the beginning of the Anthropocene is most generally considered to be circa 1800 CE, around the beginning of the Industrial Revolution in Europe (Crutzen's original suggestion); other potential candidates for time boundaries have been suggested at both earlier dates (within or even before the Holocene) or later (e.g., at the start of the nuclear age). A formal Anthropocene might be defined either with reference to a particular point within a stratal section (i.e., a Global Stratigraphic Section and Point, GSSP) colloquially known as a 'golden spike'; or by a designated time boundary (a Global Standard Stratigraphic Age). The Anthropocene has emerged as a popular scientific term used by scientists, the scientifically engaged public, and the media to designate the period of Earth's history during which humans have had a decisive influence on the state, dynamics, and future of the Earth system. It is widely agreed that the Earth is currently in this state.

Nature Is Us

Having discussed the Anthropocene as a distinct geological epoch and its potential starting point, let us focus more closely on it characteristics. The discussion presented in this section derives from my collaboration with Christian Schwägerl (Crutzen & Schwägerl 2011).

For millennia, humans have behaved as rebels against a superpower we call 'Nature.' In the 20th century, however, new technologies, fossil fuels, and a fast-growing population resulted in a 'great acceleration' of our own powers. Albeit clumsily, we are taking control of Nature's realm, ranging from climate to DNA: we humans have become the dominant force for change on Earth.

Altering the climate for millennia to come is just one aspect of our new role. By cutting down rainforests, plowing through savannas, and acidifying coral reefs we drive other species to extinction. At the same time, we create new life forms through gene technology and (soon) through synthetic biology. With our expanding population—estimated to grow further to 9–10 billion individuals by 2050, we have already altered most of the available land. We spread our man-made ecosystems, including degraded lands and recreational landscapes, and 'mega-regions' with more than 100 million inhabitants. We infuse huge quantities of synthetic chemicals and persistent waste into Earth's metabolism. Where wilderness remains, it is often only because exploitation is currently unprofitable. Conservation management turns wild animals into new forms of pets.

Geographers Erle Ellis and Navin Ramankutty (2007) argue that we are no longer disturbing natural ecosystems; instead, we now live in "human systems with natural ecosystems embedded within them": Earth is thus being 'anthroposized.' The long-held barriers between nature and culture are breaking down: It is no longer us against Nature; instead, it is we who decide what 'Nature' is and what it will be.

To master this huge shift, we must change the way we perceive ourselves and our role. School students are still taught that we are living in an age called the Holocene, an era that began roughly 12,000 years ago at the end of the last Ice Age. But this term masks the powerful role of our own species in determining Earth's future. It is suggested that students should instead learn that they are living in the 'Anthropocene,' or the Epoch of Man.

Rather than representing yet another sign of human hubris, this name change would emphasize the enormity of humanity's responsibility as stewards of the Earth. It would highlight the immense power of our intellect and our creativity, and the opportunities they offer for shaping the future.

What, then, does it mean to live up to the challenges of the Anthropocene now and in the future? Three avenues for consideration should be mentioned:

First, we must turn away from our current hyper-consumption. What we now call economic 'growth' amounts too often to a Great Recession for the web of life upon which we depend. Gandhi pointed out that, "The Earth provides enough to satisfy every man's needs but not every man's greed." To accommodate 9 billion people within the current Western lifestyle, we would need the resources of several more planets. With countries world-wide striving to attain the 'American Way of Life,' citizens of the West should redefine its meaning and pioneer a modest, renewable, mindful, and less materialistic lifestyle.

Second, we must far surpass our current investments in science and technology. Our troubles will deepen exponentially if we fail to replace the wasteful fossil-fueled infrastructure of today with a system fueled by solar energy in its many forms, from artificial photosynthesis to fusion energy. We need bio-adaptive technologies to render 'waste' a thing of the past, among them compostable cars and gadgets. We need innovations tailored to the needs of the poorest. Agriculture must become high-tech and organic at the same time, allowing farms to benefit from the health of natural habitats. We also need technologies that recycle substances like phosphorus—a key element for fertilizers and therefore for food security.

To prevent conflicts over resources, and to progress towards a durable 'bio-economy' will require a collaborative mission that dwarfs the Apollo program. Global military expenditure reached 1531 billion US dollars in 2009, an increase of 49% compared to 2000. We must invest at least as much in understanding, managing, and restoring our 'Green Security System'—the intricate network of climate, soil, and biodiversity.

Finally, to become good stewards of the Earth, we should adapt our culture to sustaining what can be called the 'world organism.' This phrase was not coined by an esoteric Gaia guru, but 200 years ago by eminent German scientist Alexander von Humboldt. It suggests we should shift our mission from crusade to management, from electronic diversion to contemplation of the natural world, from anthropocentric ignorance to long-term thinking.

Until now, our behaviors have defied the goals of a functioning and fruitful Anthropocene. Living up to the Anthropocene means building a culture that grows with Earth's biological wealth instead of depleting it. Remember: in this new era, 'Nature' is us.

LITERATURE CITED

Crutzen, P.J. (2002): The Anthropocene. In: Journal de Physique IV France 12/10: 1–5.

Crutzen, P.J., Schwägerl, C. (2011): Living in the Anthropocene: Toward a New Global Ethos. New Haven, CT: Yale University.

Crutzen, P.J., Stoermer, E.F. (2000): The Anthropocene. IGBP Newsletter 41: 17–18. International Geosphere–Biosphere Programme.
[http://www.igbp.net/download/18.316f18321323470177580001401/ 1316517410973/NL41.pdf].

Ellis, E., Ramankutty, N., (Lead Authors) McGinley, M. (Topic Editor) (2007): Anthropogenic Biomes. In: Cleveland, C.J. (Ed.). Encyclopedia of Earth. Washington, DC: Environmental Information Coalition, National Council for Science and the Environment. [http://www.eoearth.org/article/Anthropogenic_biomes].

IPCC (2007): Climate Change 2007: The Physical Science Basis. In: Solomon, S., Qin, D., Manning, M., Chen, Z., Marquis, M., Averyt, K.B., Tignor, M., Miller, H.L. (Eds.). Contribution of Working Group I to the Fourth Assessment Report of the Intergovernmental Panel on Climate Change. Cambridge, UK and New York, USA: Cambridge University Press.

IUGS (undated): What is the Anthropocene? — Current definition and status. International Union of Geological Sciences Subcommission on Quaternary Stratigraphy: Working Group on the Anthropocene. [http://quaternary.stratigraphy.org/workinggroups/anthropocene/].

Loutre, M.F., Berger, A. (2000): Future climate changes: Are we entering an exceptionally long interglacial? In: Climatic Change 46/1–2: 61–90.

McNeill, J.R. (2000): Something New Under the Sun: An Environmental History of the Twentieth-Century World. New York: W.W. Norton and Company.

Smith, S.J., van Aardenne, J., Klimont, Z., Andres, R.J., Volke, A., Delgado Arias, S. (2011): Anthropogenic sulfur dioxide emissions: 1850–2005. In: Atmospheric Chemistry and Physics 11: 1101–1116.

United Nations (2010): Resumed Review Conference on the Agreement Relating to the Conservation and Management of Straddling Fish Stocks and Highly Migratory Fish Stocks. New York, 24–28 May: United Nations Department of Public Information: DPI/2556 D.

Vitousek, P.M., Mooney, H.A., Lubchenco, J., Melillo, J.M. (1997): Human domination of Earth's ecosystems. In: Science 277: 494–499.

Wilson, E.O. (2002): The Future of Life. New York: Knopf Doubleday Publishing Group.

Maheswar Rupakheti and Mark Lawrence

From Buddha Air to Dirty Air to Clean Air: The ABCs of South Asia

The Himalayas:
Beauty, Compromised by a Brown Cloud Burden?

The serene ambience provided by majestic Himalayan mountains, lush green rolling foothills, and the vast Indo-Gangetic plains was an inspirational setting for *Rishis* (sages of insight) who attained *samādhi* (realization of the independence of soul and body, and realization of oneness with all) through *Yogic* concentration. In Vedic time, they used their wisdom to scribe the large body of nature hymns and spiritual science known as the *Vedas* and the *Upanishads*. Lord *Buddha* attained enlightenment in this very region some 2500 years ago. The beautiful Himalayan Mountains span countries in South Asia: Afghanistan, Pakistan, India, Nepal, Bangladesh, Bhutan, China, and Myanmar. Besides providing a tranquil setting, the mountains are endowed with rich natural resources, biodiversity hotspots, and cultural diversity and cultural heritage of global importance. The Himalayan Mountains as well as the nearby rivers and seas have profoundly shaped the cultures of South Asia. For centuries they have attracted a wide range of people including philosophers, meditators, and Yogis, scientists and researchers, adventure seekers and recreation tourists alike.

In recent decades, the greater Himalayan mountain regions have gained global attention not only because they are truly a global resource in terms of the goods and services they provide in the form of water, hydroelectricity, timber, biodiversity, niche products, mineral resources, recreation, etc., but also because of new challenges posed by recent rapid population growth, urbanization, migration, economic development, degradation of natural resources, increased natural disasters, and climate change within and beyond the region. In the near future, climate change is the most prominent anticipated driving force of global change, both environmentally and socioeconomically. The greater Himalayan region bears the brunt of climate change, especially

Figure 1: *River of haze. Satellite view of the atmospheric brown cloud over a large area of South Asia, covering the lowlands south of the Himalayas with gray-brown haze stretching over the eastern Himalayas, southeast part of Nepal, northeast India, Bangladesh, and northern Bay of Bengal. Image from 4 January 2002.*
Source: http://modis.gsfc.nasa.gov

Maheswar Rupakheti and Mark Lawrence

through impacts on mountain glaciers and snowpack. The ice reserve of the Hindu Kush-Himalayan-Tibetan (HKHT) region is the largest besides the North and South Poles, and therefore truly represents the 'Third Pole' of the Earth. As the source of ten major Asian river systems, the Greater Himalayan mountains provide water, ecosystem services, and the basis of livelihoods for a population of more than 210 million people living in the HKHT region; they also provide indirect benefits to more than 1.3 billion people living downstream and nearly 3 billion people at large, via the food and energy produced in the river basins that find their source in the Greater Himalayas.

Until recently, the global, regional, and national agendas of discussion and actions have been mainly focused on what happens upstream of the heavily populated regions—notably the melting of glaciers and snowpack in the mountains due to global warming; the potential impacts downstream in terms of resources, environmental and socioeconomic development; and how the sustainable development of the region can be achieved within the context of climate change. For nearly two decades now, there has also been growing concern about what happens upwind of the Greater Himalayan region, over Southern Asia; and about how the changes upwind, especially emissions of atmospheric pollutants, are linked to environmental changes in the region and their socioeconomic implications. The first major step in developing this increasing awareness was made by the INDOEX (Indian Ocean Experiment), a multi-million dollar, multi-institutional international atmospheric characterization campaign conducted over the northern Indian Ocean in 1999 (Ramanathan et al. 2001), following a pre-campaign phase of measurement cruises that started in 1995. The campaign was led by Nobel Laureate Prof. Paul Crutzen and distinguished climate scientist Prof. V. Ramanathan. The INDOEX project discovered plumes of atmospheric pollution covering much of the region. These were dubbed 'Atmospheric Brown Clouds (ABC)' and were interpreted as an indication that regional-scale air pollution (see Figure 1) is another major dimension of human influence on the environment, with likely substantial impacts on regional air quality, public health, agriculture, regional climate change, hydrological cycle, and ecosystems.

INDOEX made several major findings, including: (i) the widespread nature of atmospheric brown clouds over South Asia, extending hundreds of kilometers over the Indian Ocean; (ii) approximately 75% of atmospheric aerosols over the Indian Ocean are of anthropogenic origin; (iii) the major redistribution of solar radiation by both scattering and absorption of downwelling radiation by the man-made aerosols in the ABCs, further heating the atmosphere and greatly reducing the solar radiation reaching the Earth's surface; (iv) man-made aerosols influence regional monsoon precipitation via a large north–south heating gradient over the Indian Ocean, with considerable cooling of the northern Indian Ocean (the Arabian Sea and Bay of Bengal) and minimal cooling south of the Equator, and also through changes in cloud properties (Ramanathan et al. 2001). Subsequent to INDOEX, the availability of new global

Impacts of Atmospheric Brown Clouds (ABC)

Atmospheric Brown clouds are regional-scale plumes of air pollution. Through studies initiated under the ABC project (summarized in UNEP's 2008 Atmospheric Brown Clouds: Regional: Assessment Report with Focus on Asia. Ramanathan et al.), scientists now have an overview of the major sources and the global nature of the brown cloud problem. Recent studies show that the aerosols in ABCs reduce the amount of sunlight reaching the Earth's surface by as much as 10−15%, and enhance atmospheric solar heating by as much as 50%. Thus, ABCs, on the one hand, partly mask the perceived greenhouse warming by surface dimming, while on the other hand they enhance the greenhouse warming of the atmosphere. While confirming that ABCs may have masked global warming by 10−20%, ABC studies have led to new findings on regional climate changes such as: (i) a slowing of the monsoon circulation and reduction in monsoon rainfall; (ii) an increase in the strength and frequency of winter and springtime temperature inversions; (iii) regional warming of the atmosphere, primarily by black carbon; (iv) atmospheric warming and surface darkening by black carbon, both contributing to glacier melting; and (v) a substantial impact on agriculture and human health. A global assessment of black carbon and tropospheric ozone carried out by UNEP and WMO (2011), and another global assessment carried out by a group of prominent scientists in early 2013 (Bond et al.) re-confirm the findings of the ABC project: that black carbon is the second-strongest contributor to global warming after the greenhouse gas carbon dioxide.

South Asia, especially the vast Indo-Gangetic Plain region, is now considered to be one of the most polluted yet least studied regions of the world. Air pollution is linked to more than a million premature deaths and substantial crop loss every year in South Asia. It is also linked to changes in the monsoon circulation and rainfall, melting of Himalayan snow packs and glaciers, strong atmospheric warming, and thus to regional climate change. South Asia is in the midst of a growth process that is likely to exacerbate the already notorious air pollution problems unless current policies and practices are steered towards supporting widespread and early implementation of solutions that are firmly grounded in science and yet based on local specifics.

aerosol data and images acquired since December 1999 by the MODIS instrument on the Terra satellite revealed brown clouds in- and downwind of other major population regions of the world, and therefore established ABCs as a trans-boundary, trans-continental, and trans-oceanic phenomenon—a major global problem (Kaufman et al. 2002). The South Asian ABCs persist over large parts of South Asia and the Indian Ocean for almost six months of the year (during the long dry season from November to April), which is conducive to the accumulation of pollution in the region. During the rainy summer monsoon, ABCs still persist over the continent but are less intense than during the dry season (Ramanathan et al. 2008).

To the Rescue

The findings of INDOEX, as well as subsequent atmospheric characterization campaigns and atmospheric modeling exercises gained the attention not only of the global scientific community, but also of environmental agencies, NGOs (nongovernmental organizations) working on environmental issues, development agencies, and political leaders. ABCs are seen as a recurrent feature of the region, and it is recognized that they would likely worsen in response to rapidly growing population, industrialization, and urbanization, leading to impacts on public health, climate change, and water and food security.

Figure 2: *The meeting in Kathmandu, Nepal, in March 2001 that conceived the UNEP Atmospheric Brown Cloud (ABC) project. Prof. Klaus Töpfer (3rd from right) with Nobel Laureate Prof. Paul Crutzen (far right), atmospheric scientists Prof. V. Ramanathan (2nd from right) and Prof. A.P. Mitra (3rd from left), Surendra Shrestha (far left).*
Photo: V. Ramanathan.

From Buddha Air to Dirty Air to Clean Air: The ABCs of South Asia

Figure 3: *Prof. Klaus Töpfer (center right), Prof. V. Ramanathan (center left), Prof. Paul Crutzen (front left, only partly seen), and Mr. Surendra Shrestha (rear left) on a chartered Buddha Air Flight in Nepal to see the Atmospheric Brown Clouds in the region in March 2001.* Photo: V. Ramanathan.

Klaus Töpfer, the then Executive Director of the United Nations Environment Programme (UNEP), was one of those who took note of the issue. Along with Mr. Surendra Shrestha, UNEP Regional Director and Representative for Asia and the Pacific, Prof. Töpfer met with several distinguished atmospheric scientists, including Prof. Paul Crutzen, Prof. V. Ramanathan, and Prof. A.P. Mitra in Kathmandu, Nepal in March 2001 (Figure 2). They discussed the new scientific findings that were unfolding, assessing the severity of the ABC issue from the scientific point of view, and considering how to take timely action to reduce the impacts. During the meeting, the group took a charter flight across Nepal (Figure 3) to get a first-hand view of the regional scale of the ABC, which normally peaks in the region during March and April. One of the participants, Surendra Shrestha, recently recalled that the view to the north side of the airplane overlooking the Himalayan mountain range was thrilling, whereas the view to the south over the Nepalese foothills and the vast Indo-Gangetic Plain was shocking: the vast area, as far as one could see, was covered with a thick atmospheric brown cloud.

In recognition of these major scientific findings, and the realization of the need to further strengthen the understanding of the science and impacts of ABCs, the participants decided to address the issue in a more coordinated manner, resulting in the idea of a UNEP Project on Atmospheric Brown Cloud (ABC). UNEP formally established the ABC project in 2002, with a steering committee headed by the UNEP Executive Director, and a science team led by Prof. Ramanathan, comprising 17 internationally distinguished atmospheric scientists from Asia, Europe, and North America, including Dr. Mark Lawrence, the Scientific Director of the Institute for Advanced Sustainability Studies (IASS). The project represented a concerted effort on the part of UNEP, national governments in Asia, the scientific community, and development agencies. The first focus of the ABC project was on Asia, home to about 60% of the world's 7 billion population. However, it was recognized that the ABC problem is common to all areas of the world, and the project was also expanded to Africa and Latin America in 2009. More than a decade later, the foresight of these leaders in 2001 to address the issue of ABCs in Asia, to establish the ABC project, and to encourage research towards better understanding the science, impacts, and possible mitigation measures has been proven to be timely—even perhaps ahead of its time. The work of the ABC project has been foundational in establishing a political platform known as the Climate and Clean Air Coalition to Reduce Short-lived Climate Pollutants (CCAC) [www.unep.org/ccac], which was inaugurated in February 2012, the Secretariat of which is managed by UNEP.

Mitigation Potentials

New analyses by UNEP and the World Meteorological Organization (UNEP/WMO 2011) and more recent studies (for example Bond et al. 2013) show that fast and wide-spread implementation of already available measures that would globally address short-lived climate-forcing pollutants (SLCP) such as black carbon, methane, and hydrofluorocarbons (HFCs) would cost-effectively save human lives, increase agricultural productivity, reduce atmospheric warming and melting of ice and snow, and also help address other socioeconomic and developmental challenges associated with these pollutants. The benefits of SLCP mitigation are greatest in- and near areas where SLCP emissions are reduced, such as the Himalayan region, where the average rate of warming is higher than the global mean. But substantial benefits also extend to the rest of the world through reduced long-range transport of pollutants, and reduced climatic and economic impacts. Needless to say, SLCP mitigation measures should be implemented simultaneously with those for long-term climate change, which require deep and rapid cuts in carbon dioxide emissions at a global scale. Carbon dioxide, in contrast to SLCPs, is a long-lived species with an atmospheric lifetime of a century or more.

The ABC project and other studies have built a powerful case suggesting an urgent need to mitigate emissions of SLCPs. This has begun receiving greater attention at the national, regional, and global level, and has prompted action to reduce SLCP emissions. The CCAC partnership represents the first global initiative to treat these pollutants together as a collective challenge, and to support rapid action that will make a difference on several fronts at once: protecting public health, improving food and energy security, and mitigating near-term climate change. Since its launch, initially with only six countries and UNEP, it has grown to include at the time of this writing 33 countries, the European Commission, 8 intergovernmental organizations, and 30 leading NGOs and research institutes, including the Institute for Advanced Sustainability Studies (IASS).

Measures to reduce SLCP emissions, which largely comprise general air pollution control measures, are most effective if they are country- and/or region-specific and integrated with existing policies to address air pollution, climate change, and other socioeconomic and developmental concerns. In other words, the transfer and replication of policies and practices always requires careful examination of the local context (e.g., physical, economic, social, and political realities, including current policies and practices) and, if needed, the introduction of innovative approaches that fit well with local requirements and hence enhance the potential for sustainability of the interventions.

Back to the Origins of the Buddha: the Case of Nepal

Nepal is currently ranked 4th among countries that are extremely vulnerable to the effects of climate change but are least prepared to deal with them. It is also increasingly affected by local and regional air pollution, especially from the south. Kathmandu, the capital of Nepal, is one of the most polluted cities in the world. Thousands of inhabitants are exposed to unhealthy levels of air pollutants. The few available local and regional studies suggest that air pollution can have substantial harmful impacts on human health, crop productivity, and tourism income in Nepal. Kathmandu Valley's population and urbanization will increase in the coming years, as will energy consumption, motorization, and traffic congestion, normally expected to lead to increasing levels of chronic and severe air pollution. At present, the limited knowledge of emissions, transport, transformation and removal of pollutants gained from previous studies hinders the quantification of these impacts in the Kathmandu Valley. Although it is possible to identify several main sources of air pollutants—notably diesel trucks and buses, small diesel power generators, brick kilns, cooking stoves, open burning of trash, and inflow of pollution from the Indo-Gangetic Plain—the proportional contributions of the various sources remain unknown. Without this information, it is not possible to design effective mitigation measures.

SusKat

The Kathmandu Valley has significant levels of pollution, yet is of manageable size for potential interventions. It was therefore chosen as the site for an end-to-end case study of clean solutions, called the *Sustainable Atmosphere for the Kathmandu Valley (SusKat)*. SusKat aims to achieve a comprehensive understanding of the science of air pollution in the Kathmandu Valley and the broader region, as well as assessment of the mitigation options, thereby transcending science to engage key players in supporting local implementation of mitigation measures. Since a key requirement for designing pathways to improve local air quality is to characterize the magnitude and sources of each major pollutant, SusKat began with a 6-month field campaign providing detailed observations of pollutants. From December 2012 to June 2013, more than 40 scientists representing nine countries and 18 research groups deployed more than 160 instruments, including the first deployment in South Asia of the highly complex Proton-Transfer-Reaction Time-of-Flight Mass Spectrometry (PTR-TOF-MS) technique for intensive ground-based monitoring at an urban supersite (now a continuous station) and a network of 22 additional regional sites. The SusKat field campaign was adopted by the UNEP ABC Project as SusKat-ABC field campaign. It stands now as the second-largest international campaign ever conducted in South Asia. Airborne sampling will be performed during autumn 2013 to winter 2014. SusKat provides the most detailed data for the region to date, and also supports on-going modeling, long-term observations of key species, and collaboration with follow-up studies that support the objectives of the SusKat project. For instance, the reason behind the clean and polluted days observed in the Kathmandu Valley (Figure 4) can now be better explained with observational data.

The implementation of SusKat, which is led by the IASS, will help design realistic measures (e.g., sector-based technological solutions) that are firmly grounded in sound science and local specifics. In other words, this will result in informed decision- and policy making. With an enabling policy and institutional framework, Nepal would stand a good chance of joining appropriate schemes to receive global support for customizing national strategies and action plans. It could also argue for special provisions to meet the financial, technical, and capacity-building requirements essential for rapid and widespread implementation of clean solutions—for instance, doubling the share of renewable energy by 2030, and a clean kitchen for every household by 2017—that would address the socioeconomic and environmental challenges associated with air pollution in Nepal, and thus assist the transformation to a green economy.

Through our end-to-end study and implementation effort, we aim to demonstrate a pathway for knowledge–solution–action, which can be emulated in other regions of

Figure 4: *Pictures taken from the SusKat supersite at Bode in the Kathmandu Valley.*
Upper panel: on 20 March 2013, a highly polluted day (with an atmospheric aerosol optical
depth of 1.5); lower panel: on 28 February 2013, a rare clear day with an atmospheric aerosol
optical depth of 0.05. SusKat aims to reduce air pollution in the Kathmandu Valley
so that the majestic mountains are again normally visible, returning the Kathmandu Valley
to the true Shangri-La that it was in the 1970s — an inspiring place to visit or live.
Photo: Dipesh Rupakheti.

Maheswar Rupakheti and Mark Lawrence

the world. SusKat aims to generate scientific knowledge to develop sustainable solutions to air pollution. SusKat is therefore perfectly aligned with the philosophy of the IASS and consistent with the legacy of international sustainable policy and science, of which Klaus Töpfer has been at the forefront for decades. The high-level recognition of the vast and growing problem of air pollution in South Asia, and the first steps towards developing lasting solutions, all began with a visionary group of leaders onboard a Buddha Air flight that is now legendary within the ABC-Asia community.

LITERATURE CITED

Bond, T.C. et al. (2013): Bounding the role of black carbon in the climate system: A scientific assessment. In: Journal of Geophysical Research: Atmospheres 118: 5380–5552, doi:10.1002/jgrd.50171.

Kaufman, Y.J., Tanre, D., Boucher, O. (2002): A satellite view of aerosols in the climate system. In: Nature 419: 215–223.

Ramanathan, V. et al. (2001): The Indian Ocean experiment: An integrated analysis of the climate forcing and effects of the great Indo-Asian haze. In: Journal of Geophysical Research 106 (D22): 28371–28399.

Ramanathan, V. et al. (2008). Atmospheric Brown Clouds: Regional Assessment Report with Focus on Asia. United Nations Environment Programme (UNEP), Nairobi, Kenya.

UNEP/WMO (2011). Integrated assessment of black carbon and tropospheric ozone. Summary for Decision Makers. United Nations Environment Programme (UNEP), Nairobi, Kenya.

Veerabhadran Ramanathan

The Two Worlds We Inhabit:
The Top Four Billion (T4B)
and the Bottom Three Billion (B3B)

The nexus between population, energy, development, environment, and human well-being has to be understood, both conceptually and empirically, for making practical advances into the sustainability issue. Scientific studies of this nexus must recognize that there are two separate but co-dependent worlds or planets: The bottom three billion (B3B) live in a world with minimal access to fossil fuels, whereas the top four billion (T4B) live in a world with a seemingly inexhaustible supply of affordable fossil fuels. Consumption of fossil fuels by the T4B has created the biggest threat to sustainability for both T4B and B3B, which is the planetary-scale warming of unprecedented magnitudes that will be witnessed during this century. Destruction of local habitats and ecosystems (forests) by B3B is also a threat affecting both worlds. Among economists, political scientists, and global leaders interested in mitigating climate change, much of the emphasis is on decarbonizing the economy and reducing the per capita carbon foot print—issues that are of relevance to T4B. Here I make the case for an

Figure 1: *T4B: Bangkok at night.*

Figure 2: *B3B: Traditional cooking stove.*
Photo taken by the author.

equal emphasis on enabling sustainable and clean energy access (a mix of biomass, solar, and fossil) for the B3B to avoid amplifying the global warming that is already set into motion. In order to avert unsustainable climate changes in the coming decades, the decarbonization of the T4B economy as well as the provision of modern energy access to B3B must begin now.

Preamble

A fateful chartered flight over the Eastern Himalayas with Klaus Töpfer set me on my current path of enquiry into the fundamentals of the sustainability issue. The flight took place on 25 March 2001, aboard a small aircraft operated by Buddha Tourist Airlines of Nepal. Prof. Töpfer was then the Executive Director of UNEP. To the north side we were presented with breathtaking views of Mount Everest, but I had directed Klaus' attention to the south side—to the widespread brown clouds shrouding the more modest Himalayan mountain ranges bordering Nepal. I knew, with the juxtaposition of Mount Everest on one side and the vast brown clouds on the other, that we had his full attention on the subject. Nevertheless, a big surprise awaited me when we disembarked and settled into the back seat of the waiting car. Before it started, Klaus turned towards me, held my hand firmly, and said: "I am going to do my best to address this problem." A day earlier on 24 March, the two of us met with my colleagues, Drs. Paul Crutzen based in Germany and A.P. Mitra of India. We all flew into Kathmandu from different parts of the world to meet Prof. Töpfer and persuade him to start a major UNEP initiative on the brown clouds problem. He did not need any further persuasion.

True to his word, Klaus started the Atmospheric Brown Clouds (ABCs) project and appointed Paul Crutzen and I as Co-Chairmen in 2002. The team included scientists from China, Germany, India, Italy, Japan, Korea, Maldives, Sweden, Thailand, and USA. Klaus' successor, Achim Steiner, continued the program with equal vigor and interest. After six years of intensive field experiments and modeling studies, we released a regional assessment report in 2008, focusing on the impacts of air pollution on health, water, agriculture, and the climate of Asia. The report was the first of its kind and had a big impact. Its main conclusion was: ABCs threaten the health and the water- and agriculture-security of Asia; furthermore, ABCs were linked with millions of deaths outdoors, the melting of glaciers, and disruption of the monsoon. This report (UNEP 2008), which I chaired, set me on a path beyond scientific enquiry, for it convinced me that we have to get rid of these pollutants for no other reason than saving millions of lives and slowing the rapid retreat of the Himalayan/Tibetan glaciers.

A year earlier, the IPCC released its AR4 report. Using the data in that report on greenhouse forcing and climate sensitivity, my post-doctoral colleague Yan Feng and I came to an alarming conclusion, which was published in the Proceedings of the National Academy of Sciences (PNAS) in 2008 (Ramanathan & Feng 2008). We showed that the manmade greenhouse blanket, comprising CO_2 and several non-CO_2 gases, was already thick enough to warm the planet by as much as 2.4 °C (1.2 °C to 3.6 °C). It merited a commentary by Schellnhuber (2008) in the same issue of PNAS, titled: *Global warming: Stop worrying and start panicking.* My introduction to the non-CO_2 warming pollutants began in 1975, when I identified (Ramanathan V. 1975) the super-greenhouse effects of a class of halocarbons, chlorofluorocarbons (CFCs), then known as *Freons*.

Two corollaries from the 2008 PNAS study led me to study the short-lived climate pollutants (SLCPs), which are basically non-CO_2 warming pollutants with lifetimes of a decade or less:

First, the cooling effect of aerosols from air pollution (in brown clouds) has masked the 2.4 °C greenhouse warming thus far and kept the planet from experiencing it. Once the air pollution is cleaned up, the planet will warm rapidly beyond 2 Celsius. But not all air pollutants cause cooling: ozone gas and particles of black carbon lead to warming. In fact, that same year I teamed up with Greg Carmichael (also with the ABC project) to conclude that black carbon was the second-largest contributor to global warming. However, contemporary air-pollution laws were instead targeting sulfates, mainly from coal combustion. Sulfates were one of the major cooling aerosols. If we had viewed both air pollution and climate change with one lens, we would have sought to cut black carbon and ozone at the same time we were tackling sulfates from coal combustion. *Second*, if the greenhouse blanket has already committed the planet to a warming in excess of 2 Celsius, the only way to reduce the committed warming is to thin that blanket; but, because of the long lifetimes of CO_2 (of the order of a century and longer), cutting down emissions of CO_2 (which we must do) can only prevent it from thickening more, but can not thin it. We therefore need to target climate warming gases and particles that are short lived, in addition to targeting CO_2.

Teaming up with my student Xu, we published (Ramanathan & Xu 2010) a hybrid climate mitigation strategy in PNAS in 2010 that will stabilize CO_2 at 440 ppm to limit long-term warming and mitigate the emission of four SLCPs (methane, black carbon, HFCs, and ozone precursors in addition to methane) to limit near-term (mid-century) warming. The important point is that mitigation of SLCPs did not require development of new technologies but rather the maximum use of available technologies, as recommended by the IIASA in Austria (International Institute for Applied Systems Analysis). The surprising findings were that limiting SLCPs reduced near-term (until 2050) warming by about half, and that the mitigation of CO_2 and SLCPs together was sufficient to limit global warming to within 2 °C until the end of this century. UNEP, under Dr. Steiner's leadership, took up the proposal and formed an international committee that released a report in 2011, basically supporting the Ramanathan–Xu (RX) hybrid mitigation strategy for CO_2 and SLCPs. This report was followed by the formation of the Climate and Clean Air Coalition which, as of this writing, has been joined by 30 countries and several NGOs.

Now, I am ready to describe what led me to the 'Two Worlds' approach to sustainability. I realized that the science behind our RX hybrid mitigation strategy was not part of the lexicon of mainstream climate change community. It became clear to me that it has to be demonstrated via real-world trials or experiments. In addition, data published by various groups pointed to the burning of biomass in traditional cooking stoves as a major source of the black carbon concentrations in the brown clouds. I saw this as a great opportunity to address not only a climate change problem but also a vexing problem faced by the millions of poor in South Asia. After all, I witnessed how my grandmother suffered with the traditional mud stoves, burning dung and firewood in our ancestral village of Eraharam in South India, about 200 km south of the famous city of Chennai (Madras). This realization gave birth to Project Surya in 2007 under the UNEP ABC Program (www.projectsurya.org). Teaming up with The Energy Resources Institute of India and Nexleaf Analytics of USA (both NGOs), we started field studies in northern Indian villages to replace the mud stoves with improved designs and to document their impact on human health and air pollution. The two major outcomes so far are the utilization of cell-phones for collecting vast amounts of data from individual homes (Ramanathan N. et al. 2011), and identification of the forced-draft biomass cooking stove as the most effective way to reduce black carbon and CO_2 emissions (Kar et al. 2012). Five years into this program, in early 2013, I spent eight weeks living in villages in India (my grandmother's village in the south and other villages in central and northern India). In between, I would seek some reprieve from the harsh, almost brutal living conditions by retreating into nearby cities with air-conditioned rooms and cars to ward off the oppressive tropical heat. It was then that I discovered the two worlds we live in. I had no inkling, during that March 2001 flight with Klaus Töpfer, that it would ultimately lead me through various unusual but exciting pathways to discover the two worlds we inhabit.

Setting the Stage

Let us start with an overly simplistic view of how humans interact with the environment and the Earth system (Figure 3).

Homo sapiens began as an integral part of the ecosystem, i.e., as an internal component. In other words, *Homo sapiens* and the ecosystem constituted a closed system, with incoming solar energy as the sole external driver. Some time during the last millennia, humans evolved into an external driver, leaving behind enormous quanti-

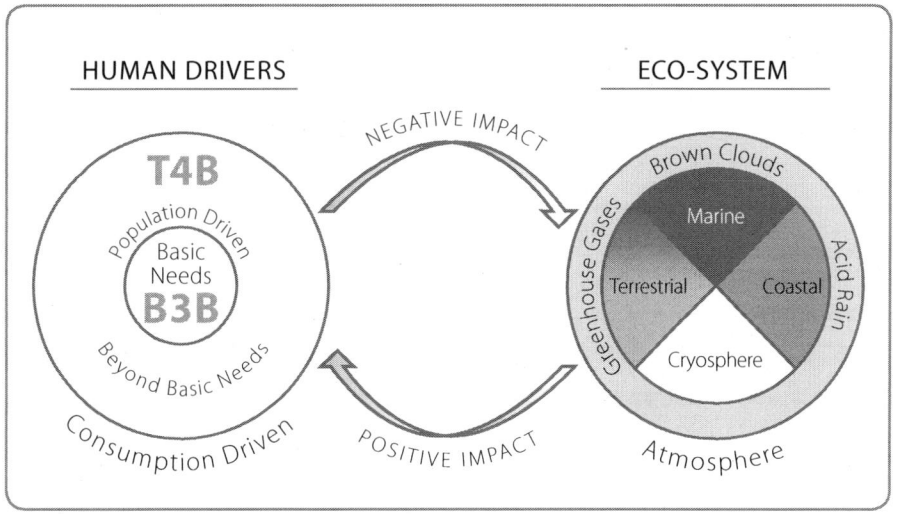

Figure 3: *Schematic of human/environment interaction.*
The B3B live in the smaller inner circle and the T4B in the larger outer circle.
The areas of each circle qualitatively reflect the magnitude of resource consumption
(Reproduced from Ramanathan V. 2010).

ties of unrecyclable waste either in the atmosphere or in the land–ocean–cryosphere system. The atmosphere alone contains about 1000 billion tonnes (1000 gigatonnes, Gt) of manmade CO_2; widespread brown clouds of toxic SO_2, CO, NOx, ozone, and black carbon; hundreds of organic compounds and acids; a depleted ozone layer, etc. Similar waste and destruction of the ecosystem have been chronicled elsewhere and need no repetition here (e.g., Schellnhuber et al. 2004). It is this period that was named the Anthropocene by Crutzen.

The Two Worlds We Inhabit

Referring back to Figure 3, there are two basic human drivers of change: overall population and per capita consumption. Human well-being is dependent on ecosystem services that meet basic human needs: Food, water, shelter, health. The ecosystem stress resulting from meeting those basic needs is basically driven by the scale of human population. All other activities that fall outside are, for lack of a better term, referred to as 'beyond basic needs.' This category must include activities that are critical for human development (e.g., transportation, information technology, refrigeration, space exploration, recreational activities, etc.). The environmental stresses that result from meeting 'beyond basic needs' are driven more by consumption than population growth. I will give examples of this later. The usual categories, such as 'developed' and 'developing' nations, are not that helpful in the current context. Many hundreds of millions living in developing nations have living standards and carbon footprints comparable (at least in the last decade) to those in the industrialized nations such the USA and Western Europe. The categorization of all human drivers into two developmental areas (population and consumption) is an overly simplistic way of describing an incredibly complex pattern of human intervention with the Earth's life-support systems; but the thesis developed here does not depend on the number of categories.

The B3B Perspective

Approximately three billion human beings are still struggling to meet their basic needs and they live in the inner world, B3B, shown in Figure 3; about 1.2 billion lack electricity even for lighting; about 2.7 billion earn less than $2/day and burn solid biomass (firewood, dung, and crop waste) for cooking and home heating with rudimentary mud stoves. From personal experience, I can say the food tastes authentic and delicious—particularly if it is cooked by your grandmother and served hot from the burning stove, with the flames not only keeping the food warm but also your face, hands, and feet on a cold morning. But the delicious food comes at an enormous cost. About 3 million people (mainly women and children) die each year from inhaling the toxic pollutants (carbon monoxide, volatile organic compounds [VOCs], black carbon, organic acids, etc.) contained in the flames. My grandmother was not part of this statistic—in part because our house (not a hut) was well ventilated. But I did not realize then that the ventilated smoke is transported thousands of kilometers in a week or less, and contributes to air pollution in distant cities (the world of T4B).

The Co-dependence of B3B and T4B

The two worlds are co-dependent. The indoor biomass smoke, when transported outdoors, additionally kills more than 1 million people annually (both T4B and B3B are victims), bringing the premature mortality from this source of air pollution to 4 million each year. It is also transported vertically, contributing to the 3-kilometer-thick ABCs prevalent over much of Asia. In regions such as South Asia, 30–60% of the black carbon (soot) in ABCs derives from smoke produced by biomass cooking/heating. The rest is from fossil fuels burned by the T4B population living in the region. Absorption of solar radiation by this black carbon directly heats the elevated air of the Himalayas and when it is deposited on the ice/snow of the mountains (by snowfall) reduces its reflectivity and enhances melting. The combined warming of the air

and land surface by black carbon is a major threat to the stability of the Himalayan/
Tibetan glaciers that feed famous rivers such as the Indus and the Ganges in South
Asia, and the Yangtze and the Mekong in East Asia. The other destabilizing influence
on glaciers is global warming caused by greenhouse gases (largely emitted by T4B in
the developed nations).

The T4B Perspective

Now let us discuss the T4B perspective. The most vivid and also most vexing example
of unsustainable growth is the human impact on climate change, which is likely the
most potent and catastrophic sustainability issue we now face. There is rancorous
exchange between developing and developed nations about who is responsible for
global warming. The developing nations point out that about 70% of the CO_2 in the
atmosphere was dumped by about 30% of the global population in developed nations.
The developed nations respond, in turn, that as the developing nations industrialize
using fossil fuels, their emissions in the coming decades will far exceed levels that can
trigger dangerous climate changes and mass extinction of species.

Much of the world's focus with respect to mitigation of climate change is on the
T4B consumption problem. We are now dumping about 36 Gt of CO_2 annually. We
need to reduce this to 18 Gt (50% reduction) by 2050, for us to have any chance of
limiting global warming below 2.5 Celsius; and must then achieve zero or even negative emissions (sequestering excess CO_2 from the air) by 2100. The per capita emission of CO_2 by the B3B is less than 1 t/year and the total B3B annual CO_2 emission
is less than 2 Gt. The global average per capita fossil CO_2 emission is about 4.5 t/yr;
US per capita is 18.5 t/yr. We hope that the living standards of the B3B catch up with
those of the T4B; but if they achieve this by climbing up the fossil ladder to the global
average per capita CO_2 emission of 4.5 t/yr by 2050, the emissions of the B3B will
increase to 14 Gt/yr. For us to still meet our goals of limiting CO_2 emission to 18 Gt/
yr by 2050, the emission by the T4B has to come down from 34 Gt (now) to about
6 Gt by 2050—a reduction of 80% in 35 years! Clearly, it is to our (i.e., T4B) own
advantage to help the B3B climb the cleaner renewable energy ladder rather than the
fossil ladder. Under some scenarios, global population is projected to reach about
9 billion during this century, and it is a good guess that most of the additional 2 billion population will be among the B3B: therefore, the B3B will, during this century,
morph into the B5B.

My proposal is for the T4B to help the B3B morph not into the B5B but instead into the M5B: the middle world of 5 billion with modern but sustainable energy access and aspirations of well-being similar to those in T4B. The basic energy needs for the B3B are: cooking, lighting, and heating. Such energy access is crucial to lift the three billion out of energy poverty as well as monetary poverty. It is for this reason that the United Nations initiated the Universal Energy Access Program in 2012. Technologies are available off-the-shelf to provide access to clean, renewable energy without increasing their CO_2 emissions.

Two examples are given to justify this claim:

The biomass used for cooking leads to deforestation equal to the emission of 1 billion tonnes of CO_2; and another 1 to 2 billion tonnes of non-CO_2 warming pollutants (black carbon, methane, and ozone). The smoke from the cooking kills over 4 million annually. It is the second- to third-largest source of outdoor air pollution; destroys millions of tonnes of crops; exacerbates the melting of Himalayan/Tibetan glaciers; and weakens the monsoon. Deforestation combined with monsoon disruption depletes water availability; and worse, women have to walk about 1 to 2 hours per day to collect firewood. Project Surya (www.projectsurya.org) has demonstrated that improved forced-draft biomass cooking stoves can drastically reduce emissions of black carbon, CO_2, and other pollutants (Kar et al. 2012). But there are huge problems related to the adoption of new technology, for example the lack of: good business models; supply chains; infrastructure; user-friendly technologies; and poor understanding of the choices the B3B population make with respect to technologies—all of which hinder scale-up.

The second example is electricity. Distributed solar photovoltaic micro-grids can provide electricity for lighting and small-scale industry, replacing highly polluting (and expensive) kerosene lamps and diesel generators.

Environmental economists from IIASA (Pachauri et al. 2013) have estimated the B3B energy access market (or cost) to be about 65 to 86 billion US dollars per year. What does society stand to gain by solving this energy access problem?

1. Saving 4 million lives (the majority among women and children) lost to air pollution each year;
2. Reducing poverty and improving quality of life among rural women and children;
3. Mitigation of 1 billion tonnes of CO_2 emissions per year, and of the short-lived climate pollutants (black carbon, tropospheric ozone, methane);
4. Saving tens of millions of tonnes of crops lost to air pollution;

5. Slowing the melting of the Himalayan/Tibetan glaciers;
6. Providing energy access to farmers for improving agricultural output;
7. Avoiding massive emissions of CO_2 by the B3B, which could result if they climb the fossil ladder rather than the renewable energy ladder.

Proposal for a Way Forward

We need to develop and demonstrate a scalable model for providing clean energy access to the B3B. Towards this objective, I suggest conducting a pilot project with a million homes in a contiguous location, with the goal of providing sustainable access to clean and renewable energy; and documenting the impacts on air pollution, health, climate mitigation, local economy, and human well-being. The terms 'scalable' and 'sustainable' refer to both natural resources and to economics. The inclusion of 'economics as criteria' precludes donation (giving-away) of the energy access. It requires sustainable *business models, a value chain, and a supply chain*. If the pilot can be conducted in *one contiguous location*, we can capture the pollution-hole created by the intervention, via a combination of mass-scale in-situ data collection (using cell-phone-based sensors; see Ramanathan N. et al. 2011) and high-resolution satellite data (resolution of tens of meters). Imagine how impressive that will be to show to the rest of the world. A project of such massive scope should include partnerships between natural and social scientists, technology innovators, entrepreneurs, industry, and civil society.

Acknowledgement: Supported by the Alderson Foundation, the Vetlesen Foundation, and the US National Science Foundation.

LITERATURE CITED

Kar, A., Rehman, I.H., Burney, J., Puppala, S.P., Suresh, R., Singh, L., Singh, V.K., Ahmed, T., Ramanathan, N., Ramanathan, V. (2012): Real-time assessment of black carbon pollution in Indian households due to traditional and improved biomass cookstoves. In: Environmental Science and Technology 46/5: 2993–3000.

Pachauri, S., van Ruijven, B.J., Nagai, Y., Riahi, K., van Vuuren, D.P., Brew-Hammond, A., Nakicenovic, N. (2013): Pathways to achieve universal household access to modern energy by 2030. In: Environmental Research Letters 8/2. doi:10.1088/1748-9326/8/2/024015.

Ramanathan, N., Lukac, M., Ahmed, T., Kar, A., Praveen, P.S., Honles, T., Leong, I., Rehman, I.H., Schauer, J.J., Ramanathan, V. (2011): A cellphone based system for large-scale monitoring of black carbon. In: Atmospheric Environment 45/26: 4481–4487.

Ramanathan, V. (1975): Greenhouse effect due to chlorofluorocarbons: Climatic implications. In: Science 190: 50–52.

Ramanathan, V. (2010): Measuring and monitoring progress toward sustainability. In: Levin, S.A., Clark, W.C. (Eds.). Toward a Science of Sustainability. Conference at the Airlie Center, Warrenton, Virginia. November 29–December 2, pp. 91–94: http://www-ramanathan.ucsd.edu/files/brt26.pdf.

Ramanathan, V., Feng, Y. (2008): On avoiding dangerous anthropogenic interference with the climate system: Formidable challenges ahead. In: Proceedings of the National Academy of Sciences of the United States of America 105: 14245–14250.

Ramanathan, V., Xu, Y. (2010): The Copenhagen Accord for limiting global warming: Criteria, constraints, and available avenues. In: Proceedings of the National Academy of Sciences of the United States of America 107/18: 8055–8062.

Schellnhuber, H.J. (2008): Global warming: Stop worrying, start panicking. In: Proceedings of the National Academy of Sciences of the United States of America 105: 14239–14240.

Schellnhuber, H.J., Crutzen, P.J., Clark, W.C., Claussen, M., Held, H. (Eds.) (2004): Earth System Analysis for Sustainability. Dahlem Workshop Reports. Cambridge, MA: The MIT Press.

Ramanathan, V., Agrawal, M., Akimoto, H., Auffhammer, M., Autrup, H., Barregard, L., Bonasoni, P., Brauer, M., Brunekreef, B., Carmichael, G., Chang, W.-C., Chopra, U.K., Chung, C.E., Devotta, S., Duffus, J., Emberson, L., Feng, Y., Fuzzi, S., Gordon, T., Gosain, A.K., Hasnain, S.I., Htun, N., Iyngararasan, M., Jayaraman, A., Jiang, D., Jin, Y., Kalra, N., Kim, J., Lawrence, M.G., Mourato, S., Naeher, L., Nakajima, T., Navasumrit, P., Oki, T., Ostro, B., Panwar, Trilok S., Rahman, M.R., Ramana, M.V., Rodhe, H., Ruchirawat, M., Rupakheti, M., Settachan, D., Singh, A.K., St. Helen, G., Tan, P.V., Tan, S.K., Viet, P.H., Vincent, J., Wang, J.Y., Wang, X., Weidemann, S., Yang, D., Yoon, S.C., Zelikoff, J., Zhang, Y.H., Zhu, A. (2008): Atmospheric Brown Clouds: Regional Assessment Report with Focus on Asia. Nairobi, Kenya: United Nations Environment Programme: http://www.rrcap.ait.asia/abc/impact/index.cfm

Hans Joachim Schellnhuber

Climate Change,
the Monarch Butterfly,
and Intergenerational Contracting

Introduction

Back in 1987, I was awarded one of the prestigious Heisenberg Fellowships. This scheme, established by the German Science Foundation (DFG), allows 'high potentials' in science to pursue (for a maximum of 5 years) whatever research in whatever location they prefer. I chose to go first to the Santa Cruz campus of the University of California (UCSC) to join the Nonlinear Physics group. Chaos science, as complex systems analysis was called in those days, had one of its main roots at UCSC, where a group of graduate students once started to fiddle around with an analog computer to study the amazingly strange behavior of iterated nonlinear maps (Gleick 2008).

I was also interested in such maps and the beautiful fractal patterns (Julia sets) they generate (Nauenberg & Schellnhuber 1989). Incidentally, my interest in those topics later led me into the field of environmental studies and, eventually, towards climate-impacts research. But that is a different story...

When my late wife Petra and I arrived in Santa Cruz, which is located on the Pacific Coast south of San Francisco, we rented an apartment on Western Drive. This choice was made for convenience, since the gorgeous UCSC campus was just two miles uphill; yet it turned out that we had picked a unique spot indeed: the apartment building faced a deep canyon, densely covered with maquis shrubbery, eucalyptus, and mimosa trees, and this very canyon was part of the western trail pursued by the annual Monarch butterfly migration. The Monarch is a beautiful insect with large black–orange–white wings that inhabits, for instance, the Rocky Mountain valleys during the summer and travels many hundreds of miles towards its hibernation sites on the Pacific coast during autumn. In certain years, more than a million members of the 'Western population' of that species (Urquhart 1987) join in the biblical exodus, which is among the greatest wonders of the natural world.

Many of these phenomenal butterflies settled in *'our'* canyon for the winter—we easily spotted them on the eucalyptus trees, which were in full bloom and therefore provided lots of nectar. Most of the insects in the area, however, took shelter several miles downhill on the Natural Bridges State Beach. Motivated by these direct encounters, I started to read about the Monarch and learned about the stunning complexity and vulnerability of this species. Ever since, the Monarch migration has served me as a powerful metaphor for cultural sustainability. I will elaborate on that below, but let me emphasize here that the intergenerational cooperation of these beautiful animals provides a narrative that is quite compelling in an ecological as well as an ethical way. The Monarch tale may actually teach us how to manage the *'intractable'* problem of anthropogenic climate change.

Global Warming

Thousands of scientific articles have been written about man-made global warming over the last decades (as evaluated, in particular, by the IPCC 1990, 1996, 2001, 2007), so I do not have to go into any detail in this essay. I will, instead, highlight several crucial aspects that characterize the challenge involved and its singular nature.

The Fundamentals

Time and again, more or less serious 'climate skeptics' argue that the projections of climate change in response to emissions from human activities (such as power generation from coal burning) are 'only' based on computer simulation models, which they hold to be notoriously unreliable. I will deal with this sweeping statement later, but would like to emphasize here that anthropogenic enhancement of the natural greenhouse effect had already been analyzed in the pre-computer century by Fourier, Tyndall, and Arrhenius, from the first principles of thermodynamics, fluid dynamics, and radiation physics in combination with well-interpreted observations. Later investigations have broadened and refined the theory, and later measurements have augmented the empirical evidence. Based on these findings, it is scientifically warranted to project a warming of our planet of 3–4°C by 2100 and up to 8°C by 2300, if the burning of fossil fuels keeps going down the 'business-as-usual' road. However, climate science does not predict a smooth, quasi-linear rise in global mean surface temperature, since the lower troposphere is just a thin spherical layer of the hyper-complex Earth System, dwarfed, e.g., by the gigantic ocean waters and their immense heat-storing capacity. The global 'fever curve' is therefore likely to exhibit some decade-long plateau, especially during certain episodes when the deeper seas absorb the excess energy from the anthropogenic greenhouse effect in an accelerated manner (Balmaseda et al. 2013).

The best way to put to rest the largely spurious debate about the reality of man-made climate change would be by cautious high-precision monitoring of the radiation-energy balance at the top of the atmosphere. If one can determine, year by year, that more energy entered the system than left it, then it would become evident beyond reasonable doubt that our planet is being transformed. How exactly the Earth System digests the extra heat through a multitude of intricate processes remains a major question, yet one of predominantly academic nature. Therefore, establishing a network of satellites to monitor global radiation balance (extending the current, unsatisfactory observation methods) might be one of the most important human projects in the medium-term future.

The Impacts

What are the consequences for our civilization of rapid global warming? The more classic effects (like sea-level rise, ecosystem shifts, or crop-yield changes) were reviewed in May 2013 in Potsdam, at the first ever world conference on these topics (IMPACTS WORLD 2013). The meeting also tried to set an ambitious agenda for the next decade, of research in the pertinent fields and particularly of advanced schemes to ensure the comparability of individual studies across sectors and regions. This orchestrated approach could eventually lead climate-impacts science beyond 'patchworking' to robustly assess what a warming of 2, 3, 4, or more degrees Celsius really means for our world.

The emerging 'big pictures' will only be able to guide us (towards appropriate adaptation strategies, for instance) if they encompass the regular as well as the singular aspects of climate change. The term 'singular' stems from mathematical analysis, where it means 'ill-behaved' in a broad sense. For example, a function 'misbehaves' at a given point if it is discontinuous, non-differentiable, or even diverges to infinity there. If we carry over this terminology to physical processes (like climate dynamics), singular behavior could mean that a system ceases to respond gently to an external forcing but instead undergoes extreme excursions or even flips into a completely novel state. There is quite some scientific evidence (especially derived from paleo-studies) that anthropogenic climate change will display a number of singular features indeed. Recent analysis has focused especially on the so-called 'tipping elements' in the climate system (Lenton et al. 2008; Schellnhuber 2009), i.e., large-scale components of the planetary machinery that may change their character (in an abrupt or a more retarded way) if the 'red line' thresholds of certain parameters are transgressed. Iconic examples include ice sheets that might collapse beyond specific warming thresholds, monsoon regimes that might go chaotic under major humidity change, or vast coral systems that might die back under too acidic ocean conditions.

A tipping element directly related to extreme weather events is the Northern Hemisphere jet stream, a high-speed wind field 8–12 km above the ground. This flow pattern circles the Earth from west to east and separates cold Arctic air from milder mid-latitude and sub-tropical air. The jet stream normally has a rather straight propagation pattern but occasionally develops southward or northward bulges called Rossby waves. These perturbations bring unusually warm or cold air masses, respectively, to the temperate zones. As a rule, these Rossby waves last only a few days; however, under very specific conditions, they may lock into quite persistent states, causing extreme-heat or heavy-precipitation episodes with disastrous consequences. The underlying mechanism—quasi-resonance of stationary and travelling planetary waves of a certain frequency—was described in 2013 by a team from the Potsdam Institute (Petoukhov et al. 2013). Consistent conditions were actually realized quite a few times in the Northern Hemisphere during recent decades, when severe heat waves (e.g., Western Europe 2003; Russia 2010), droughts (e.g., USA 2011 and 2012), or floods (e.g., Central Europe 1997 and 2002; Pakistan 2010) occurred. As a matter of fact, a quasi-frozen pattern of Rossby waves also generated the recent deluges in southern and eastern Germany, which caused economic damage in the multi-billion Euro range.

Two reports commissioned and released by the World Bank (Schellnhuber et al. 2012, 2013) attempted to encompass the crucial regular as well as singular effects of a projected 4°C warming of the globe and to provide integrated assessments for several regions at peculiar risk (Southeast Asia, India, Sub-Saharan Africa). One of the key messages of these analyses is that the impacts of unbridled climate change will be distributed very differently in space and time: A 60-year-old Swedish citizen, for example, may experience nothing unusual during the rest of their lifetime, whereas a person born in Namibia today is likely to suffer heavily from environmental hardships by the time they become elderly and infirm. This is precisely one of the reasons why global climate protection is an almost impossible mission for humanity.

A Diabolical Management Problem

Imagine that you are driving back from work to your suburban home, when suddenly a young child runs into the street, chasing after a football. Undoubtedly, you would hit the brakes—probably irrespective of the risks of that maneuver to your vehicle or yourself—it could be your own child, after all…

By way of contrast, imagine that you wish to buy a new, stronger car, but a climate change scientist tells you that the extra emissions from that vehicle are likely to contribute to the acceleration of global warming which might, quite generally, increase the severity of tropical cyclones, thereby potentially harming a child on the other side of the planet in the distant future. Would you now refrain from purchasing the car you fancied? The answer seems obvious …

This little gedankenexperiment captures several tantalizing aspects of the climate-protection challenge in a nutshell. More systematically, I would like to characterize the problem of confining global warming to a tolerable level by reference to three human fallacies, namely (i) the infinity illusion, (ii) causal myopia, and (iii) genetic selfishness.

The first point refers to the tacit assumption that harmful things 'thrown away' will be sufficiently quickly diluted and thereby rendered harmless by the natural processes in our vast environment. This was a good working hypothesis for a hunter-gatherer clan roaming the savannahs, but it is an ill-founded proposition for seven billion people sharing a small planet. In particular, CO_2 molecules released from local sources seem to vanish into the big, blue nothing—but yet they accumulate, persist, and operate at a global level.

The second fallacy refers to the human inability to imagine causality cascades that transcend continents and centuries. A brilliant chess player might anticipate ten moves or so, but this is an exceptional expertise applicable only within a narrow context. Politics, business, and private life are rather dominated by considerations of tangible and immediate return on whatever investment. Worrying about the more or less likely impacts of anthropogenic global warming at a huge causal distance is not precisely what our visceral instincts might instigate. Unfortunately, climate change mechanisms work inexorably across such scales of space and time.

The third fallacy may also be perceived as a major strength, driving the human species to ever higher evolutionary levels—without any teleological plan devised by some superior entity, as the renowned Oxford scientist Richard Dawkins has repeatedly emphasized (Dawkins 1976). It means, in essence, that a given genetic make-up strives to replicate by outcompeting its slightly different fellow make-ups. One crucial aspect thereof is the direct provision for offspring, which also encompasses, in modern societies at least, various sophisticated types of intergenerational investments.

For instance, parents struggle to fund the best education for their children, and migrant workers send remittances to families left behind on distant shores. This illustrates that large spatiotemporal distances between costs and benefits can be overcome if the genetic distance is sufficiently small. However, it does not remove a fundamental dilemma of climate protection, since people—especially those in rich countries (that have the highest per capita emissions)—tend to think (perhaps rightly) that their descendants will easily cope with global warming—with a little help from their contemporary kin. Never mind what the grandchildren of the exotic poor are going to do…

Several years ago, I was serving on a highly distinguished advisory panel on climate change. One colleague (a former chief executive of a leading oil company) declared with a deep sigh that the global warming problem was *"simply intractable"* for the reasons I have elaborated in the previous sub-section.

Is this it? Do we have to surrender to a self-inflicted predicament that is too big for self-therapy? My answer is *"no,"* based on two principles that may still save the day, namely (i) scientific inference, and (ii) species solidarity.

The first principle basically refers to our ability to harness the insights of science in order to cover huge causal distances and to unravel intricate relationships that defy everyday intuition. For instance, inference chains can be crafted that connect the pleasures of contemporary people with the suffering of future generations in a statistical yet compelling manner that precludes 'looking the other way.' The scientific method enables us to land a vessel at a preselected spot on Mars on a preselected day during a multi-year mission; and also to calculate (with still poor numerical precision but high systemic confidence) the changes in environmental conditions as caused by fossil-fuel burning over the next century. The physics behind those calculations is so powerful that the long-term result will not be affected by short-term natural climate variability or other transient effects. This implies, in particular, that one should not rush to revise global-warming projections with every episodic slowing-down of the increase in planetary surface temperature, as mentioned above (Otto et al. 2013). Empirical evidence is weaker than mature theoretical analysis, especially in non-analog situations—and complex climate models are largely based on that analysis.

The second principle is most sophisticated in some sense, while quite elementary in others. It has to do with the observation that human compassion does not necessarily decay linearly with genetic distance, i.e., with decreasing hereditary proximity. For illustration, consider the following two examples: Many women stubbornly resist all recommendations to stop smoking despite the overwhelming evidence that it reduces female life expectancy by at least 10 years on average. However, once these women become pregnant they immediately overcome the addiction for the sake of their unborn offspring. For another instance, people often display a peculiar empathy for strangers and can be extremely moved by their fate. By the way, this is why sentimental films (like 'Titanic') are so exceedingly popular, while the mundane predicaments of one's long-term partner tend to be acknowledged with a shrug. A more general conclusion is that close familiarity does not automatically foster empathy or even solidarity. It rather seems that we recognize a transindividual *conditio humana* in our species fellows, no matter how different they are in complexion, character, and culture. The strong desire of couples from rich countries to adopt babies from the least-developed world provides another hint in this context. And think of that slightly out-of-date, yet still touching post-WWII fashion of 'town twinning,' which arranges blind dates between communities across cultural divides as big as the Earth–Moon hiatus.

I am neither a psychologist nor an anthropologist, yet I feel that a latent but powerful species solidarity pervades much of our doing. There is an anecdote about the early days of game theory and behavioral economics, when scientists (at the Institute for Advanced Studies in Princeton, I think) designed pedestrian social experiments to explore the rational-choice hypothesis. It maintains that individuals 'naturally' act in order to maximize their personal benefits. The (male) researchers employed their (female) secretaries as guinea pigs, and were utterly dismayed to learn that those women behaved not selfishly (according to the theory) but rather collegially, even compassionately. Therefore, besides egoism, altruism appears to be part of our genetic disposition; and the transcendence of long causal distances by species solidarity is much more than a cultural code, as demonstrated in a mind-boggling way by that beautiful butterfly I first encountered in California.

The Monarch

In the introduction I referred to the Western population of the Monarch butterfly, which is already an amazing group, yet nothing in comparison to their Eastern relatives. The latter branch consists of some 100 million individuals, which live between the Rocky Mountains and the Atlantic Coast during the warmer part of the year. The highest population density occurs around the Great Lakes, where the insects find milkweed (*Asclepias* spp.), their preferred food plants. During autumn, the major part of the community starts its migration of more than 3000 miles towards the Sierra Nevada in Central Mexico. There, they hibernate in patches of fir forest that cover an area of less than 20 hectares! This concentration on an extremely specific and narrow habitat comes with a high vulnerability to all sorts of perturbations. Accordingly, the annual insect census estimated that the number of Mexican butterflies was at a record low in 2013 (Tuckman), a development that environmental organizations like the WWF blame on the local use of herbicides that wipe out milkweed, the plant that provides the Monarch with food and also serves as a breeding ground.

While the migration of these butterflies is a stunning achievement in itself, the intergenerational organization of the full wandering cycle is even more impressive. As mentioned already, the first generation sets out between September and November, and hardly any individual member of this community will return to their home ground. After hibernation in Mexico the insects of that generation return north and reach the South of the US (Texas, Oklahoma, Arkansas, etc.) towards the end of April, where the females lay their eggs and thereby generate the second generation. The latter migrate further north in May and June to eventually arrive in North Dakota, Minnesota, and the Great Lakes territory, where they, in turn, lay their eggs. The third generation appears in late June and early July and moves northeast into Canada and even Newfoundland. One reason for this migration leg is that the preferred food plants in the southern US have meanwhile withered in the summer heat. Depending on the respective environmental conditions, the fourth and fifth generations arise in various places of the migration space during late August/early September to form the mature summer population. Once they begin to move southward again, the miraculous phenomenon comes full circle.

The unraveling of the mysteries surrounding the Monarch—and these are not restricted to the wandering of the insect—has been called the "greatest entomological story of the 20th century" in various publications. The butterfly is a true global vagabond, which has meanwhile colonized places as distant as the Philippines, New Zealand, and Spain. Yet the most remarkable feature of this species remains its eco-dynamic ballet, performed across the North American semi-continent. The generations comprising the seasonal insect population act as one single clockwork mechanism, wherein each small wheel and spring has a task to perform within a collective act of perpetual motion. In particular, each generation builds upon the previous one and paves the way for the subsequent one. If one of these generations fails, the entire population is bound to collapse. Is there such a thing as 'individual pursuit of happiness' in the evolution and sustenance of that species? Don't get me wrong: I am in no way suggesting that humans should behave like the population of the Monarch butterfly. But perhaps personal happiness and population survival are not contradictory after all—especially not for the *Homo sapiens sapiens*.

A Social Tele-contract

Acting as a community according to a long-term strategy is not unusual in the animal world, although little compares to the Monarch tale. However, in all those cases (including the organization of a beehive), the spatiotemporal choreography of the individuals unfolds according to an intrinsic genetic program that is to some extent elastic to accidental circumstances (like extreme weather conditions or food scarcity). Human beings, by way of contrast, are able—yet not always willing—to realize something that might be called 'collective rationality,' which appears to be a unique feature in our universe. The two most important ingredients have been mentioned already in the previous section, namely species solidarity (as a complex emotion) and scientific inference (as a cognitive capacity).

The Enlightenment (as epitomized by thinkers such as John Locke, Jean-Jacques Rousseau, and Immanuel Kant) greatly progressed the corresponding intellectual debate that culminated in the notion of the 'Social Contract,' which means, in the broadest sense, a restriction of the action space of individuals in order to maximize the benefits and liberties of the entire community. This is predominantly a form of generational contracting, especially with regard to delegating to some mandated power (like kings or parliaments) the right to use force. Yet there are many other articles that may be part of a social contract, e.g., the obligation to notify the authorities of individual cases of certain infectious diseases; such information facilitates an effective containment strategy based on scientific analysis.

It is evident that the climate protection challenge, with all its diabolical characteristics discussed above, can only be met via a social contract of unprecedented quality and range. The necessary convention has to be intergenerational in essence, and it has to be extraordinarily smart in implementation. In other words, climate stabilization requires a tele-contract, reaching across distant generations, continents, causes, and effects. This means that the principles of species solidarity and scientific inference have to be stretched to the limits. As a precondition, we have to resist those voices that maintain that humans are purely selfish and that climate science is too immature to provide reasonable guidance for action. The first assertion is falsified daily by the deeds of great philanthropists and numerous individuals, the second one by the stunning advances made in circulation pattern modeling since the early attempts initiated by John von Neumann (Edwards 2010).

So 'all' we need is science and solidarity. Based on these key ingredients of humanism, we may yet make the right decisions today for the sake of tomorrow's children. Like not purchasing that cool car. Keep on flying, Monarch…

Acknowledgements

I would like to thank Ricarda Winkelmann for reminding me of the power of the Monarch parable, and my wife, Margret Boysen, for the critical reading of the draft text and her valuable suggestions for improvement.

LITERATURE CITED

Balmaseda, M.A. et al. (2013): Distinctive climate signals in reanalysis of global ocean heat content. In: Geophysical Research Letters 40: 1754.

Dawkins, R. (1976): The Selfish Gene. New York: Oxford University Press.

Edwards, P. (2010): A Vast Machine. Cambridge, MA: MIT Press.

Gleick, J. (2008): Chaos: The Making of a Science. New York: Penguin.

IPCC AR1 (1990): Climate Change: The IPCC Scientific Assessment. Cambridge, New York, and Melbourne: Cambridge University Press.

IPCC AR2 (1996): Climate Change 1995: The Science of Climate Change. Cambridge and New York: Cambridge University Press.

IPCC AR3 (2001): Climate Change 2001: The Scientific Basis. Cambridge and New York: Cambridge University Press.

IPCC AR4 (2007): Climate Change 2007: The Physical Science Basis. Cambridge and New York: Cambridge University Press.

Lenton, T. et al. (2008): Tipping elements in the Earth's climate system. In: The Proceedings of the National Academy of Sciences of the United States of America 105: 1786.

Nauenberg, M. & Schellnhuber, H.J. (1989): Analytic evaluation of the multifractal properties of a Newtonian Julia set. In: Physical Review Letters 62: 1807.

Otto, A. et al. (2013): Energy budget constraints on climate response. In: Nature Geoscience 6: 415.

Petoukhov, V. et al. (2013): Quasi-resonant amplification of planetary waves and recent Northern Hemisphere weather extremes. In: The Proceedings of the National Academy of Sciences of the United States of America 110: 5336.

Schellnhuber, H.J. (2009): Tipping Elements in Earth System. In: Special Feature: The Proceedings of the National Academy of Sciences of the United States of America 106: 20561.

Schellnhuber, H.J. et al. (2012): Turn Down the Heat – Why a 4°C Warmer World Must be Avoided. A Report commissioned by the World Bank.

Schellnhuber, H.J. et al. (2013): Turn Down the Heat – Climate Extremes, Regional Impacts, and the Case for Resilience. A Report commissioned by the World Bank

Tuckman, J. Mexican monarch butterfly numbers at record low, scientists say. The Guardian: 14.05.2013 [http://www.theguardian.com/environment/2013/mar/14/mexican-monarch-butterfly-numbers] Accessed 31 July 2013.

Urquhart, F.A. (1987): The Monarch Butterfly: International Traveler. Chicago: Nelson-Hall.

Reinhard F. Hüttl

Caring for the
'Skin of the Earth'—Soils as a
Critical Component of Global Development

Soil as a Scarce Geo-resource

Soils are one of the fundamental resources for life on Earth. They are the basis for food and feed production, and supply a number of indispensable services: Soils provide the physical and nutritional support system for plants; they hold and release water, provide flood control and water purification benefits. As such, they are an essential basis of the 'human habitat.'

Furthermore, soils are a critical component of the global biogeochemical cycles. The pedosphere is one of the key components for processes that influence the global climate. Soils hold significant carbon-storage potential, exceeding that of above-ground vegetation cover. In addition, soils directly and indirectly affect the albedo of land surfaces and hence interact with global radiation regimes. Soils are important components of hydrological cycles by storing water and releasing it to aquifers, surface water bodies, or vegetation. Soils are also one of the most important sources of the world's biodiversity, as they provide habitat to a vast number of organisms including fungi, algae, bacteria, lichens, and articulate animals.

Thus, the Earth's surface in general—and soils in particular—can be regarded as the crucial interface between the lithosphere, hydrosphere, atmosphere, and biosphere; the latter includes the anthroposphere, or in other words, that part of 'System Earth' which has been created or affected by humans.

However, one decisive fact has yet not sufficiently entered the public awareness: Soils are finite resources. In this respect, they are comparable to fossil fuels: they re-form only over long geological timescales. Nevertheless, soils have been disproportionately used for quite some time, resulting in widespread soil degradation. The

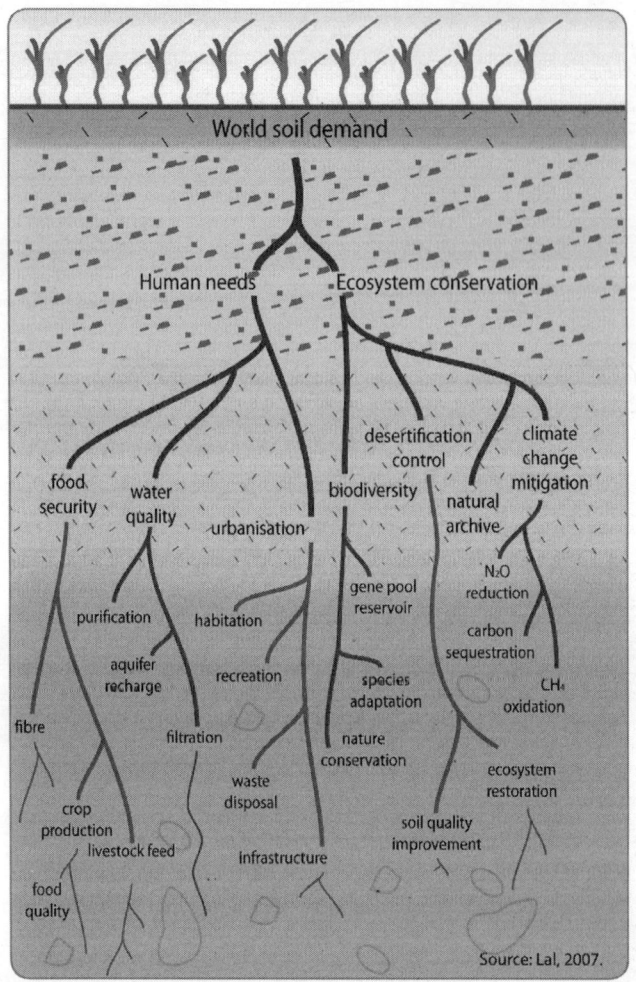

Figure 1: *World Soil Demand: Human needs and ecosystem conservation*
Source: Lal 2007; design: Riccardo Pravettoni – UNEP/GRID-Arendal,
http://www.grida.no/graphicslib/detail/world-soil-demand_149b

world population, which is expected to grow to nine billion people by 2050, will impose ever greater and more diverse demands on the soil as a resource, particularly with regard to food, raw material, biodiversity, and water supply (see Figure 1). Therefore, soils, as the boundary layer of 'System Earth' will undoubtedly attract ever greater attention as a potential field of conflict and as a focal point of various environmental challenges. Science will have to play an important role in providing the necessary information for decision makers and society to ensure appropriate utilization of soils.

Reinhard F. Hüttl

Linking the Compartments of 'System Earth':
The 'Critical Zone' Concept

The term 'critical zone' is used to describe the boundary layer of the Earth's surface. It is the outermost part of the crust, from the top of the unweathered rock layer to the top of the Earth's vegetation cover. Most terrestrial, chemical, physical, and bio- or microbiological exchange, conversion, and turnover processes take place within this 'critical zone.' These processes are increasingly affected by humans. A central component of the 'critical zone' is the pedosphere, i.e., the soils. Soils not only control the global cycling of organic and inorganic matter, they also act as a buffer, have a cleansing effect on the hydrosphere and atmosphere, and play a major role in food and biomass supply. River valleys and deltas contain soil erosion products and are important human habitats.

At the same time, soils are also a highly vulnerable component of our planet. Within the scope of global change, humans are having an increasing effect on the processes of landscape development, and mostly in a negative way. Sustainable management of

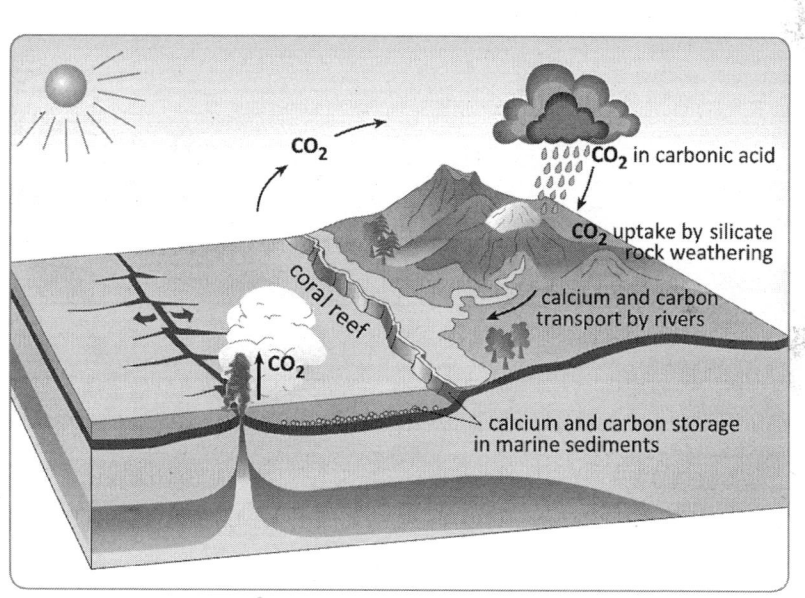

Figure 2: *The geological cycle of carbon dioxide. Rock-weathering chemically combines the CO_2 that is continuously emitted by volcanoes. Rivers transport this material to the oceans, where it is bound for long periods in calcium carbonate deposits such as coral reefs or foraminiferal muds. Large amounts of CO_2 are also disposed indirectly, via photosynthesis, in sediments rich in organic material.*
Source: GFZ.

Caring for the 'Skin of the Earth'—Soils as a Critical Component of Global Development

soils is one of the major tasks of the future. Above all, this means the development of new options for improved utilization of the various functions of soils, including production, transformation, and as a buffer and a place for biological processes.

Soils are mainly formed by weathering of rock and by accumulation of organic material. Water, in turn, is an essential medium in these processes, which also control the global cycling of elements such as carbon, nitrogen, sulfur, and oxygen (see Figure 2 for a graphical representation of the geological cycle of carbon dioxide). Many soil properties—especially soil fertility—are characterized to a large extent by these weathering and mineralization processes.

In principle, the scientific differentiation of water and soils must be put in relative perspective, because both components act directly together: soils are only fertile in the presence of water. Transport of materials, especially pollutants, can only be reconstructed and understood when the flow paths of water in the ground are known. Water transports these substances, during which the material loads often change. To date, only rough estimates of these mechanisms are available, especially at the landscape scale. Some pollutants penetrate deep into the ground and probably remain there for centuries or millennia. The sustained atmogenic deposition of an increasing number of toxic and persistent substances, due to traffic, industry, and land use, leads to contamination of soils. Compared to point sources, the absolute levels of pollutants distributed over large areas are generally low. However, the input of pollutants from the atmosphere implies that there is now virtually no place on our planet that remains completely unaffected by human activities. In addition, such substances can accumulate considerably at specific sites, for example in river sediments.

The Role of Science

Soils are a scarce resource and must be used sustainably. As our knowledge of soils and their development is still limited, scientific advancements are needed for a better understanding of our soils. Hence, some examples are presented for cutting-edge research approaches into the pedosphere of planet Earth.

Remote Sensing and Imaging Spectrometry

Remote sensing methods can be used to record quantitative and qualitative data of rock, soil surfaces, and areas covered with vegetation. Today, this information is also available at different spatial scales.

Imaging spectrometry is currently the most innovative and future-oriented method for the visual observation of the Earth's surface. This approach is based on the observation that all materials—plants and minerals—have unique spectral properties.

Hyperspectral sensors are used for identification and analysis of materials, and for quantitative recording of surface components such as soils, rocks, and vegetation. Multispectral systems measure the reflection of the Earth's surface within a few distinct spectral bands (n < 10). As these systems have already been used for some years, the results allow the establishment of longer time series. Hyperspectral systems, on the other hand, provide signals with a much higher resolution, as they have a large number of bands (n > 100). The hyperspectral satellite EnMAP, which will be launched in 2017, will provide the first high-quality hyperspectral data on a global scale.

EnMAP will scan the Earth's surface with the help of 228 bands within the visible spectrum as well as near- and short-wave infrared (0.42–2.45 μm) at a surface resolution of 30 m × 30 m. Unlike multispectral data, hyperspectral signals allow unambiguous diagnostic derivation of a large number of biochemical, geochemical, and geophysical parameters of plants, minerals, and human-made materials.

Satellite-based hyperspectral methods thus also provide data for detailed analysis and better understanding of the processes taking place on the Earth's surface. These data are not only relevant for agriculture, forestry, or geology, but also for the evaluation of rivers, lakes, and coastal areas, as well as in the context of desertification and erosion. The use of modeling approaches to perform repeated analyses of biophysical, biochemical, and geochemical parameters recorded over key regions provides new, globally comparable results. In turn, these data can be used to optimize modeling concepts.

Agricultural management is generally characterized by high vegetation dynamics and periodic changes of the cultivated plants. In recent years, remote sensing methods have enabled us to reproduce these dynamics to a large extent. However, aspects such as plant row spacing, row alignment, and plant density still cause problems for the exact classification of a specific crop type from satellite images. The effects of these parameters on reflection characteristics must be studied further, and adjustment methods are needed to obtain more reliable spatial information about vegetation type and respective development status. These issues led to the development of virtual three-dimensional inventory models, which can be used to develop new analysis methods. They allow near-natural modeling of radiation flows within vegetation stands while also permitting individual parameters to be varied in order to examine their effect on the reflection by a specific plant stand. In this way it is possible to study the data qualities associated with biomass, chlorophyll content, plant water content, photosynthetically active radiation, soil water availability, organic content of the topsoil, maturing time, and harvest yield. Owing to the growing pressure to use all available land areas for biomass production, under the conditions of climate change it will be necessary to manage our soils as efficiently and sustainably as possible. In this respect, utilizing remote sensing data for long-term observation of soils available for specific land use practices is of great importance.

Caring for the 'Skin of the Earth'—Soils as a Critical Component of Global Development

In the same way as the human skin is able to convey specific information about the whole organism, the Earth's surface is also capable of providing specific information about geological processes of planet Earth. Huge matter cycles are active on the Earth's surface. Large quantities of sediment are continuously eroded and transported by riv-

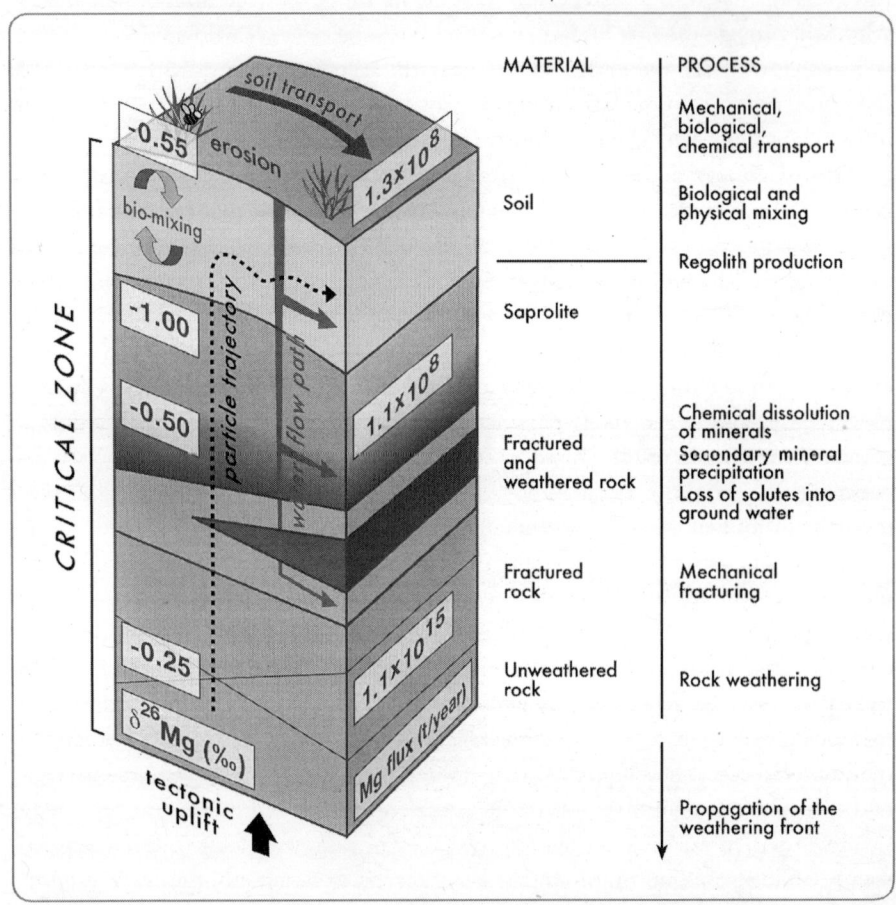

Figure 3: *Schematic diagram of the 'critical zone,' consisting of fresh rock, weathered rock, and rock detritus (saprolite), soil, and vegetation. The numerals on the left show how magnesium isotope composition (in parts per thousand) differs between the various compartments; the numerals on the right indicate the global flow of magnesium (in tonnes of Mg per year) between the various compartments. Weathering preferentially releases the lighter magnesium isotopes; these are transported in groundwater. Plants, on the other hand, preferentially absorb heavy isotopes from soil water. These isotope 'fingerprints' can be used to precisely characterize metal-transfer processes within the compartments of the 'critical zone.'*
Source: v. Blanckenburg, GFZ.

Reinhard F. Hüttl

ers. Around two billion tonnes of chemical elements derived from rocks are mobilized annually by weathering and transported into the oceans. Microbes and plants produce remarkable biogeochemical material flows by the uptake of metals and their release into the biosphere. For certain elements, biogeochemical cycles move many times the amounts that are transported in rivers. In this way, chemical elements such as potassium can circulate up to 50 times through higher-plant systems before they leave this system and are eventually transported into the sea. In the different compartments of the 'critical zone,' each cycle leaves behind a geochemical isotope 'fingerprint' (Figure 3). Only in the past few years have modern analytical methods been developed that allow highly precise studies into these mechanisms that are so relevant to shaping the surface of our planet.

For example, chemical, physical, and biological processes that take place at the boundary between the lithosphere, hydrosphere, biosphere, and atmosphere can change the relative proportions of stable isotopes of metals and semi-metals. This so-called isotope fractionation is generally very small and thus requires highly accurate measurement. This challenge can be compared to measuring the perimeter of a football field to the same accuracy as half the length of a box of matches. For about ten years it has been possible to measure previously unrecordable isotope fractionation of metals and semi-metals using multi-collector ICP (inductively coupled plasma) mass spectrometry. However, as a large number of reactions that cause isotope fractionation occur at the micro-scale, it was necessary to develop suitable micro-analytical methods for the relevant stable isotopes.

Processes in the 'critical zone' that produce characteristic isotope fingerprints are related to a specific biogeochemical cycle: i.e., fresh rock is brought to the Earth's surface by mountain uplift. As a consequence, this rock material is exposed to physical, chemical, and biological weathering. Primary minerals in the rock dissolve and the resulting ions accumulate, e.g., within groundwater. Secondary minerals may then form (e.g., clay minerals and iron oxides), which characterize the process of soil formation. Plants may absorb metals and other elements (i.e., plant nutrients) via roots and transport them into branches, leaves, and fruits.

Plant residues are broken down in the soil, where they are subject to various processes (e.g., mineralization, formation of soil organic matter, erosion). However, this organic material may also be transported into the deeper lithosphere, where it may remain for very long periods. Eventually, increased temperature and pressure may cause chemical changes and spatial redistribution of this material. Through geodynamic processes, these organic compounds may be returned to the Earth's surface where they are oxidized and may re-enter the atmosphere.

For isotope fractionation, various element-specific properties play a role. Elements that naturally exist in more than one redox state exhibit a particularly high degree of isotope fractionation when they change their oxidation state. Therefore, iron, chromium, and molybdenum isotopes can be used to reconstruct redox processes in the environment, particularly in soil or lake sediments. Silicon, magnesium, and lithium isotopes fractionate during rock weathering. The resulting isotope fractions are characteristically influenced by a number of factors, including the type of weathered rocks, different chemical weathering and soil formation rates, or even different plant species.

However, it is also noteworthy that those isotope systems which have been known for longer also tell much about Earth surface processes. For example, hydrogen isotopes in soil clay minerals and plant substances provide information about where the precipitation originated; carbon isotopes in organic matter reveal plant types; and oxygen isotopes can be regarded as 'paleo-thermometers' that shift in relation to the temperature at the time of precipitation.

The scientific challenge of this still-young geo-scientific approach lies in acquiring a better understanding of the chemical, physical, and biological processes on the surface of the Earth by identifying and quantifying geochemical isotope fingerprints over a wide range of the different spatial and temporal scales.

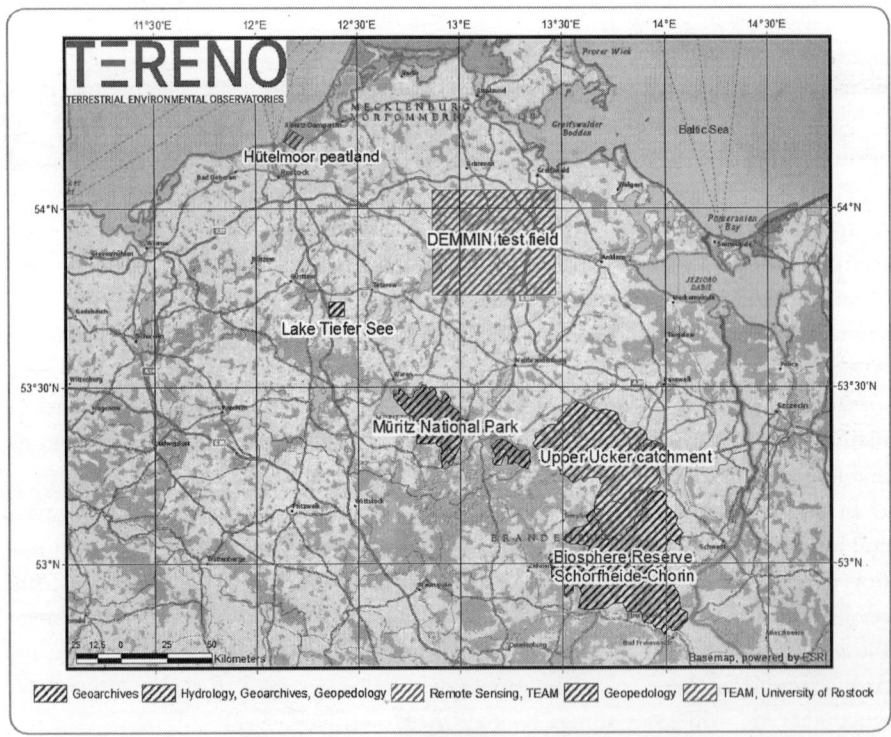

Figure 4: *The TERENO Northeastern Lowland observatory is situated in a region shaped by recurring glacial and periglacial processes over at least half a million years.*
Source: TERENO.

The TERENO (**Ter**restrial **En**vironmental **O**bservatories) network demonstrates how different research and modeling techniques can be combined with a longer-term monitoring approach. TERENO is an interdisciplinary research program involving six research centers of the German Helmholtz Association, spanning an Earth observation network across Germany that extends from the North German lowlands to the Bavarian Alps.

The TERENO observatory 'Northeastern German Lowland' (Figure 4) is coordinated by the GFZ German Research Centre for Geosciences and focuses on a region that is considered to be affected by climate change. The observatory covers the catchment area of the Uecker River, the Müritz National Park, the Schorfheide-Chorin biosphere reserve, and the DEMMIN calibration and validation test site operated by the German Aerospace Center (DLR). Particular emphasis in this observatory is placed on geoarchives and landscape development.

The Soil–Water Nexus: Experiences from Central Asia

Several functional linkages exist between the Earth system compartments of soil and water. Just like soil, water is undeniably one of the most important factors for human livelihoods and a fundamental requirement for life. The UN Millennium Development Goals assign high priority to access to sanitation facilities and clean drinking water. Due to its uneven distribution—both geographically and in terms of seasonal supply—the provision of sufficient amounts of water for consumption and irrigation as well as for energy production is one of the great global challenges. It is important to understand that, in many cases, the increasing need for water storage derives from anthropogenic soil degradation and depletion as well as unsustainable land management practices.

In various regions of the world, the availability of water has a political dimension and is the cause of social conflicts. The Fergana Valley in Central Asia is one such setting for conflicting interests regarding water utilization. This valley was uniformly administered until 1991. Upon the collapse of the Soviet Union it was divided between the autonomous states of Uzbekistan, Kyrgyzstan, and Tajikistan. Today, water countries such as Kyrgyzstan, located in the upstream region of the large river basins, border countries in the downstream region, such as Uzbekistan. Hence, this region has long been a geo-political hotspot.

In tsarist Russia at the beginning of the 20th century, there were already plans for a large-scale irrigation network for this region. During the Soviet era, large channels and reservoirs were constructed for water from the two large rivers, the Amudarja and Syrdarja. With the help of this infrastructure, one of the world's largest cotton production areas was established in this region, which was formerly characterized by deserts. Today this system is required to provide water for one of the most densely populated areas of Central Asia. In addition, huge dam cascades were built to provide hydro-electricity to meet the growing energy demand. However, this massive interference with the natural water balance led to extremely negative effects: The most prominent is the desertification of the Aral Sea triggered by massive abstraction of water from its tributaries, which today covers only a fraction of its former extent. In addition, the Fergana Valley is faced with further environmental challenges: about 80 percent of the soils in this area are saline as a result of irrigation, and the effects of uranium mining and aluminium smelting impose severe burdens on the soils of this region.

Adequate scientific knowledge is a prerequisite to overcome these problems. As the political changes in 1991 brought about a decline in systematic observations of mountainous Central Asian headwaters, better data provision may be one important step in this respect. Therefore, in cooperation with Central Asian specialists, GFZ researchers have installed a regional hydro-meteorological and geodetic Earth observation network to monitor parameters of the water cycle in Central Asia. These activities are part of the CAWa project (Central Asian Water: www.cawa-project.net). By the end of 2011, CAWa project partners had implemented five automatic low-maintenance multi-parameter stations, which collect hydro-meteorological, GPS, and seismic data. The satellite-transferred data from these new stations provide high temporal resolution and are transmitted in near-real-time. The data will be used for weather and runoff forecasting and the assessment of climate change, including monitoring high-altitude glaciers. In addition, GFZ will use the ground-based station data for the validation and calibration of new remote sensing technologies related to the CryoSat, EnMAP, and GRACE satellite missions.

An integrated overview of the water- and soil-related problems in this region—also utilizing the findings and data provided by research projects such as CAWa—is adopted by the interdisciplinary research group (IRG) 'Society–Water–Technology' at the Berlin-Brandenburg Academy of Science and Humanities. This group closely examines the effectiveness, efficiency, and sustainability of major water projects. The overall goal of the IRG is to provide scientific policy advice to decision makers and stakeholders by means of recommendations for action that will result in technically capable, ecologically modern, and socially equitable use of water resources.

A New Global Challenge:
Bioenergy and Diverging Claims on Soil Utilization

An important field of conflict with regard to land use is the global utilization of bio-energy crops and the implications of their cultivation for soils.

Worldwide energy consumption is continuously growing. In various parts of the world, the only available source of energy is biomass, mainly used for cooking or heating. The demand for firewood will continue to increase dramatically due to population growth—particularly in Asia and even more pronounced in Africa. Hence, there is a need to increase the availability of bioenergy in a sustainable way. At the same time, the ambitious goals to reduce the global emissions of greenhouse gases call for alternative energy sources to substitute for fossil fuels. Bioenergy has the potential to play an important role in the future energy mix. However, respective land use systems need to integrate biomass supplies for both food and energy without compromising the sustainable fertility of soils or biodiversity conservation goals.

Well-managed and -cultivated wood-based biofuels can provide a number of ecological advantages in addition to merely providing a renewable energy resource; for example, the positive synergies of specific woody biomass production systems can enhance carbon sequestration in soils. With regard to climate change, sustainably managed forests, short-rotation coppice, and agroforestry systems are land use options that can contribute to both mitigation and adaptation strategies. Figure 5 refers to these and other systemic advantages of integrated agricultural management schemes such as agroforestry.

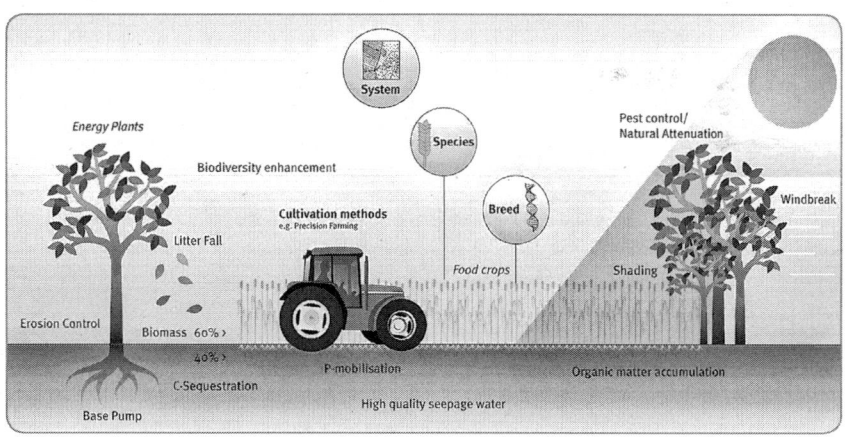

Figure 5: *Potential systemic advantages of combined cultivation of food crops and bioenergy plants in agroforestry plots.*
Source: Hoechstetter / Schneider / Schwalbe, GFZ.

Caring for the 'Skin of the Earth'—Soils as a Critical Component of Global Development

The production of woody biomass on degraded land may become part of a long-term cultivation process during which periodic conversion of woodlots into arable land may allow for cyclic improvement of soil organic carbon stocks, thereby gradually restoring soil fertility and potentially facilitating investment in soil remediation.

Frequently, a lack of data represents an important problem for sustainable soil management, e.g., when attempting to assess soil organic carbon content. Therefore, advanced remote sensing tools and specific criteria are needed for mapping, selecting, and monitoring degraded land when used for bioenergy production. The information provided by these approaches is a prerequisite for developing decision-support systems that can be utilized by all relevant stakeholders.

In addition, greater emphasis is required on the development of technologies for the cascading use of biomass. There is a need for basic research on soil/plant interactions to facilitate assessment of relevant ecosystem processes and structures as well as the resilience of such systems. Also in this context, the transfer of knowledge is indispensable. It is important to realize that this knowledge transfer should not be a 'one-way street' from developed to less developed countries, but will offer its full potential only via the mutual exchange of skills and ideas. Bioenergy is neither 'good' nor 'bad': rather, it is appropriate management that matters.

A New Research Agenda and the Course of Action

A new awareness is needed, that soils are among the most valuable and at the same time the most severely endangered of natural resources. Soils have just begun to enter the public and political spotlight. Science and technology will play a key role in this endeavor. Present-day circumstances require strategic coordination of research topics and comprehensive, interdisciplinary responses—on both a national and international basis.

In general, the economic and social importance of soils as a finite geological resource at a national, European, and global level should be highlighted. Furthermore, land management practices should be adjusted to ensure a rapid response to the effects of global change. Innovative approaches need to be developed for managing competition between different soil and land use concepts, and additional measures should be taken to ensure the transfer of knowledge and technology from the scientific community to practitioners. Initiatives to develop capacity in all regions of the globe, and the establishment of long-lasting partnerships for scientific and administrative exchange will be crucial in this regard.

In terms of the political implementation of soil conservation goals, the Outcome Paper of the first *Global Soil Week* in Berlin (November 2012) suggested the international adoption of a zero net land- and soil-degradation target. It also proposed that soil policy should form part of global endeavors towards food security. This requires operationalization in the form of a sustainable development goal on food security that emphasizes the link between development and environment. Only such an integrated view of our soils and openness to new technological, social, and management-related advances can offer potential progress towards solving the most urgent problems in this field.

Acknowledgements

Parts of this text represent a condensed and revised extract from the book 'Ein Planet voller Überraschungen: Neue Einblicke in das System Erde / Our Surprising Planet: New Insights into System Earth,' edited by Reinhard F. Hüttl (Spektrum Akademischer Verlag, 2011). This book and the article at hand are also based on the expertise and commitment of the staff of the GFZ German Research Centre for Geosciences. Particular gratitude goes to Bernd Uwe Schneider and Sebastian Hoechstetter.

Joachim von Braun

Guiding Urban–Rural Linkages Toward Sustainable Development

To Klaus Töpfer,
the man who fosters sound linkages—always seeing the whole,
not just the parts that shape
sustainable development—for the benefit of people and nature.

Introduction

Urbanization is part of a healthy economic development process and can certainly provide many opportunities for innovation and efficiency (Töpfer 2005); however, when unguided and too rapid, it may often bring about market- and other institutional failures, resulting in adverse effects on people and the environment (idem.). Although poverty remains largely a rural phenomenon, the urban share of poverty is increasing, from around 19 percent in 1993 to almost 25 percent by 2002 (Ravallion et al. 2007), and 28 percent in 2008 (IFAD 2010). Unsustainable urbanization and rural stagnation also cause negative environmental externalities (von Braun & Virchow 2001) such as degradation of land, soil, and water; air pollution; water and sanitation challenges; health hazards—exacerbating the issues of poverty, inequality, and marginalization. Therefore, policies must address the market failures in urbanization dynamics and in rural stagnation, involving failures in labor, services, and goods markets that are attributable to misguided expectations, information gaps, and missing markets (e.g., finance); government failures due to biased taxation, pricing, and investment; as well as local elite capture of public goods and policies.

Against this broad context, this paper seeks to address a more specific question: how to guide urban–rural linkages toward sustainable development, and more narrowly for eradicating extreme poverty by better managing scarce natural resources through research and innovation, addressing market failures, improving infrastructures, and promoting policies for rural transformation. The key premise is that the lack of economically optimal urban–rural linkages impedes poverty reduction and economy-wide growth. It also divides societies, leads to inefficiencies and resource degradation, and is a root cause of inequality, which is in itself growth-inhibiting (World Bank 2005). Conversely, strong linkages enhance people's welfare and growth because they facilitate the flow of resources to where they have the largest net economic and social benefits. However, such linkages cannot be taken for granted in development; they require optimal investment, both to help reduce transaction costs related to the diversity of linkage types and also to stimulate positive externalities and spillover effects. As such, urban–rural linkages need greater policy attention, which requires that adequate institutional and organizational structures be put in place, necessitating appropriate coordination mechanisms between central and local governments (Birner & von Braun 2013).

The paper starts with a brief synthesis of conceptual frameworks of urban–rural linkages so as to identify points of entry for sustainable development policy. Thereafter, megatrends in urban–rural linkages are reviewed. Next, policies facilitating urban–rural linkages and some criteria for setting policy priorities are identified. Finally, areas for related economic research are mentioned.

Conceptual Frameworks

The economics profession has shown cyclical interest in the issue of geography and spatial distribution of economic activity. Such waves have in part been driven by fluctuating beliefs and disbeliefs in planning tools and in the role of government in regional economic policy.

An early analysis of the spatial distribution of economic activity was reported by J. H. von Thünen in 1826. Using the example of demand and supply of agricultural products, von Thünen showed how the interplay of market processes and geography shaped land use decisions in specific locations. Given (the then prevailing) market prices, production costs, and transport costs (the latter influenced heavily by the value, bulk density, and perishability of individual commodities), dairy and intensive farming activities were predicted to be located closest to the city, encircled by timber and firewood in the second zone, grain production in the third, and finally ranching and livestock activities in the fourth circle. Already in this early model of the spatial distribution and patterns of rural space, urban demand was demonstrated to be a key driver, shaped by the potential marginal returns on assets and labor.

Another breakthrough came in 1933, when Walter Christaller developed *central place theory* to explain how urban settlements are formed and spatially distributed relative to each other. This model, later refined by Lösch (1954), predicted an urban

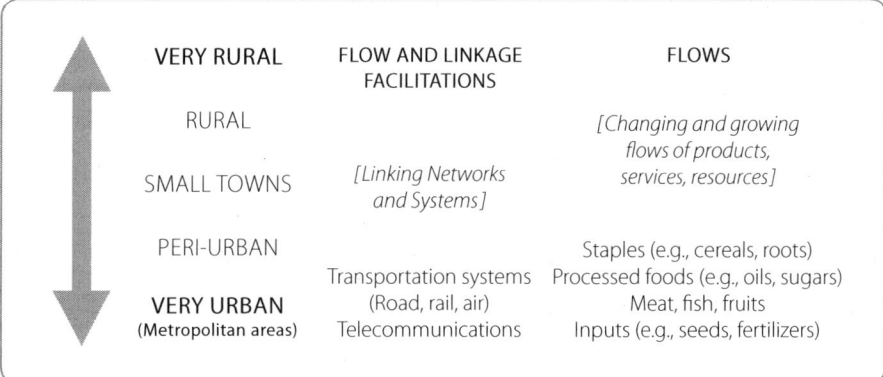

VERY RURAL	FLOW AND LINKAGE FACILITATIONS	FLOWS
RURAL		*[Changing and growing flows of products,*
SMALL TOWNS	*[Linking Networks and Systems]*	*services, resources]*
PERI-URBAN		Staples (e.g., cereals, roots)
	Transportation systems	Processed foods (e.g., oils, sugars)
VERY URBAN	(Road, rail, air)	Meat, fish, fruits
(Metropolitan areas)	Telecommunications	Inputs (e.g., seeds, fertilizers)

Figure 1: *Stylized rural–urban continuum with its spatial flow-facilitating elements, and flows of products, services, and resources.*
Source: Devised by author.

hierarchy of human settlements around hexagonal shapes with centers of varying sizes. The size of the center is determined by the types of goods and services it provides, whereby larger settlements provide more sophisticated and specialized goods and services, and smaller settlements provide goods and services of a 'lower order.' In this framework, since some of the demand for the goods produced in the centers (such as manufacturing) comes from consumers on the periphery, production is tied to agricultural land distribution (Krugman 1991).

However, these early models were based on strong assumptions such as homogeneous spaces, uniform consumer preferences, and proportionality of transport costs to distance. Therefore, the applicability of such models to real settings is limited. Nevertheless, they do clarify the gradual nature of the differentiation between urban and rural areas. In reality, the 'very rural' and the 'very urban' coexist along a continuum with many in-between stages, varying from small towns to peri-urban areas and patterns of rural urbanization (Figure 1), and the sharp conceptual separation of 'urban' vs. 'rural' areas is not productive in terms of achieving sustainable development goals (Töpfer 2001). In general, two dimensions can be conceptually distinguished here: flow and linkage facilitators; and actual flows (Figure 1). The first includes infrastructures (broadly defined) in addition to government and other public and private actors; the second includes flows of people, goods, money (such as in the form of remittances), knowledge, information, and waste. In biophysical perspectives, flows of water, biomass products, and nutrients are relevant, as are land and soil utilization.

Although goods and factors can move from one area to another, such movements incur costs. Such costs may be information costs, transport costs, or policy-induced costs such as tariffs and restrictions on movements of goods and factors. Costs may also result from non-economic and/or historical factors; as these costs are reduced,

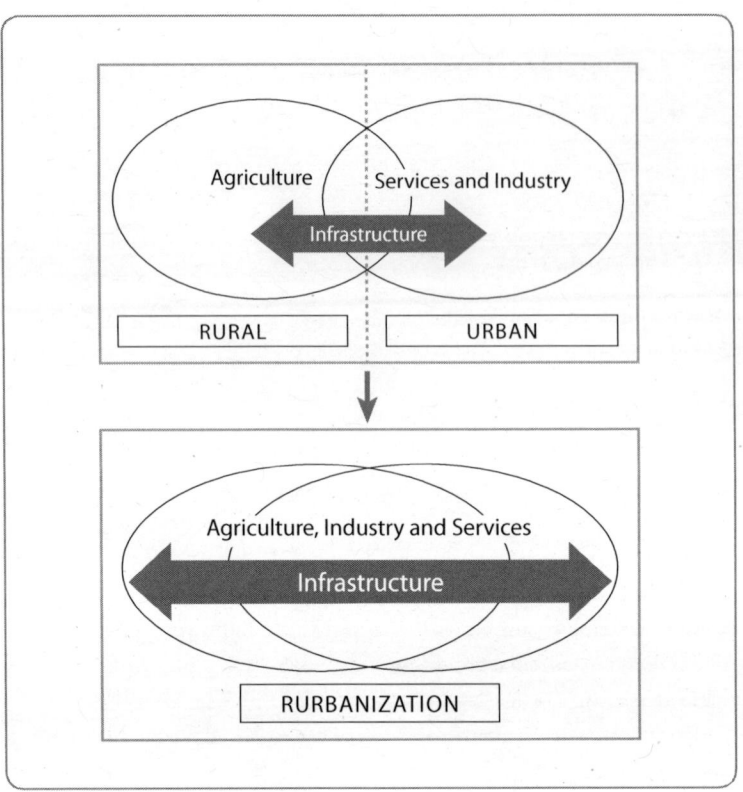

Figure 2: *Changing dynamics of urban–rural distinctions.*

spatial integration will increase, facilitating trade between rural and urban areas and, subsequently, an increased level of urban–rural linkages (Chowdhury & Torero 2007).

Moreover, it has also been shown that previously held distinctions between urban and rural livelihood activities (with rural areas engaged only in agriculture and urban areas in services and industry) are less sharp than imagined, pointing at strong sectoral interactions (Tacoli 2004). Denser and faster infrastructure networks, advancement of information and communication technologies, and the extensive application of industrial zoning in urban planning are further blurring these sectoral distinctions (Figure 2), to the extent that sharp distinctions between rural and urban areas are already gradually being replaced by the notion of 'rurbanization,' whereby the rural areas will increasingly be less distinguishable from urban in terms of key sources of livelihoods.

Mega-trends and Policy Domains Facilitating
Urban–Rural Linkages

A major trend of the last two decades was the historically unprecedented acceleration of economic growth in the developing countries worldwide. To illustrate, from
2000 to 2010 the developing countries as a whole experienced average growth rates
of 4.6 percent per annum, with African countries growing by around 2.7 percent
per annum during the same period (UNCTAD 2012). At the same time, the level
of interaction between urban and rural areas has intensified, with both positive and
negative implications.

Flows between Rural and Urban Spaces,
and Implications for Rural Transformation

Driven by technological progress, improvements in infrastructure, and liberalization
and creation of markets, globalization has facilitated rapid rural transformation across
the developing world.

Resource and Environmental Flows: Urban Ecological Footprint

Even though it is often believed that economies of scale grant urban areas a smaller
environmental footprint per capita than in rural areas (Töpfer 2005), the overall magnitude of the footprint imposed on rural areas remains overwhelming. The intensification of rural–urban linkages with respect to environmental flows has occurred as
a result of increased urban demands for rural resources such as land, water, and air.
The most visible change is associated with the physical expansion of urban areas, as
urbanization has led to the extension of urban space onto rural space to accommodate
growing populations and levels of economic activity. Demand for land around cities
has increased in order to build residences, industries, and transport corridors such as
roads and highways, as well as for the disposal of urban waste (both industrial and
household) (McGranahan et al. 2004).

Urbanization also creates pressure on agriculture production as urban demands
grow in terms of both quantity and diversity of agricultural outputs needed, but also
as urban expansion encroaches into often highly productive tracts of agricultural land.
Such urban-induced pressure can impose a significant environmental footprint upon
rural areas as the agricultural frontier is expanded through land conversion, or as production on existing agricultural land is intensified (Millennium Ecosystems Assessment 2005). Both areal expansion and the unsustainable intensification of production
often result in the loss of natural biodiversity, increased greenhouse gas emissions,

reduced quantity and quality of available freshwater resources, and accelerated soil erosion and nutrient cycling (impacting soil fertility and water quality). By degrading the rural natural resource base (i.e., overdrawing on natural capital), the negative environmental footprint and externalities of urban-induced demand for greater exploitation of rural resources imposes sustainability risks on both rural livelihoods as well as on the future food security of both rural and urban populations. Moreover, cross-sectoral aspects of such urban–rural tradeoffs are revealed, such as when enhancing agricultural output diminishes the contribution of rural areas to the supply of other ecosystem services and products that are also required in increasing amounts by urban populations (i.e., fresh water supply, flood protection, fuel wood, and lumber). Furthermore, Töpfer (2001) highlights that globalization has added a new dimension to the urban footprint, especially for the prosperous megacities around the world, which absorb resources from the entire planet, making it ever more challenging to manage the environmental impacts of these megacities within the standard framework of urban–rural linkages.

Urban areas impose especially large footprints on water- and land resources. Throughout the world, urban diets have been rapidly shifting to include more meat-based products (Romanik 2007). Meat-based diets require significantly more land and water to produce the same amount of calories (Pimentel & Pimentel 2003). As a result, rapidly increasing demand for land and water resources has led to multiple increases in land prices around the world. The expansion of agriculture to deforested and marginal lands has brought about serious degradation of land, soil, and water resources and their related ecosystem functions in many areas around the world (von Braun et al. 2012).

Labor, Financial, and Knowledge Flows

Urbanization is accelerating across the developing world—from 2005 to 2010, the rate of urban population growth among developing countries averaged 2.6 percent per annum, compared to 0.3 percent for rural population growth (UNDESA 2013). The reclassification of areas from rural to urban plays an important part in this change. The average annual rate of urban population growth is even higher for Sub-Saharan Africa, at 3.7 percent, compared to 1.8 percent for rural population growth (ibid). This trend is expected to continue over the coming decades, with urban populations in less-developed regions surpassing rural populations by 2020. In Sub-Saharan Africa, this will occur around 2040, when the urban and rural populations are predicted to reach 810 million and 777 million respectively (UNDESA 2013).

The causes and dynamics of rural-to-urban migration are complex. The economic thinking behind migration decisions dates back to the Harris–Todaro model (1970), which asserts that an individual's decision to migrate is based on the expected income differential between one's rural home and that of the formal urban sector. Subsequently, economic theory has evolved to focus on families as a unit of analysis, as opposed to just the individual. Stark and Bloom (1985) found that migration is a household decision, and that families invest in a migrant (or migrants) in return for future receipt of remittances. As such, migration is a source of income diversification for households facing income risks and is also circular, in that it entails continued (rural–urban) interaction between migrant(s) and their families who remain in the area of origin. More broadly, however, migration is determined by push and pull factors. Push factors include droughts, land scarcity, and low wages or the absence of wage labor in out-migration areas, and pull factors include better job opportunities and/or the possibility of higher income, and lower or different risk profiles in destination areas (von Braun 2005). On the one hand, if people migrate because they are pushed away by the unavailability of work in rural areas, they risk joining the already high number of unemployed in urban areas (Garrett 2005). On the other hand, if people migrate because they have found better jobs, then migration is welfare-enhancing (i.e., migrants would be better off and would be able to send remittances back to their communities).

At the macroeconomic level, the practice shows that moving from rural areas to cities in search of jobs does not always bring about economic growth (World Bank 2013). Population movement from rural to urban jobs was associated with high levels of economic growth in East Asia, but not so in Sub-Saharan Africa (ibid.). The decision by rural households to migrate to urban areas may also result in gender-biased outcomes, with increasing working burden on women (ibid.). Moreover, the massive growth in the urban employment of rural migrants is not always accompanied by formalization of these jobs, but may instead be associated with informal and precarious employment in urban areas, as in Bangladesh (ibid.).

Rural migration is not always restricted to large urban centers. For instance, in the Philippines, migration to smaller towns in rural areas that offer comparable 'urban-like' opportunities in education and employment for migrants is common. This counters the migration flow to more congested metropolitan centers of the country (Quisumbing & McNiven 2005). In addition, migration is not always permanent. There is a strong component of seasonal migration in developing countries (especially in Asia and Africa), whereby people are 'pulled' into urban areas as a result of strong growth in manufacturing and services. One of the advantages of such migrations, beyond increased earnings, is that the availability of these urban jobs is not tied to the agricultural season, which entails that people can work in both rural and urban areas (Deshingkar 2005). Seasonal migration can be welfare-enhancing; for instance, a study in Vietnam found that seasonal migration resulted in an increase of about 5 percent in annual household expenditure, and a 3 percentage point decrease in the poverty headcount (de Brauw & Harigaya 2007). One of the main outcomes of increased migration (including international migration) linkages is growing remittance receipts in many developing countries (World Bank 2013). Such remittances can play a very important role in supplementing incomes in receiving households. Additionally, the increased purchasing power of receiving households can stimulate the local economy and, in the particular case of rural areas, increased remittance receipts can stimulate the rural non-farm economy (Thanh et al. 2005).

Table 1: *Global employment change, 2005 to 2020 (in billions).*

	Farm	Services and industry: rural areas	Services and industry: urban areas	Total
2005	0.9	0.6	1.5	3.0
2020	0.6	1.0	1.9	3.5
Change 2005 to 2020	−0.3	+0.4	+0.4	+0.5

Source: Author's estimates of sector shares based on ILO projections of economically active population.

Much of the global change in labor allocation is related to inter-sectoral shifts due to enhanced growth in other sectors (manufacturing, industry, and services) in rural and urban areas. Between 2005 and 2020, the economically active population is projected to increase from 3 billion to 3.5 billion, and while farm employment may decline by approximately 300 million, employment in services and industry—both in urban and rural areas—is estimated to grow by an additional 400 million people each. It is noteworthy that much of the employment growth is expected in rural (including small town) services and industries (see Table 1). Such significant decrease in rural employment will necessitate radical increases in farm labor productivity if the food demands of the growing world population are to be met. However, progress in labor productivity within the agricultural sector has so far been uneven (World Bank 2013).

The failures of development strategies based on import-substituting industrialization (e.g., in many Latin American and African countries) and the successes of countries that pursued agricultural-led growth (e.g., China) have demonstrated that agricultural productivity growth is essential to launching economy-wide growth, especially in predominantly agrarian societies. Indeed, agricultural growth engenders both backward linkages in the form of increased demand for farm inputs such as fertilizers and farm equipment; and forward linkages, as the increased income of farm households translates into increased demand for consumption goods and services (Mellor 1995; Hazell & Röell 1983; Diao et al. 2007; de Ferranti et al. 2005, World Bank 2013). These linkages can subsequently lead to rural transformation, with an expansion of the rural non-farm economy (RNFE) and better linkages with the rest of the economy, with increasing sectoral and spatial flows between rural and urban

areas. Better infrastructural connectivity between urban and rural areas can significantly contribute to the development of the rural non-farm economy (Deichmann
et al. 2008)

The Rural–Urban Divide is Still Relevant

Despite increasing levels of rural–urban interaction, major rural–urban disparities
persist across the developing world (Liu et al. 2013). As a result of adverse terms of
trade between agricultural and nonagricultural product prices—as well as urban biases
in government spending on health, education, and physical infrastructure across the
developing world—major inequalities between urban and rural areas persist, not only
in terms of income but also in asset endowment and human development (Eastwood &
Lipton 2004). Thus, while inequality exists separately within the rural and urban
spheres, the largest differences are between urban and rural areas; most of the poor
live in rural areas and depend for their livelihoods on agriculture and related trade,
services, and processing activities. Additionally, in many countries, rural inhabitants
do not have the same level of access to social services, such as health and education
facilities and infrastructure, as their urban counterparts, thereby further perpetuating
existing inequalities while marginality becomes also a phenomenon of both rural and
urban spaces (see Figure 3).

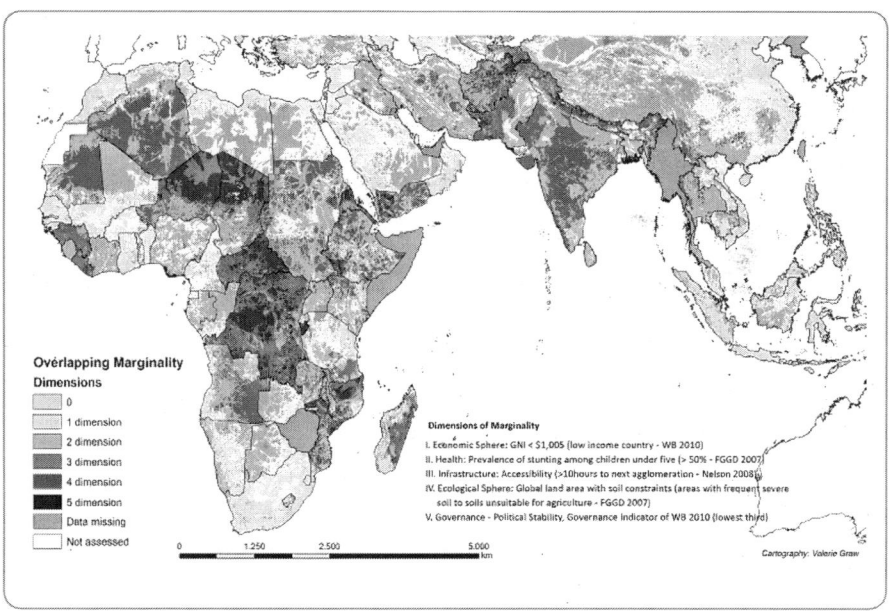

Figure 3: *Marginality in Sub-Saharan Africa and Asia.*
Source: Graw (2010).

Guiding Urban–Rural Linkages Toward Sustainable Development

An issue of even greater concern is that the rural–urban divide seems to be widening in parts of the developing world (Eastwood & Lipton 2004). China and India provide illustrations: both countries have experienced sustained economic growth over the last decade (on average 10.3 percent annually for China and 7.6 percent for India between 2003 and 2013) and have achieved major success in poverty reduction. However, economic growth and poverty reduction have been distributed unevenly. In both countries, the bulk of the poor still live in rural areas and are concentrated within certain regions. In China, the majority of the poor are concentrated within the interior of the country, and in India half of the poor are concentrated within just three states—Uttar Pradesh, Bihar, and Madhya Pradesh. Moreover, spatial inequality in both countries seems to be increasing. In China, the difference in the average monthly per capita income between urban and rural areas almost doubled between 1994 and 2004, from US$99 to US$161, and the percentage of total inequality (measured using general entropy) due to inequality between inland and coastal areas increased from 6.5 percent in 1990 to 11.6 percent in 2004. Similarly in India, the difference between average monthly per capita income in urban and rural areas rose from US$21 to more than US$27, and the percentage of total inequality attributed to North–South disparity increased from 2.6 percent in 1990 to 15.9 percent in 2003 (Gajwani et al. 2006). At the same time, this trend of growing urban–rural income disparities exacerbates perceptions of relative deprivation, from which violent political unrest can result.

Increasing inequalities are also a central feature of agricultural production in many developing countries, especially in terms of access to land. Indeed, approximately 85 percent of the world's farms are smaller than two hectares, and of those 90 percent are in low-income countries. For instance, farm sizes in Sub-Saharan Africa remain predominantly smaller than one hectare, and there is evidence that farm size is still gradually shrinking over time due to population growth and density (von Braun 2005).

Policy Domains for Facilitating Urban–Rural Linkages for Sustainable Development

Three major areas alluded to in the conceptual discussion above—R&D combined with technology, infrastructure, and market institutions—play key roles in stimulating rural–urban linkages to promote sustainable development, create employment, and reduce poverty. Urban–rural linkages constitute "a fundamental policy lesson that we must carry into the 21st century" (Klaus Töpfer, quoted by Tweitdal 2004).

R&D and Technology

Technologies work through factor- and output markets; processing; and consumption linkages. Here, two types of technologies that have had a substantial impact on rural growth and poverty reduction are explored: innovations arising from agricultural research and development (R&D), and improvements in information and communication technologies (ICTs).

Agricultural R&D Knowledge-flows

Science and technology are fundamental to rural–urban linkages, and in this context, agricultural research is fundamental. The Green Revolution experience, especially in Asia, has shown that agricultural R&D can result in technological breakthroughs that enable considerable improvement in agricultural productivity, resulting in agricultural growth, which in turn can translate into substantial rural development and poverty reduction. Today, technological innovations in agricultural production continue to be significant sources of growth in agricultural productivity, which can in turn translate into rural growth and poverty reduction. For instance, it is estimated that in Asia and Latin America, for each additional dollar of agricultural income, an additional $0.6–0.9 and $0.4–0.6 respectively is generated in the local rural non-farm economy (Haggblade et al. 2007). The multipliers are lower for Sub-Saharan Africa, due to agro-climatic conditions and the lack of infrastructure and sound policies.

Nevertheless, while agricultural performance has been relatively high in recent years, there is cause for concern. Eighty developing countries together spend only about $1.4 billion on agriculture R&D, which represents only 6 percent of global expenditure. Furthermore, together, the agricultural R&D expenditures of China and India represent 22 percent of the total investment by developing countries (Pardey et al. 2006). Many small and medium-sized developing countries are not investing enough in agricultural R&D. In effect, as the positive spillovers derived from the previous R&D programs of industrialized countries dry up, and because even the capacity for adapting technologies is constrained by the lack of expenditure among small and medium-sized developing countries, many of these countries have only limited access to available growth-enhancing technologies. As a consequence, rural–urban linkages become weaker.

ICTs can lower transaction costs by reducing information asymmetries[1] and opening-up market possibilities for rural inhabitants, which can result in additional network externalities. Indeed, at the macro level, tele-density is positively associated with growth. Waverman et al. (2005) found that 10 more mobile phones per 100 people increased GDP by 0.6 percent. But there seems to be a minimum threshold of about 1 percent coverage to achieve the strongest growth effects (Torero & von Braun 2006).

At the micro level, the welfare gains derived from access to ICTs are large, because the alternatives (sending a messenger or letter) are much costlier and more time consuming. For instance, in Bangladesh and Peru, the effective welfare gains from a telephone call range between US$1.62 and US$1.91. As such, the willingness to pay for access to telephones is also relatively high and typically exceeds the actual prevailing tariff rates (Torero & von Braun 2006).

If information asymmetries persist between producers and consumers based in two spatially separated locations, intermediaries emerge who facilitate transactions between urban and rural areas; therefore, any change in information asymmetry can lead to a change in the intermediation process, and can lead to the demise of existing (traditional) intermediaries and the rise of new (modern) intermediaries, as is currently happening in the modern food value chains in many developing countries. If not corrected, the lack of or differential access to market information can create direct barriers to mutually beneficial exchange and greatly increase the costs associated with trade. The consequences of asymmetric information are that equilibrium may or may not exist; or if equilibrium exists, resources are used less efficiently than they would be if there was symmetric information. Thus, the availability of efficient and reliable market information is key to fostering rural–urban linkages. Information and communication technologies (ICTs) are also providing new opportunities for improving local governance and increasing the benefits of decentralization for the poor (Birner & von Braun 2013).

Infrastructure

Infrastructure works as a bridge between the rural and urban worlds, and between agriculture and others sectors of the economy. In particular, in situations characterized by a wide dispersion of production and consumption centers, transport costs account for a significant proportion of the total costs of linking urban and rural areas. For sustainable development and inclusive green growth, it is therefore critical to develop

---

1 Information bottlenecks hinder effective rural–urban linkages by raising transaction costs comprising search, screening, and bargaining costs.

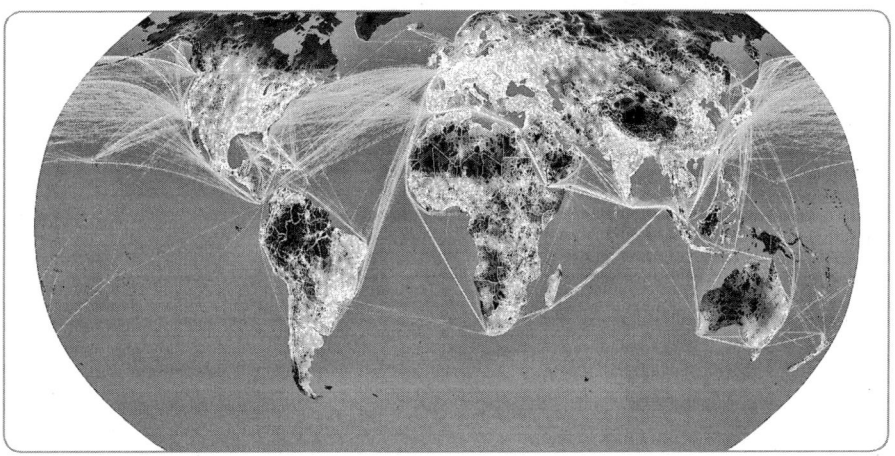

Figure 4: *Travel time to major cities.*
Source: World Bank (2009). Note: lighter areas have better access to urban centers.

new infrastructures with environment-friendly characteristics from the outset, so as to avoid costly technological lock-ins to unsustainable forms of infrastructure (World Bank 2012).

An improvement in rural road quantity (length or density) and quality reduces travel time and vehicle operating and maintenance costs, which in turn lowers the actual costs of marketing produce and of delivering inputs, thereby facilitating inter-linkages between urban and rural areas. But beyond reduced transport costs, infra-structure improvements have important indirect benefits for the flow of goods, ser-vices, and information. The large returns in terms of growth and poverty reduction from investment in rural roads are well known. For example, in China, in terms of national income, the return on investment in rural roads is more than three times that for urban roads—for every yuan invested in rural roads, the return is around 6 yuan, versus 1.55 yuan for urban roads. This investment in road infrastructure produces even greater disparities in terms of poverty reduction: 5.67 persons per 10,000 yuan invested in rural roads versus 0.31 persons for urban roads (Fan & Chan-Kang 2005). Similarly, Mogues et al. (2007) find that investments in roads have the highest returns compared with other investments considered.[2] However, the study also finds that returns on road investments vary by region, with those regions with better road net-works benefiting most. In the last decade, although many developing countries have invested heavily in rural roads, leading to better access to markets composed of more than 50,000 inhabitants, overall market access from rural areas in developing coun-tries remains patchy and uneven (see Figure 4).

---

2   The study also considers public investment in agriculture, health, and education.

As globalization evolves, the consumer-driven agri-food chain is becoming more integrated, incorporating more small farmers through arrangements such as producer-marketing cooperatives, which facilitate horizontal cooperation; and contract farming, which facilitates vertical cooperation. Such arrangements can substantially boost the income of poor rural households by helping reduce transaction costs and variability in prices of agricultural products. Additionally, such arrangements give farmers better access to markets for their produce and to technological innovations in agriculture.

A study looking at the impact of a large Ethiopian dairy cooperative on the commercialization of smallholders found that, on average, farmers in cooperatives had better market access, higher productivity, and better quality milk relative to individual farmers (Francesconi & Ruben 2007). However, such arrangements are usually information-intensive and require adequate legal frameworks and organizational capacity. Thus, to maximize the potential gains for farmers from integration within the globalized agri-food system, it is necessary to provide farmers access to communications technologies, as well as training and capacity building. An opportunity here is in commodity exchanges appropriately adapted to the infrastructure and institutional environments of low-income countries. In addition, access to insurance and credit in rural areas can potentially prevent 'stress migration.' Thus, development of these markets—for instance, fostered by transaction-cost-cutting ICTs—can deliver efficient gains in labor markets. In relation to migration and increased remittances to rural areas, investment opportunities and enhanced banking and savings institutions need to be developed in many countries.

Policies Facilitating Transformation

Diversification of Rural Economies

The development paths taken by many countries have shown that it is inaccurate to simply associate urban with industry, and rural with agriculture. As stated earlier, rural economic activities outside the agricultural sector are major sources of income and employment, and therefore the rural non-farm sector is an important contributor to economic growth and poverty reduction during the economic transformation of many developing countries. Rural non-farm activities are especially important in countries where landlessness prevails, offering the rural poor important economic alternatives to traditional land-dependent activities. However, the rural non-farm sector has limited capacity to absorb part of the agricultural labor force—a situation which is particularly pressing, given the global decline predicted in agricultural employment. Diversification of rural economies is greatly helped by denser infrastructure networks linking them with urban and other rural areas.

Development of Small Towns

The majority of urban dwellers in developing countries do not live in a megalopolis but rather in medium-sized cities. Consequently, small and medium-sized towns play an important role as an intermediary point along the rural–urban continuum, linking and benefiting both rural and urban areas through consumption, production, and employment patterns as well as various types of economic and social provisions (e.g., Satterthwaite & Tacoli 2003; Wandschneider 2004). More specifically, small and medium-sized market towns and cities are extremely important to the economic activities of rural households because they provide the economic space for rural households both to purchase their inputs and household items as well as to sell their final products at local markets, thereby linking rural producers to the national and global economies.

For example, apart from remittances, rural households in Ethiopia were found to have few direct links to more distant urban centers or the capital, with intermediary cities being the main urban locations where rural households undertook economic activities (Hoddinott & Dercon 2005). Consequently, the development of small and medium-size town infrastructure has the potential to reduce transportation costs and improve access to markets for both urban and rural consumers and producers. Small towns can also serve as a stepping-stone or an end-point for rural residents seeking opportunities outside the agricultural sector, by absorbing some of the agricultural labor, thereby alleviating the pressure on already congested metropolitan centers while at the same time contributing to the growth of the national economy and transformation of agriculture.

Furthermore, many higher-level rural services in health and education depend on urban locations. Access to such services depends on infrastructure that links rural and urban areas. This affects, for instance, access to secondary education, and many of the more complex health services in rural areas are delivered through hospitals and clinics located in small and medium-size towns. For instance, people in eastern Africa mainly gain access to TB and antiretroviral (ARV) HIV/AIDS treatment through hospitals located in towns; and in some countries, the cost of transportation is currently a greater barrier to accessing treatment than are the availability of treatment and the cost of drugs.

This specific example of HIV/AIDS-related rural–urban linkages is of a two-way nature over time: whereas the source of the disease was at first largely urban and along transregional infrastructure axes (transit roads), the disease later became more rural;

the secondary feedback is now about the linkages within the health services, because access to such services requires well-functioning rural–urban linkages. Otherwise, access to treatment at urban health centers is impaired.

Decentralization for Poverty Reduction

Decentralization can potentially serve as a powerful means of rural transformation and poverty reduction (Birner & von Braun 2013). The eventual impact of decentralization on rural economic development, however, depends on local characteristics (ibid.). Birner and von Braun (2013) conducted a meta-analysis of studies that assessed the impact of decentralization on public services that are relevant for the poor in Asia (Ghuman & Singh 2013). Of 32 studies reviewed in the meta-analysis, 13 documented a positive impact of decentralization on public services, 11 revealed a negative impact, and eight studies had mixed results. Increasing the dynamism of local rural economies through decentralization could be especially challenging in remote, marginalized areas with poorer infrastructure connections, low educational levels, and low local government capacity (Birner & von Braun 2013). Therefore, there is a need for context-specific solutions for such areas. Technological opportunities though widespread dissemination of information and communication technologies (ICTs) are providing new opportunities to make decentralization work for the poor (ibid.).

Conclusions

The paper highlights the need for renewed attention to the spatial dimensions of development and to urban–rural linkages for sustainable development. The nature of such 'attention' by policy and advisory communities includes:
- Distinguishing the various types of dynamic flows that exist between rural and urban spaces;
- Reviewing the transaction costs of all economic activities between rural and urban areas, with an eye toward their optimal reductions; and
- Focusing on the nontrivial positive and negative externalities of spatial allocation and concentration of economic activities, including services supporting them.

Four types of public policy actions are crucial for enabling better urban–rural linkages:
1. Scaling-up of transport and communication infrastructures toward optimal densities;
2. Development of market institutions that enable the participation of rural areas and the poor in the national economy;

3. Reduction of environmental footprints of resource flows via incentives and appropriate regulations;
4. Reduction of policy barriers to effective and efficient services in decentralized participatory political systems.

One must keep in mind that policy and investment priorities for fostering urban–rural linkages cannot be 'one size fits all.' They depend greatly on initial conditions, and require a dynamic analytical framework.

These policy issues pose new challenges for research:

Much progress has been made in regionally disaggregated analysis and economic modeling. Integration of spatial analysis through, for example, the use of GIS technologies can be useful for the visualization and understanding of changing realities (Wood et al. 1999). Many of the economic models on which the rural–urban framework is based are static, simplistic, and do not take into consideration spatial realities such as ecological conditions and growth potentials.

The development analyses of practitioners also need a broader perspective. Agriculture programs should not be planned and evaluated in isolation from infrastructure—the planned incremental output may go nowhere; Vice versa, infrastructure investment, such as roads, should not be planned and evaluated in isolation from agriculture and industry investments—the road might lead nowhere.

In addition, consideration is required of historical, social, and cultural settings, as well as the types of institutions governing space (Martin 2003). Blending aggregate modeling with information systems that capture local knowledge is a challenge. Sector-specific and domain-oriented economic research (e.g., agriculture economics, infrastructure economics, and services-related economics research) need to come together to jointly address the opportunities of urban–rural linkages via a nexus-perspective.

LITERATURE CITED

Birner, R., von Braun, J. (2013): Decentralization and Poverty Reduction. In: Ahmad, E., Brosio, G. (Eds.). Handbook on Fiscal Federalism, 2nd edition. Palgrave, forthcoming.

Chowdhury, S., Torero, M. (2007): Urban rural linkages in Bangladesh: Impact of infrastructure and the food value chain on livelihoods and migration of landless households, women in the Northwestern region. International Food Policy Research Institute. Discussion paper, forthcoming.

CSA, EDRI, IFPRI (2006): Atlas of Ethiopian Rural Economy. Central Statistical Agency of the Federal Democratic Republic of Ethiopia, Ethiopian Development Research Institute, and International Food Policy Research Institute. Addis Ababa and Washington, DC: CSA and IFPRI.

de Brauw, A., Harigaya, T. (2007): Seasonal migration and improving living standards in Vietnam. In: American Journal of Agricultural Economics 89/2: 430–47.

de Ferranti, D., Perry, G., Foster, W., Lederman, D., Valdés, A. (2005): Beyond the city: The rural contribution to development. World Bank Latin American and Caribbean Studies. Washington, DC: World Bank.

Deichmann, U., Shilpi, F., Vakis, R. (2009): Urban proximity, agricultural potential and rural non-farm employment: Evidence from Bangladesh. In: World Development 37/3: 645–660.

Deshingkar, P. 2005. How rural is rural? ODI Opinions no. 52. London: Overseas Development Institute.

Diao, X., Fekadu, B., Taffesse, A.S., Wamisho, K., Yu, B. (2007): Agricultural growth linkages in Ethiopia: Estimates using fixed and flexible price models. IFPRI Discussion Paper no. 695. Washington, DC: International Food Policy Research Institute.

Eastwood, R., Lipton, M. (2004): Rural and urban income inequality and poverty: Does convergence between sectors offset divergence within them? In: Cornia, G.A. (Ed.). Inequality, Growth, and Poverty in an Era of Liberalization and Globalization. Oxford: Oxford University Press.

Fan, S., Chan-Kang, C. (2005): Road development, economic growth, and poverty reduction in China. IFPRI Research Report no. 138. Washington, DC: International Food Policy Research Institute.

Francesconi, G.N., Ruben, R. (2007): Impacts of collective action on smallholders' commercialisation: Evidence from dairy in Ethiopia. Paper prepared for presentation at the I Mediterranean Conference of Agro-Food Social Scientists, 103rd EAAE Seminar: Adding Value to the Agro-Food Supply Chain in the Future Euromediterranean Space, April 23–25, Barcelona.

Gajwani, K., Kanbur, R., Zhang, X. (2006): Comparing the evolution of spatial inequality in China and India: A fifty-year perspective. Development Strategy and Governance Division Discussion Paper no. 44. Washington, DC: International Food Policy Research Institute.

Garrett, J. (2005): Beyond rural urban: Keeping up with changing realities. Washington, DC: International Food Policy Research Institute.

Ghuman, B.S., Singh, R. (2013): Decentralization and delivery of public services in Asia. In: Policy and Society 32/1: 7–21.

Graw, V. (2010): Marginality hotspots in Sub-Saharan Africa. Digital map, available at http://131.220.109.10/geonetwork_zef/srv/en/main.home

Haggblade, S., Hazell, P.B.R., Reardon, T. (Eds.) (2007): Transforming the Rural Nonfarm Economy. Baltimore: Johns Hopkins University Press.

Harris, J., Todaro, M. (1970): Migration, unemployment, and development: A two-sector analysis. In: American Economic Review 60/1: 126–42.

Hazell, P. B., Röell, A. (1983): Rural growth linkages: Household expenditure patterns in Malaysia and Nigeria. Research Report no. 41. Washington, DC: International Food Policy Research Institute.

Hirschman, A.D. (1958): The Strategy of Economic Development. New Haven, CT: Yale University Press.

Hoddinott, J., Dercon, S. (2005): Livelihoods, growth, and links to market towns in 15 Ethiopian villages. Food Consumption and Nutrition Division Discussion Paper no. 194. Washington, DC: International Food Policy Research Institute.

IFAD (2010): Rural Poverty Report 2011. New realities, new challenges: new opportunities for tomorrow's generation. Rome: International Fund for Agricultural Development.

Krugman, P. (1991): Increasing returns and economic geography. Journal of Political Economy 99/3: 483–99.

Liu, H., Fang, H., Zhao, Z. (2013): Urban–rural disparities of child health and nutritional status in China from 1989 to 2006. In: Economics and Human Biology 11/3: 294–309.

Lösch, A. (1954): The Economics of Location. New Haven, CT: Yale University Press. (Originally published 1939).

Martin, R. (2003): Putting the economy in its place: Economics and geography. Paper presented at the Cambridge Journal of Economics Conference, Economics for the Future: Celebrating 100 Years of Cambridge Economics, September 2003.

McGranahan, G., Satterthwaite, D., Tacoli, C. (2004): Rural-urban chance, boundary problems, and environmental burdens. Working paper series on rural-urban interactions and livelihoods strategies. Working Paper no. 10. London: International Institute for Environment and Development.

Mellor, J. W. (Ed.) (1995): Agriculture on the Road to Industrialization. Baltimore: Johns Hopkins University Press for IFPRI.

Millennium Ecosystem Assessment (2005): Ecosystems and human well-being: Biodiversity synthesis. World Resources Institute, Washington, DC.

Mogues, T., Ayele, G., Paulos, Z. (2007): The bang for the Birr: Public expenditure and rural welfare in Ethiopia. IFPRI Discussion Paper no. 00702. Washington, DC: International Food Policy Research Institute.

Pardey, P.G., Alston, J.M., Piggott, R.R. (Eds.) (2006): Shifting ground: Agricultural R&D worldwide. Issue Brief no. 46. Washington, DC: International Food Policy Research Institute.

Pimentel, D., Pimentel, M. (2003): Sustainability of meat-based and plant-based diets and the environment. In: The American Journal of Clinical Nutrition 78/3: 660S–663S.

Quisumbing, A., McNiven, S. (2005): Migration and the rural-urban continuum: Evidence from the rural Philippines. FCND Discussion Paper no. 197. Washington, DC: International Food Policy Research Institute.

Ravallion, M., Chen, S., Sangraula, P. (2007): The urbanization of global poverty. Background paper prepared for the World Bank's World Development Report, 2008. Washington, DC: World Bank.

Romanik, C. (2008): An Urban-Rural Focus on Food Markets in Africa. Washington, DC: The Urban Institute.

Ricardo, D. (1951): An essay on the influence of a low price of corn on the profits of stock. In: Sraffa, P. (Ed.). The Works and Correspondence of David Ricardo: Volume IV, Pamphlets and Papers 1815–1823, (reprinted from 1815). Cambridge: Cambridge University Press.

Satterthwaite, D., Tacoli, C. (2003): The urban part of rural development: The role of small and intermediate urban centres in rural and regional development and poverty reduction. Rural-Urban Working Paper no. 9. London: International Institute for Environment and Development.

Stark, O., Bloom, D.E. (1985): The new economics of labor migration. In: American Economic Review 75/2: 173–78.

Tacoli, C. (1998): Rural-urban interactions: A guide to the literature. In: Environment and Urbanization 10: 147–166.

Thanh, H.X., Anh, D.N., Tacoli, C. (2005): Livelihood diversification and rural-urban linkages in Vietnam's Red River Delta. Food Consumption and Nutrition Division Discussion Paper no. 193. Washington, DC: International Food Policy Research Institute.

Töpfer, K. (2000): Rural poverty, sustainability and rural development in the twenty-first century: a focus on human settlements. Zeitschrift für Kulturtechnik und Landentwicklung, 41/3: 98–105.

Töpfer, K. (2001): The crucial importance of urban-rural linkages. In: Virchow, D., von Braun, J. (Eds.). Villages in the Future. Berlin/Heidelberg: Springer, pp. 21–24.

Töpfer, K. (2005): Editorial on Green Cities. Our Planet, 16:1. United Nations Environmental Program. Nairobi, Kenya.

Torero, M., von Braun, J. (2006): Information and communication technologies for development and poverty reduction. Washington, DC: International Food Policy Research Institute.

Tweitdal, S. (2004): Urban-Rural Interrelationship: Condition for Sustainable Development. Speech during the 2nd FIG Regional Conference for Africa and the Arab Countries Urban-Rural Interrelationship for Sustainable Environment. Marrakech, Morocco, December 2–5.

UNCTAD (2012): Development and Globalization: Facts and Figures 2012. Geneva: United Nations Conference on Trade and Development.

UNDESA (2013): Population Division of the Department of Economic and Social Affairs of the United Nations Secretariat, World Population Prospects: The 2010 Revision and World Urbanization Prospects: The 2011 Revision Wednesday, June 26, 2013; 11:40:48 AM. United Nations Department of Economic and Social Affairs.

von Braun, J., Virchow, D. (2001): Village Futures: Concept Overview and Policy Implications. In: Virchow, D., von Braun, J. (Eds.). Villages in the Future Berlin and Heidelberg: Springer, pp. 3–20.

von Braun, J. (2005): Agricultural economics and distributional effects. In: Agricultural Economics 32 (s1), 1–20. Malden, MA: Blackwell for IAAE.

von Braun, J., Pandya-Lorch, R. (Eds.) (1991): Income sources of malnourished people in rural areas: Microlevel information and policy implications. Working Paper on Commercialization of Agriculture and Nutrition no. 5 (May). Washington, DC: International Food Policy Research Institute.

von Braun, J., Gerber, N., Mirzabaev, A., Nkonya, E. (2012): The Economics of Land Degradation. An Issue Paper for Global Soil Week. Berlin, 08–22 November.

von Thünen, J.H. (1826): The Isolated State. Jena: Gustav Fischer.

Waverman, L., Meschi, M., Fuss, M. (2005): The Impact of Telecoms on Economic Growth in Developing Countries. Vodafone Policy Paper Series no. 2.

Wood, S., Sebastian, K., Nachtergaele, F., Nielsen, D., Dai, A. (1999): Spatial aspects of the design and targeting of agricultural development strategies. EPTD Discussion Paper no. 44. Washington, DC: International Food Policy Research Institute.

World Bank (2005): World development report, 2006: Equity and development. New York: Oxford University Press.

World Bank (2006): World development indicators, 2006. Washington, DC.

World Bank (2007): PovcalNet Database. Washington, DC. Online access http://iresearch.world-bank.org/PovcalNet/jsp/index.jsp (last accessed 2 May 2007).

World Bank (2009): World development report, 2009: Reshaping economic geography. Washington, DC.

World Bank (2012): Inclusive green growth: the pathway to sustainable development. Washington, DC.

World Bank (2013): World development report, 2013: Jobs. Washington, DC.

Ernst Ulrich von Weizsäcker

Klaus Töpfer at 75

In 1985, my British friend and colleague Nigel Haigh advised me to meet the Parliamentary State Secretary at the Ministry of the Environment in Rhineland-Palatinate. Returning from America, I had recently become Head of the Institute for European Environmental Policy (IEEP/IEUP: Institut für Europäische Umweltpolitik), and Nigel Haigh was Director of its London branch. So I set off to Mainz in order to meet the much-vaunted advisor. His name was Klaus Töpfer. After just a few minutes I was sure of one thing: I wanted to recruit him for my institute's International Advisory Committee. Although our institute was  highly political, it was party-neutral. And I was a Social Democrat, so I definitely wanted to enlist a Christian Democrat to the board. But he would have to be open-minded, undogmatic, and think internationally. Is there anybody who could be more fitting than Professor Klaus Töpfer? Hardly!

Klaus Töpfer said yes. But soon afterwards he became a minister in his own federal state. And two years later he even became a federal minister in Chancellor Kohl's cabinet. He was therefore no longer able to devote so much time to the IEUP. He was usually represented by his highly competent assistant Cornelia Quennet-Thielen, and that was fine. She later made an illustrious career in the Environment Ministry, Office of the Federal President, and in the Ministry of Education and Science.

As the Federal Environment Minister, Klaus Töpfer probably reached the peak of his popularity with his announcement of the Packaging Ordinance. The public were inspired by the idea that you could simply leave behind unwanted packaging in the shops. This was not even a central aspect of the ordinance, but merely a threat to those companies who refused to pay for the disposal costs. The initially government-controlled Green Dot scheme, known as the German Dual System, was responsible for the actual disposal. The Green Dot on the packaging meant that the manufacturer had paid their dues for the disposal costs. And the collection system using yellow bins and bags ensured that the material was recycled as much as possible. Rather ingenious — if it wasn't for the fact that many households used the yellow bins as convenient overflow containers for residual waste, and some people simply refused to grasp the concept of waste separation. However, none of this diminished the popularity of the minister.

There was one political snag with the Green Dot scheme. Outside of Europe, the system was viewed as protectionist: a Chilean fruit producer felt that he was now forced to buy packaging with the Green Dot in order to comply with the German market. This was although only a fifth of his goods were actually sent to Germany. For the Chileans, the costs did not really provide any benefits. German manufacturers and packing companies, on the other hand, at WORLD TRADE least had the advantage of a precise target audience. The international ORGANIZATION Green Dot dispute was one of the first in which a broad segment of legal practitioners realized that there can be structural contradictions between the environment and free trade. This was, of course, a source of considerable irritation for the proponents of free trade, since they believed—and still do believe—that any liberalization of trade is, by its very nature, good for all. And so, during the Uruguay Round of the GATT (1996–2004), they invented the myth that free trade also served the environment. This myth, which has become a mantra in the World Trade Organization (WTO), was based on two claims: firstly, that environmental technologies would now easily and freely cross borders and, secondly, that free trade would accelerate the development of prosperity and only affluent countries and social strata could afford to worry about the 'luxury' issue of the environment.

The latter claim is, of course, highly problematic at a time when climate, biodiversity, and natural resources are at the forefront of the environmental debate. In these cases, it is clear that affluent societies are mainly responsible for the harm. So if free trade serves prosperity, it would also heighten worries about climate, biodiversity, and resources.

Politically, Klaus Töpfer was also a very important pioneer regarding climate issues. As Federal Environment Minister, he was a congenial supporter of the courageous Bundestag Enquete Commission on Preventive Measures to Protect the Earth's Atmosphere. This confronted the politically active public in Germany and beyond with the new challenges. There was a need for long-term, global ideas and actions that changed structures. Traditional pollution policy, however, was short term, national, and preserved structures. The initiative at the UN for a Convention on Climate Change emerged during Töpfer's tenure as the head of the German Environment Ministry (BMU) and at the time of the Enquete Commission. With the approach of the Earth Summit in Rio de Janeiro (1992), the BMU became a central partner of the German Foreign Office for the first time in its history. Chancellor Helmut Kohl recognized this new challenge and put the climate issue onto the agenda of the G7. In Rio de Janeiro, he also invited the parties to the Framework Convention on Climate Change to Berlin for their first Conference of the Parties.

After an intermezzo as the Federal Minister for Regional Planning, Civil Engineering, and Urban Development (with responsibility for moving the Bundestag and federal institutions from Bonn to Berlin), Klaus Töpfer received probably the most important opportunity of his life: as Executive Director of the United Nations Environment Programme (UNEP) in Nairobi. He became Under-Secretary-General of the United Nations and head of a UN organization with a global remit.

However, conflicts were the rule, not the exception at international environmental conferences, almost always in the form of a North–South dispute. This is particularly evident with the Convention on Biological Diversity (CBD), but — mutatis mutandis — also with climate protection. The North typically wants to implement nature conservation outside of its own territory so as to protect nature from people and their demand for settlements, food, transport, and raw materials. Conversely, the South first of all wants to satisfy exactly that demand and wants the North to limit its own space requirements and to help finance biodiversity protection in the South. The latter refers to the CBD principle of a fair and equitable share of the benefits arising from the utilization of biodiversity for producing, for example, new medicines. Negotiations about that principle have been constantly delayed, ignored, and sabotaged by the North, in particular by the USA, which is not even party to the Convention. US scientists and commercial companies systematically collected biodiversity and then declared the loot to be the property of the US biotechnology companies or botanical gardens. During this time, Klaus Töpfer became one of the leading protagonists for the creation of a CBD anti-biopiracy protocol. It finally came into being in 2010 as the Nagoya Protocol (on access to genetic resources and equitable sharing of benefits), after Töpfer had already left the UNEP. The protocol came very watered-down and very late, pleasing the pharmaceutical and seed giants in the North.

In parallel, a transatlantic dispute has raged between Europe and the USA for decades over the use of precautionary or 'scientific' principles as the legal bases. At first sight, this does not seem to be a contradiction, but it is — particularly for the Americans. They accept ecological constraints only after scientific evidence is established of the alleged damage. We Europeans, on the other hand, have for the last forty years made the precautionary principle a core component of environmental policy: allowing legal constraints upon suspicion of severe damage, meaning to act before it is too late. Precaution marks the trans-Atlantic divide in particular on genetic engineering in agriculture. Relying on scientific evidence can be seen as problematic at a time when the relevant scientific community draws most of its funding from the genetic engineering industry.

Even before assuming office at UNEP, Klaus Töpfer closely familiarized himself with these lines of conflict and, particularly among developing countries, has earned considerable respect as somebody from the North who is absolutely fair when taking into consideration (and, where appropriate, representing) the concerns of the South. In addition, we Europeans were always able to rely on his perspicacity regard-

ing the precautionary principle. Fully in line with the UNEP's mandate, Töpfer would always base his fight for the precautionary principle on the 'Rio Principles' from 1992, which have been signed by all UN member states, including, perhaps inadvertently, by the USA. (Regretting this 'mistake,' the USA tried very hard during the Rio+20 Conference in 2012, to make the Rio Principles obsolete by not reiterating them, but fortunately the guardians from the other side, notably from developing countries, outwitted that attempt.).

UNEP's main task has never been the legislation—that is discussed and fought over by the member states during the international negotiations. Rather, UNEP is mainly concerned with projects that show the South how the environment can be conserved or regenerated while simultaneously improving the economic living conditions of local people.

Töpfer has recorded his insights into the global environmental situation, and in particular into what we Europeans need to do, in a wonderful book entitled 'Arche in Aufruhr' (Ark in Turmoil: Töpfer & Bauer 2007).

He has been back in Germany for some time now, and the German Government has very wisely enabled him to take up a new leading role—at the IASS, the Institute for Advanced Sustainability Studies in Potsdam. Sustainability is the most important issue worldwide. At the aforementioned Rio+20 Conference in 2012, the most important issue was the development of Sustainable Development Goals built upon the Millennium Development Goals that expire in 2015. And, once again, we see the same old familiar themes: climate, biodiversity, resources, and the developing countries' constant desire to catch up with the North in terms of prosperity. Within a short time the IASS has therefore developed into a highly sought-after international partner.

Perhaps it would be expedient for the IASS if the sustainability challenge was formulated constructively: all people want a reasonable level of prosperity. An ecological dictatorship that, based on presumed or proven limits, restricts the lifestyles of people is politically insane. As a consequence, the international competition between nations and companies is essentially geared towards producing as much prosperity as possible. However, it is precisely this competition-driven, blind economic expansion that is leading us headlong into the ecological abyss. We have a chance if we can demonstrate how to increase prosperity while at the same time preventing the exploitation of nature. That is the objective and basic concept behind Factor Five (see von Weizsäcker et al. 2009): reducing the energy requirement of buildings by 80 or 90 percent, reducing the water consumed in agriculture by a factor of five for each kilo of cereal produced, increasing five-fold the recycling rates for hi-tech metals, or drastically reducing the distances involved in the production chain of raincoats or strawberry yogurt—these are all technically achievable goals.

So why is this not done, or only in small measures? Because under the prevailing conditions more profits are made by continuing to waste resources than by stopping this. This is where sustainability policies need to be applied. I am thinking of a policy that makes the consumption of energy, water, and minerals more expensive each year in proportion with the increase in energy or resource efficiency. The cost of resource use then remains stable on average, but from year to year it becomes increasingly lucrative to further improve efficiency and/or reduce waste. The historical model for this proposal has been the Industrial Revolution with its dramatic increase in labor productivity. Whenever productivity increased, the workers were able to command higher wages. And the ping-pong effect continued: the higher wages forced industry to enhance labor rationalization. Following one hundred years of this ping-pong effect, labor productivity increased by a factor of 20!

That is, of course, an oversimplified depiction of the idea. In reality it will be contentious to implement such policies—perhaps a lovely new challenge for people of Klaus Töpfer's stature.

LITERATURE CITED

Töpfer, K., Bauer, F. (2007): Arche in Aufruhr: was wir tun können, um die Erde zu retten. Frankfurt am Main: S. Fischer Verlag.

von Weizsäcker, E.U., Hargroves, K., Smith, M. (2009): Factor Five: Transforming the Global Economy through 80 % Improvements in Resource Productivity. London: Earthscan (Taylor & Francis).

Mario Tobias

Translating Knowledge into Action: How Do Innovative Technologies Enable Sustainability?

Introduction

We live in a globalized world that faces unprecedented challenges. Global phenomena of our time such as rapid climate change, ecosystem imbalances, population growth, demographic change, urbanization, globalized markets, and scarcity of energy and resources pose a major threat to the sustainable development of our planet.

Consequently, we need to find global solutions to all major issues that may jeopardize sustainable development. Advanced research on sustainability matters must be undertaken to identify, evaluate, and implement new perspectives and pathways towards a more sustainable future. Since the influence of national governments in tackling such global issues is limited, the most appropriate approaches need to be found in cooperation with science, industry, and politics. Furthermore, these efforts must involve society at an early stage of knowledge creation in order to ensure public acceptance.

In line with this ambition, the Institute for Advanced Sustainability Studies (IASS) was founded in Potsdam in 2009 to provide research on important sustainability challenges and to stimulate the transfer of sustainability knowledge from scientists to society—under the objective of *translating knowledge into action*. Since then the IASS has been working on fundamental questions of a transformation towards sustainability: What are options for sustainable environmental and resource governance? What are suitable pathways for the transition of energy systems? How can technologies contribute to a circular economy?

A Path to a Circular Economy

In a world approaching 8 billion people, we can no longer afford the overexploitation of resources, or a throw-away society based on oversimplified business models that neglect the relationship between production and the natural environment. Instead, the role model for a sustainable future must be Mother Nature. Nature does not know waste in terms of loss of material or energy; everything is connected and interacts as a system, and resources are thus used in a circular manner. In fact, nature itself invented the principle of recycling. The important question of the 21st century is thus how to properly apply nature's own model of a circular interconnected economy in the organization of our economic processes and the handling of products along the supply chain. The goal must be to deeply embed the circular use of resources within economic reasoning.

Already, some twenty years ago, a sustainable transformation process was initiated in Germany through the establishment of a circular economy replacing the one-way waste treatment of landfilling. During his term as the federal minister of environment, Prof. Klaus Töpfer took a leading role in this implementation of the circular economy concept in the German waste legislation of the 1990s. Although it was initially considered a "crazy German idea," the legislation has proven to be one of the most important achievements of environmental policy in Germany, and an export star. While the introduction of extended producer-responsibility and internalization of costs through the 'polluter pays' principle found little sympathy on the producers' side at first, the perspective on waste has begun to change: In many ways waste has become a valuable resource. The so-called 'lifecycle' or 'cradle to cradle' principle has emerged due to increasing resource scarcity and the resulting need for process innovations, as well as public pressure from environmental stakeholders and general society. Today, the lifecycle approach lays an important foundation for the further implementation of a circular economy.

In this tradition the IASS and its research platform *Enabling Technologies for Sustainability* (ETS) are involved in numerous projects on designing and implementing technological, political, and economic solutions to optimize different circular economies: Existing recycling structures need to be improved to reduce the depletion of resources, while new circles have to be identified to further transmit the ideal of a zero-waste economy.

A Path to Sustainable Technologies

In order to find innovative solutions for urgent problems such as climate change, the destructive exploitation of natural resources, and the scarcity of strategic metals, cutting-edge research is needed to promote transdisciplinary approaches and to develop multidisciplinary networks of scientists from various backgrounds such as civil society, politics, and business. The IASS has already taken important steps in this direction. The ETS platform explores how innovative technologies can support sustainable development of the environment, the economy, and society at large. However, technological innovation by itself does not ensure this development. Innovative products and technological solutions need to be accompanied by a systemic approach that identifies 'sustainable business cases.' Therefore, in accordance with the IASS' mission, the ETS platform collaborates with partners from research institutions, industry, and civil society to determine the potentials of promising technology developments and to evaluate these from a scientific as well as the political and economic perspectives. In its alliances and collaborations, ETS serves as a communicator and partner for knowledge transfer.

Sustainable ICT Solutions:
Transforming e-waste into Valuable Resources

Information and Communication Technology (ICT) has played an important role in fostering the economic growth of all advanced economies. Modern technologies such as computers and mobile devices have rapidly permeated people's lives. Computers, the Internet, mobile phones, data banks, and 'smart networks' all play a vital role in everyday life and will be essential in its future development. ICT products and applications have become inseparable from our daily routine, both in the public domain and in our professional and private lives.

However, these fast-paced technological improvements of information and communications technology have also contributed to the general (over)exploitation of resources. Although our modern everyday lives are unthinkable without these products and appliances, it is not clear whether they are 'part of the problem' or a significant 'part of the solution.' Moore's Law describes the doubling of computing performance approximately every two years, and the resulting consequences such as the shortening of lifecycles. Such increases in performance can be attributed to utilization of new materials and the repeated miniaturization of products. Half a century ago, only a dozen elements were required to satisfy industrial production; today, almost all the elements of the periodic system are required. Contrary to expectations, the reduction in size and weight of electronic goods has not slowed the extraction of natural resources. Production processes might have become less resource-intensive; however, rising sales and increasing affordability have offset the advantages of miniaturization and increased eco-efficiency. Currently, the use of ICT technology causes approximately 2% of the planet's carbon dioxide emissions—which roughly corresponds to the emissions of the global airline industry.

Reducing raw material inputs and increasing resource efficiency are two important requirements for the green transformation of societies, because resource depletion—independent of availability—always has negative ecological and often negative social consequences. Such consequences need to be limited or avoided, e.g., through re-use of electronic e-waste circulating around the world. In general, the sustainable management of resources is an economic necessity for resource-dependent economies such as Germany, which largely depend on the availability of strategic resources in sufficient amounts and at affordable prices.

Hence, to enable information and communication technology for sustainability, a transformation leading to greater resource efficiency by means of a circular economy in the ICT industry is absolutely indispensable. This transformation can only be successful if implemented globally and if best practices are exchanged between countries. Therefore, cooperation is needed between countries with highly developed and efficient recycling infrastructures and those with less developed or unofficially organized systems for recycling.

Carbon Dioxide Utilization Technologies: Rethinking from Waste to Feedstock

Although carbon dioxide (CO_2) has always been part of our atmospheric lifecycle, it has only recently become an issue. As a result of industrialization, the concentration of the greenhouse gas CO_2 in the atmosphere has increased by almost 40 percent in the last 250 years. Overall, atmospheric CO_2 concentration has not reached today's levels for the past 650-thousand years (e.g., Lüthi et al. 2008). Furthermore, the man-made contribution to atmospheric CO_2 levels has accelerated within recent decades. In the most developed countries, including Germany, the largest proportion of CO_2 emissions originates from the energy sector. Nevertheless, a considerable share derives from other industrial processes, such as production in the chemical industry.

However, in certain industrial processes CO_2 has long been considered a resource. In addition to its use in the carbonation of beverages and the production of urea, CO_2 can be utilized as a carbon source in a number of chemical reactions. The element carbon in the form of carbo-hydrogens is one of humankind's major energy sources (e.g., coal, petroleum gas, crude oil, etc.) and also part of many materials that surround us in our everyday life, such as plastics and foams. Due to the volatile prices of fossil fuels, the idea of an alternative carbon source seems convincing. Thus, governments have offered funding and the chemical industry, among others, has been researching so-called 'carbon capture and utilization technologies' (CCU). Major technological breakthroughs have been achieved, especially with regards to the chemical catalysis of CO_2.[1] As a result, in the near future the carbon needed for various chemical products or even renewable fuels could be generated from recycled CO_2 'waste' emissions from industrial plants.

The utilization of carbon dioxide as a feedstock for the chemical industry certainly has striking advantages. Fossil fuel consumption could be reduced, thus helping to preserve the Earth's natural resources and reducing production costs for the industry. By filtering CO_2 from industrial exhausts, emissions can be retarded or, depending on the specific utilization technology, even constantly offset. In particular, highly industrialized countries with limited natural resources (such as Germany) have a vital interest in alternative approaches to meeting the raw material needs of industry and in mitigating political dependencies, as well as positioning their economies within a promising field of emerging technologies with major export potential.

In a broader context, the technological use of CO_2 as a raw material implies not only a change in perspective for the chemical and processing industry but also a necessary change in the approach to waste and resources in general. A material that has been considered a pollutant and a main driver of anthropogenic climate change is currently subject to a process of rethinking, leading it to be rebranded as a valuable asset for our economy. Moreover, developing functions for CO_2 that would other-wise be emitted into the atmosphere is an important step towards closing material lifecycles and a zero-waste society.

The ETS project 'CO$_2$ as an Asset — Potentials and Challenges for Society' is undertaken by a transdisciplinary team to establish the challenges and potentials of such promising technologies. The project focuses on societal aspects of CCU technologies, and aims to evaluate the benefits and risks for society as well as their possible contribution to a circular economy. Therefore, an essential part of the project is the lifecycle analysis of CCU processes and products as well as comparison with conventional products in the chemical industry. This research will be undertaken in cooperation with the university RWTH Aachen. Furthermore, the project is supported by Bayer Material Science as an industry partner.

---

1 Several usage alternatives for CO$_2$ are being explored via research projects at scientific institutions and within industry. The German Ministry of Education and Research is supporting these efforts as part of the 'high-tech-strategy' of the Federal Government.

Change towards sustainable development and a circular economy requires not only decisive measures such as building appropriate infrastructures that incorporate efficient collecting and effective recycling systems, but also the implementation of a political, regulatory, and social framework that supports these technologies. Society at large needs to be involved in the change towards sustainability: producers, dealers, customers, and politicians who need to promote technological improvements and cope with the challenges of a steadily changing environment. Inter- and transdisciplinary approaches that bring together universities, ministries, and industry, and which combine insights from various disciplines such as politics, law, social sciences, economics, geosciences, and engineering science can initiate important new technological developments, stimulate the exchange of ideas, and produce synergies to the benefit of all. Such approaches have already been successfully implemented at the IASS.

Moreover, in accordance with the IASS objective to translate knowledge into action, young people need to be sensitized to the issue of sustainable consumption, for instance with regards to the lifecycle and ecological footprint of electronic devices. Employing young people's interest in mobile devices, the ETS team at the IASS uses an interactive 'Raw Materials Box' to demonstrate the resource intensity of a mobile phone. The box includes nine minerals and ores that are the basic inputs for mobile phone production. The project was part of the 'raw materials expedition' by the German Federal Ministry of Education and Research. It involved approximately 1600 schools all over Germany, and 2000 boxes were sent out to schools and education institutions. The project has received very positive feedback from students and teachers alike, and current demand for the boxes is unremitting. In addition to learning about resource recycling, urban mining, and the basic principles of circular economy, users are also introduced to issues relating to environmentally-friendly product use. Focusing on young people's participation in processes of sustainable development has proven to be a successful and rewarding approach to initiating sustainable development and environmentally-friendly use of resources.

Will carbon capture and utilization (CCU) technologies be considered as an enabling technology for sustainability? It is perhaps too soon to say, but once the promising research results of today are transformed into the business cases of tomorrow, the public and consumers will decide the true potential of these technologies. Politicians will decide about technology funding and tax benefits. Residents will have their say regarding the construction of industrial facilities, pipelines, and other relevant infrastructures. The processing industry will decide between continuing 'the way it used to be' or transforming their facilities and products in line with the requirements of a more sustainable future. And finally, the new products 'made with CO_2' must be brought to market—whether it be a mattress, a car seat from foam plastics containing CO_2, a new jogging shoe, a football with a special coating from CO_2, or an innovative synthetic fuel made with CO_2.

Unfortunately, the successful implementation of innovative technologies is often inhibited by a lack of information from the start of a project, and by the distribution of 'pseudo knowledge' or other emotional obstacles. Acting on the IASS' ambition to translate knowledge into action, research on CCU is therefore accompanied by a wide range of communication activities. While communication challenges within technology innovation is an object of research itself, the project team considers itself an active communicator with stakeholders in business, politics, media, and the general public, and works to establish adequate communication channels with each of these groups. The objective is to enhance knowledge about CCU technologies and their potential advantages and, as a consequence, to soften the path for the successful implementation of a new sustainable technology. Thus, the IASS projects serve as drivers for sustainable innovation and as advocates of sustainable thinking and re-thinking.

An Innovative Pathway
of Transdisciplinary Research and Action

The 2007 Nobel Laureate Symposium 'Global Sustainability—A Nobel Cause' in Potsdam inspired the Alliance of German Science Organizations to found an interdisciplinary, interactive, and international institute for sustainability research: the Institute for Advanced Sustainability Studies (IASS). Due to a mostly specialized and mono-disciplinary research environment, there was a perceived need for new perspectives on the complex challenges of sustainability. Prof. Töpfer was chosen as the founding director of the IASS.

The IASS has since worked successfully on its mission to develop innovative, sophisticated approaches to highly relevant sustainability issues, to make outstanding contributions to scientific progress, and to shape opinions by functioning as a hub for strategic dialogue between researchers, policy makers, businesses, and society. On its way to becoming a high-profile research institute with more than 100 employees from 27 different nations, the IASS has benefited substantially from Prof. Töpfer's broad experiences and his new, innovative, and transdisciplinary approach to research and science. Prof. Töpfer never tires of convincing scientists, business people, policy makers, and civil society of his ideas on sustainability. Instead, he regularly demonstrates his conviction that the learning process must be initiated from civil society, and that creating knowledge is never a one-way road. Just like in a circular economy that preserves resources for future generations, we need to act according to the knowledge we have gained for the sake of the future. Science, politics, and civil society have to interact in order to create a sustainable future for the world.

Translating knowledge into action consequently includes the concepts of creating 'change through knowledge' and gaining new 'knowledge by changing' traditional pathways to the future. Corresponding to the principles promoted by Klaus Töpfer throughout his impressive professional career, and in accordance with his well-known personal convictions, the IASS with Prof. Töpfer as Executive Director fulfills its purpose in its various projects by enabling sustainability and initiating innovative learning processes for new ideas.

LITERATURE CITED

Lüthi, D., Le Floch, M., Bereiter, B., Blunier, T., Barnola, J-M., Siegenthaler, U., Raynaud, D., Jouzel, J., Fischer, H., Kawamura, K., Stocker, T.F. (2008): High-resolution carbon dioxide concentration record 650,000–800,000 years before present. In: Nature 453, 379–382. doi:10.1038/nature06949.

Matthias Kleiner, Caroline A. Lodemann

Science in Democracy—Knowledge Exchange in an Informed Society

Knowledge—A Basic Principle of Life

Knowledge is exchanged almost everywhere at all times. It is an accompanying effect of any communication and interaction. Ever since the exploration of the so-called 'mirror neurons,' it has become evident that certain brain reactions not only occur when performing an action oneself but also when observing others carry out movements or activities. The reactions triggered by simply watching seem to be linked to the goal of the action rather than to its performance. Mirror neurons have been suggested to account for mental traceability and the competence of learning from imitation and repetition (Stamenov & Gallese 2002). Although these findings and their consequences have been discussed controversially until now, we can surely assume that knowledge can find its way from one individual to another at only a glimpse.

In any case—and often without conscious notice, we adopt terms, actions, or ideas that are based upon knowledge of some kind. Indeed, whatever is employed by human beings is at least passively known by them, subsequently by those around them, and then stored as general knowledge for a certain period of time and at a certain place. Remarkably, a lot of financial resources and work time are invested in preserving or regaining lost or obscured knowledge in rather large research projects—to make it available for today's people, for their needs and interests.

However, the term 'exchange' does not exactly meet its intended meaning: Exchange of knowledge does not follow the business model of trade, since knowledge is a good which is not lost to the one who is giving it. Also, he or she might neither notice that something known has just been transferred to another person nor receive anything directly in return. Rather than being compensated in money or material goods, the carrier and donor of knowledge is rewarded by taking an active part in the process of knowledge circulation. In the case of a researcher who regularly publishes their findings, his or her name will be linked to the recorded discoveries and establish a copyright.

When the benefit and potential of natural and spontaneous knowledge exchange was recognized, different organized formats emerged, which support, assure, and control the conservation and use of knowledge. Among those are various network and exchange activities. They range from virtual exchange platforms to meetings that bring people together according to shared characteristics—for example their profession, gender, origin, or a certain intent—where they meet and also exchange related experiences in arranged forms. Whereas it is certainly important and fruitful to use the potential of counterparts and to learn from peers, the criteria applied to construct exchange-groups threaten to impose restrictions on the openness of the discourse.

Knowledge exchange affects science and research in particular. Above all, it is fundamental research and its findings and processes which require record and addressees, since such activity does not lead directly to apparent and available results. The following remarks may count as a statement in favor of open exchange between all individuals in society who are interested in, and in any way reliant on, information—towards a model of knowledge sharing.

Information in Democracy

As the key multipliers of information, the press and media have always been an inherent part of democracies as one important force in a system of checks and balances. They have enabled community members to live and vote responsibly by presenting information in a well-structured format and by deepening the analysis of raw data to contextual information. Thus, the press has also functioned as a filter to distinguish the important from the inconsequential. But as the world increasingly acts on global and virtual levels, information is to be found everywhere, and the individual is confronted with the boon and bane of selecting and classifying facts and figures for themself.

While it is not long ago that households kept standing orders for their (often regional) print newspaper, we are now accustomed to a large variety of global online content providers. It has quickly become an automatic procedure to choose information from different sources for different topics. So today, we face two significant developments: First and paradoxically, there is too much information accessible, and yet information in its bareness is not sufficient. Second, the presence and existing quantities of information covering all possible subjects is not manageable by a single person. At the same time, we currently experience a widening of democratic principles towards what we call participation. Moreover, the availability of information seems to lead to an explicit will of deciding and creating surroundings on subsidiary levels, or at least to involve those who are concerned. People demand accountability for political decisions such as the German Energy Transition, for public construction projects, the spiraling costs of public projects, one postponement after the other; and what is new: they do it 'as they go along' or even in advance. Political processes are not just acquiesced to or consumed as decisions from 'those up there.' In the case of natural disasters, environmental and climatic changes, people ask for guidelines and insight. Legitimately, they want to know what they must adapt to and what they can do for the benefit and well-being of society. They want to be able to challenge and judge policy strategies.

Democracy has always meant civil contribution. But as the availability of information increases, citizen engagement and involvement seem to grow proportionally and, at the same time, to bring up further needs for additional information and contextualization. Often enough, people have the feeling of 'knowing nothing' about the real backgrounds of developments and events. Who and what can be trusted and relied on? This interdependency between the free access to information and the requirements for orientation in our complex world needs to be balanced in order that information becomes practicable knowledge to as many people as possible—and this means: not less than all people. This is the desideratum.

Democracy is not only based on the division of powers, but on the division of tasks corresponding to expertise and abilities. This is where science and research also play a vital role: they already function as another form of power adjacent to the legislative, the executive, the judiciary, and the media in modern democratic state forms. Scientists and researchers not only work within interdisciplinary settings; moreover, they operate transdisciplinarily and invite other stakeholders in society to gain insight into their undertakings.

Besides all serious purpose, science and research, for instance, also carry out an entertaining function, such as through 'Nights of Science' held in many German cities, and via exhibitions, 'Science Slams,' and 'Kids Universities,' science becomes tangible. It delights and teaches at the same time. This rather ancient rhetorical maxim transferred to today's publicly financed research guides us to put the aim of well-being and development at the center of all activity, and to judge its success by the felicitous effect on the recipient. This again means: on all of us.

Science and Research in Democracy

What do these aspects imply for the role of science and research in democracies, or those who aspire to democratic systems in today's world? Science and research are sometimes still perceived and treated as a distinct sphere beside society. It might not be by coincidence that they share the destiny of being viewed as an important, yet self-dependent 'stranger' with the similarly autonomous branch of press and media. Of course, press and media are independent in content and choice of topic, but the position of science and research is—and ought to be—at the center of society. Also, both capacities are strongly associated with society, since the practice and activities of neither science and research nor press and media end in themselves. Yet, the informational function is not sufficient to describe their area of responsibility.

One of the coordinates which define their central position is quite simple, if not amusingly trivial: strange though it may sound, scientists (as well as journalists) are indeed citizens at the same time. The image of the professor absorbed in and surrounded by books, or living in a laboratory, no longer serves even as a fictional figure. In fact, these 'scientist–citizens' live in the same world as everybody else. Scientists have families, friends, and hobbies, drive cars or use trains and planes, grow plants, take part in politics; they witness global developments, experience cultural events, and natural disasters just as everybody else. And just as everybody else, scientists communicate with those around them. They talk about their work, they gain ideas and comments from others, and they discuss what they are engaged in.

It is this joint world from which questions derive and initiate research, and to where the answers return via direct or indirect paths. Thus, rather than reducing knowledge exchange to the transfer of activities from one field to another—most commonly from basic to applied research—knowledge exchange in an informed, science-based society involves more: This communication is permanent and is not bound to certain events or conference dates dedicated to networking and discussions. Research facilities of any kind are not hermetically sealed. Through these mechanisms, the continual and natural dialogue and closeness of 'scientific agents' is assured. Above personal integration, we encounter scientific findings in everything we turn to. We profit from such insights and use the results when they reach us as a product, provide evidence, or when they inform a political decision. This omnipresence might deserve greater awareness and appreciation. Then again, taking it for granted also demonstrates how scientific accomplishments are naturally incorporated within our lives today, and that they would leave a gap if excluded in the future.

Nevertheless, more and consciously-practiced forms of interchange are desirable—for example through direct communication in public hearings, round tables, and open discussions. The notion of a 'dialogue' between research and politics does not fit here, and is purposely avoided: in the aftermath of the terrible nuclear catastrophe at Fukushima and its continuing effects, it is the whole net of communication which has grown between the different stakeholders and even reaches out across national borders when, for example, members of the Science Council of Japan investigate the applicability of German measures to Japan. Thus, it becomes evident that exchange in an informed society is not only permanent but also universal, and can cover collectives as well as single persons. Seen in this light, knowledge exchange is a non-stop conversation in which anyone who wants to get involved can do so at any time.

Hence, we also need to be aware that the migration of knowledge is not a one-way process. Even between basic and applied research, as mentioned above, the direction is not solely from fundamental insights towards application; rather, by empirically testing theoretical concepts and by developing innovations, new questions arise that feed back to those engaged in more fundamental research. In this way, research can grow to be an interactive process and overcome the sometimes obstructive categorizations of any kind. Donald E. Stokes (1997) has strengthened this approach by marking 'Pasteur's quadrant,' where both fundamental and applied approaches to research gather and amalgamate to form a joint research interest and process. A similar openness is possible not only among research fields, but also among different players in national societies as well as beyond national borders. Of course, there has constantly been interaction between policy makers and researchers, which varies in its intensity according to the topic and time period.

It is an integral component of the researcher's work to publish their results in order to disseminate and discuss them, challenge them, and have them verified by others. This inner-scientific mode of conduct becomes increasingly expanded in transdisciplinary formats. Other than within strictly scientific contexts, researchers provide citizens, politicians, and public stakeholders with information to enable opinion formation, decision making, and the definition of possible approaches or even solutions. On the one hand, researchers make an offer to present their findings, which might be of interest and value to specific groups or the wider society. Open conferences, exhibitions, talks, and discussions serve this function. On the other hand, researchers are invited not only to present academic findings but to take an active part in societal developments. This happened, for example, in the course of the German 'Energy Turnaround' in 2011, when the German Government assigned the Ethics Commission for a Safe Energy Supply to chaperone the decision on the future of Germany's nuclear power plants and energy supply. The commission was composed as a mirror to society: apart from scientists, also business people, church representatives, and politicians—in some cases combined in one person—worked together on recommendations.

When researchers are asked to lead and support multifaceted decision procedures it is most likely not only with regard to their thematic expertise but also because of their methods and modes. Research follows clear principles, and those who conduct research pursue objectivity, honesty, and complete data before categorizing and judging a situation and drawing conclusions. Researchers are trained in the handling of serious information in a constructive manner, in criticizing and being criticized on a factual level, as well as being confronted with conflicting data. Especially in highly emotional issues—such as energy supply, the building, reconstruction, or expansion of public facilities such as airports and stations that affect many people, and the disbursement of tax incomes—these typical scientific virtues seem to ensure dependable and fair treatment. Yet, it would be a false or overhasty conclusion to believe that the involvement of researchers is based only on an assumed independence or neutrality. Their knowledge and insight strive for a more detailed and deeper exploration of the topic in question—even more so in order to ultimately gain firm conviction. Of course—and this is where reciprocity comes in—research itself needs to nourish its place at the center of society: that is, first of all, by speaking in common terms. No research, however ingenious it may be, can ever be better than its elucidation and accessibility to those who are referred to as the 'interested public.' Researchers and their institutions need to open up and foster a special culture of welcome. Secondly, it is the people's competence which nurtures scientific progress and research interests. Everyday experience inspires ideas. All-day practice and testing lead to advancement and stimulate new fields of investigation.

The interaction between developers, enterprises, policy, and research institutions on one hand, and the public on the other hand is sometimes limited to 'public relations' exercises, in which profiles and mission statements are presented and selected information is given. The admittance of comments by costumers and users then occurs in the context of a 'service.' But with more, faster, and better access to information as well as the opportunity to express opinions and deposit them in online-forums, for example, citizens are now in the position to take a more active, self-determined role at eye-level with expert groups. Nevertheless, this desirably strengthened civilian position does not lay the ground for a duty to report on any side. Greater awareness of those around us does not create a right to interfere. This applies to all civil participants, since an open conversation is not to be mistaken for general access to one another's material or even the adequacy of a 'know-it-all' attitude.

The democratic principle of subsidiarity guarantees self-administration—for instance, to develop and advance the codes of conduct within academic contexts. Lately, we have experienced a sometimes rather unconstructive and awkward discussion about scientific misconduct arising from a very few but prominent cases. This circumstance beset the handling of the parties involved and could not contribute much to the inner-professional discussion. Thus, excessive or misunderstood openness can become an obtrusiveness, which illustrates the other side of the coin. The solution lies in a respectful and constructive claim of others' insights as well as a wise placement of one's knowledge. In this sense, researchers will not themselves take decisions on behalf of others, but instead supply their knowledge—as needed and requested—to those who take these decisions. From their perspective, only assured and comprehensible knowledge is adequate to be presented to a greater audience.

The occasions and reasons for seeking scientific understanding are multiple, and vary from the need for existing data (and conclusions to be drawn from it) to commissioned research for the benefit of society and its essentials. Occurrences such as natural disasters or unexpected criminal acts make us turn to science to find explanations and insights, to heal damage and losses, and to prevent or at least to prepare for possible repetitions. This range of different requirements is reflected by the differentiated research system in Germany, which equilibrates the scientific stakeholders and institutions covering society's approaches, from basic research to mission-oriented research.

Exchanging and Sharing

In view of resource shortages, climate change, and rising costs, the development of local participation is accompanied by a growing culture of sharing. Car- and bike-sharing schemes have been commonly commercialized in larger cities for quite some time. In the meantime, a whole 'sharing-economy' has emerged, ranging from food-sharing, clothes-sharing, and garden-sharing to apartment-sharing and book-sharing.

There are two basic models of civilian participation nowadays—and things to learn from both their elementary constellations. In the private model there is, on the one hand, an owner who is responsible for a possession. The owner decides if and when to dispense the property for a certain period of time, sets the conditions for delivery and use, and in return receives a reward that simultaneously serves as an assurance; the other side of the scenario involves someone with a temporary need, who is willing to accept and meet the set criteria. Their motives interlock in an 'individual sharing.' In the case of food, the primary motivation of the original owner might be less of a financial interest than the conviction of not wanting to waste anything which could be of (even existential) value to someone else. The business-driven version places for public disposal those goods that are needed on larger and less individual scales. Many users share with one another in a collective manner. Again, this is based on a mutual understanding and the observation of directions for use.

How does knowledge as an uncountable, abstract factor fit into this model? Can any of the proposed models serve for the common property of knowledge? Both can and both already do: On the one hand, there is such detailed knowledge as needs to be specified between at least two or possibly finite groups of partners before being transferred. This expert knowledge must meet a certain demand or answer a relevant question. It may be an intermediate step or fill a gap in research. In this capacity, it does not need publicity and as the public does not need single pieces of the puzzle vice versa. Highly technical and specialized data require contextualization and explanation. It is the complete picture, answers, or products that may be of crucial interest and importance. This is what trustworthy division of labor according to competence is all about.

On the other hand there is, of course, knowledge that belongs to the general public—even more so against the background of democratic principles. Furthermore, it is important that its distribution is secured by collectively accessible channels and media so that relevant data becomes well known and part of daily discussions rather than depending on both constricted and constricting arrangements. Therefore, knowledge exchange may take place between experts and institutions who can define their direct and purposive necessity of information. Within society, we may make knowledge widely available to each other, as our understanding of sharing suggests.

However, sharing knowledge not only derives from the current movement towards sharing individual possessions and use. It also refers to the term 'commons,' which Elinor Ostrom (1990) convincingly addressed in her major work, 'Governing the Commons: The Evolution of Institutions for Collective Action' for which she received the Nobel Memorial Prize in Economic Sciences in 2009. Together with Charlotte Hess, she applied the model of the 'commons,' which she had originally developed from analyzing natural and environmental resources, to knowledge. Together, they hosted a workshop and subsequently edited the publication 'Understanding Knowledge as a Commons: From Theory to Practice' (Hess & Ostrom 2007), which is built upon the simple notification of knowledge as a "resource shared by a group of people" (Hess & Ostrom 2007, p. 7). Hess and Ostrom investigate conditions and changes related to digital technologies and their effects on access to information in today's world. They present 'A Framework for Analyzing the Knowledge Commons,' which offers categories to handle the differences between knowledge and physical resources. Accordingly, knowledge appears in facilities, as artifacts or ideas (Hess & Ostrom 2007, p. 47). Libraries, archives, and digital distribution channels of information count as facilities, whereas artifacts are the records of ideas such as books, articles, webpages, and so forth. Ideas are defined as the underlying thoughts, visions, or conceptions which are not concretely or explicitly mentioned but are contained in artifacts. Consecutively, the authors assess the group as the community sharing the resource. The framework suggests a differentiation between users, providers, and managers on a functional level (Hess & Ostrom 2007, p. 48).

Borrowing these considerations and transferring them to democratic cultures illustrates the central role of science and research: scientists and researchers use, give, and administer knowledge, and thus they belong to each group simultaneously. It is their profession which establishes this functional union and their preferential responsibility for knowledge. Prior to the manifestations of knowledge and its classification stands conviction: in an informed society, scientists and researchers are appointed the custodians of knowledge as a publicly shared good.

LITERATURE CITED

Hess, C., Ostrom, E. (2007): Understanding Knowledge as a Commons. From Theory to Practice. Cambridge, MA: The MIT Press.

Ostrom, E. (1990): Governing the Commons: The Evolution of Institutions for Collective Action. Cambridge: Cambridge University Press.

Stamenov, M.I., Gallese, V. (2002): Mirror Neurons and the Evolution of Brain and Language. Amsterdam: John Benjamins Publishing Co.

Stokes, D.E. (1997): Pasteur's Quadrant: Basic Science and Technological Innovation. Washington, DC: Brookings Institution Press.

Initiating
Transitions

_____

Carlo Rubbia

Innovative Scientific and Technological Developments for a Coherent Energy Policy

Traditionally, science and associated technologies have been essential elements in human development. In the presently emerging Anthropocene Era, an equally essential role will be played by science and technology in ensuring the sustainability of mankind and the planet, and in particular to ensure that adequate energy, water, and food will be widely available in the future.

Anthropocene activities are producing irreversible effects that must be urgently curbed in order to avoid the consequences of a major climatic change of large proportions and of widely unknown consequences. Since the beginning of the Industrial Revolution, about 1000 gigatons (Gt: one million, million tons) of carbon dioxide (CO_2) have been added to the atmosphere. How many of us know that the mean lifetime of the emitted CO_2 is about 30-thousand years? As a comparison, the lifetime of plutonium-239, associated with today's public perception of nuclear energy, is 26-thousand years. The immense longevity of CO_2 has been widely overlooked by many politicians, decision makers, and the public at large.

Stability of the climate is a necessary premise for human life and, in the hope to reconcile such continued growth of CO_2 emissions with measures to limit global warming, it is fundamental to explore a number of different technological options. One possibility is constituted by Carbon Capture and Sequestration (CCS): substantial underground or sub-seabed storage of CO_2. In our view, this alternative—even neglecting its considerable cost—is insufficient. Sequestration is not elimination; only a limited fraction of the otherwise accumulated 1000 gigatons of CO_2 may offer a potential recovery; we would need to ensure that CO_2 wells were safely sealed under pressure for many thousands of years; and the potential degradation of wells and subsequent leakage of CO_2 has major implications for long-term safety, since even slightly elevated CO_2 levels can be highly toxic, and can induce dilation of cerebral arteries leading to potentially fatal intra-cranial pressure.

Another hypothetical method for reduction of anthropogenic greenhouse gases is so-called geo-engineering, which is based on continuously injecting sulfur in the form of sulfur dioxide (SO_2) aerosols into the lower stratosphere at a relatively modest level of a few million tons/year, which is approximately equal to 1/1000 of the CO_2 emitted: this would produce a very large, compensatory cooling effect world-wide, for a brief period during the time of injection. However, the injection of SO_2 into the stratosphere is potentially extremely hazardous, with many adverse effects including disrupting the Asian and African summer monsoons, thereby reducing precipitation and food supply for billions of people.

So far, all practical attempts to limit increases in greenhouse gas emissions via additional ad-hoc compensatory effects have failed for a number of reasons. More efficient and environmentally friendly utilization of fossils fuels, and the development and progressive utilization of renewable energy sources therefore appear as the only—and urgent—options towards the reduction of anthropogenic emissions and seriously curbing environmental changes.

The conversion of fossil energy while achieving reduced emissions is one of the most important technological challenges of our times. As an example, concerted research is being undertaken on new methods that may achieve what presently appears to be a "dream," namely producing energy from fossil sources but without CO_2 emissions. The actual process is the spontaneous thermal decomposition, at sufficient temperature, of methane into hydrogen and black carbon. This, the so-called cracking of methane without the production of CO_2, generates no less energy than the existing reforming processes that, however, produce as much as 4 tons of CO_2 for each ton of hydrogen. The resulting black carbon can either be sequestered or sold on the market as a material commodity, as it has abundant commercial applications as a filler or construction material. The absence of CO_2 in this new process is the main attraction and reason for its development. Specific pre-industrial development is ongoing as a collaborative effort between our Institute (IASS) and leading German research institutions.

Another promising alternative is replacing oil (petroleum) with the help of the so-called "methanol economy," originally conceived by the Nobel Laureate George Olah, in which the use of hydrogen (H_2) is combined with already spent CO_2 (recovered from a previous utilization) in order to generate a liquid fuel in the form of methanol. Methanol, like the well-known ethanol from biofuels, is a convenient liquid fuel for transportation. Methanol can also be readily converted into many other industrial chemicals like ethylene, propylene, and others. The simple equation is: Carbon dioxide already emitted + hydrogen to liquid methanol.

The progressive de-carbonization of our global energy systems, which are currently largely based on fossils, necessarily passes through a stage involving the increased use and consumption of natural gas (NG). Vast additional amounts of unconventional NG are becoming exploitable, for instance as shales and clathrates. The previously mentioned alternative process of converting NG into hydrogen and black carbon is crucial in generating adequate energy from fossil sources with little or no CO_2 emissions.

The massive introduction of the inexhaustible renewable energies based either directly or indirectly on the Sun (wind, biomass, solar and so on) has witnessed remarkable progress and is advancing quite rapidly: but will renewable energies alone be able to bridge the gap at a rate quick enough to ultimately maintain global warming within the reasonable limits of, for instance, 2 °C? Two main problems must be tackled. The first is cost: the cheapest energy is always the best energy. The cost of renewable energies must be substantially reduced. The second is availability: energy must be available whenever it is needed. The intermediate storage of the produced renewable energy is a necessity that urgently demands new solutions.

It is evident that, in order to reconcile sustainable development and economic growth with the threat of environmental decay, a coherent energy policy is required, and that strategic choices must be based on truly innovative scientific and technological developments. They should play an important role in fostering, at the global level, the essential fundamental breakthroughs and in catalyzing innovation. Only through such a concentrated and coordinated effort can leadership be targeted and the objectives of creating high-quality employment opportunities and a better quality of life be met.

These goals have been successfully met already in a number of other domains, from health to mobility, from IT to nanotechnologies. But in the case of the threats associated with the emergence of the Anthropogenic era, the question persists: Whether mankind will have the common political will to act and reach the understanding necessary to recognize the urgency of avoiding these threats? These are new, global problems that humanity has, so far, been poorly equipped to handle. This is why society and the public at large have become essential actors in building the forms of resource-efficient growth and development that are so badly needed for our long-term survival.

The human capital of the most educated society is a decisive factor in establishing norms of social conduct. We must recognize the duty to society in terms of long-term actions rather than immediate interests.

In a world in which *numerical growth may become decoupled from scientific development* it is unclear whether humanity will take up the challenge or might instead evolve along a path of slower development that could lead to stagnation and decay.

Laurence Tubiana,
Andreas Rüdinger, Thomas Spencer

———————————

Evolution of the Energy Transition in Germany, France, and Europe: A Process in the Making

Political Debates and Strategies on Energy and Climate Policy in France and Germany

This article provides an exploratory study on the role of public debates and stake-holder consultations in the policy process of the energy transition in France, Germany, and the EU. The energy transition is a highly complex, multifaceted, and long-term project, and therefore allows room for different discursive framings and policy options. The article shows how the deliberative process and the struggle over meaning have affected the orientation of the energy transition in both France and Germany. The final section addresses the issue of policy coordination between national strategies in the quest for an integrated European framework.

The Energy Transition:
A 'Moving Target' in the Policy Debate

The transition to a low-emissions, sustainable energy system is unquestionably one of the main challenges of the 21st century. However, despite widespread consensus on the urgency of this transformation and its overarching objective (achieving a low-carbon economy by 2050), the energy transition can be qualified as a 'moving target,' in the sense that the various political and discursive framings of the issues at stake can imply very different policy approaches and choices. This partly explains the discursive battle over the framing of the energy transition debate within a matrix composed of various and sometimes conflicting objectives: climate change, energy security, competitiveness, energy poverty, green growth, decentralization, and local ownership to name just a few. One can easily identify the impact of these different discursive framings within the orientations of strategies for national energy transition adopted by several EU member states (PBL 2012). The strong emphasis on climate change in the UK, for example, is one factor that explains its current strategy based on a strong carbon price, development of low-carbon power sources such as nuclear and off-shore wind, electrification, and energy savings. In Germany, the energy transition was largely triggered by the nuclear phase-out and mainly focuses on the power sector. However, long-term objectives include a drastic decrease of greenhouse gas emissions by 2050 (80–95%) and a strong (50%) reduction in primary energy consumption by 2050. In Denmark, the recently adopted 2050 strategy is mainly framed in terms of energy independence from fossil fuels and is largely supply-side oriented, whereas energy savings play a rather minor role.[1]

The Role of Public Debates for the Energy Transition

Since energy policy has long been considered a matter for the state and was exclusively linked to the objectives of energy security and affordability, broad public debates on energy policy are relatively new. This first began to change in the 1970s with the emergence of environmental movements, providing a new framing of energy policy in terms of technological and environmental risks. The rise of the anti-nuclear movement in several European countries, and their rapid evolution from local, site-specific initiatives to national movements is certainly one of the most striking examples, although their impact on policy implementation has been very different depending on national institutional systems (Fach & Simonis 1987; Kitschelt 1986). More recently, the rise of climate change as a broader concern for policy makers considerably reinforced the nexus between environmental and energy policy.

Moving one step further, in recent years the all-embracing concept of an 'energy transition' has attempted to grasp the nexus between environmental, social, and economic concerns and challenges around our energy systems, as embodied in the title of the European 2020 strategy for *"competitive, sustainable and secure energy"* (Vasileiadou 2012; European Commission 2010). Because of its nature as a multifaceted strategy and the role of energy systems within modern societies, the energy transition affects all sectors of society. This increases complexity while also opening a policy arena for various stakeholders with largely different interests—some complementary, some conflicting. Another layer of complexity is added through the nexus between the techno-

---

1 The energy strategy 2050 includes a rather modest objective for energy efficiency: reducing primary energy consumption by 6% by 2020 compared to 2006, whereas France and Germany have a –20% objective. However, in relative terms (per capita, per unit of GDP), Denmark is already among the leaders worldwide.

cratic and expert approach to energy and environmental issues on the one hand, and on the other the necessary social construction of the meaning of such a transition within our society, referring to specific social, cultural, and political values.

Deliberative processes and stakeholder consultations fulfill multiple functions in the public debate on the energy transition. First, they help to define a common vision, based on pluralist knowledge and assessments of the challenges, risks, and possible solutions. The second aspect refers to the gradual shift from a technocratic to a democratic governance model, implying that the traditional science–politics interface has to include interaction with stakeholders and the public in order to improve the legitimacy of specific policy choices through a larger ownership and interconnection with societal values (Bäckstrand 2003). A third dimension is linked to the notions of complexity and uncertainty, which are particularly high within the context of the energy transition, given the timescale (three to four decades) in addition to the interactions (and pace thereof) between technological and societal change. This requires interdisciplinary approaches to qualify the uncertainties and risks associated with specific policy measures and prospective assessments, in order to provide a solid basis for decision making (Renn 2008).

However, the nature of the deliberative process itself can be subject to critical assessment, referring primarily to the degree of institutionalization: does the consultation process integrate existing channels of communication and lobbying, or does it create a new and potentially more formalized structure to enhance transparency? How can equal participation be guaranteed between actors with different resources, knowledge, and means of influence? Does the process provide strong mechanisms to ensure the linkage between the output of the deliberative process and policy making?

The following case studies illustrate how these different dimensions and questions are taken into account in recent public debates and strategies on the energy transition in France and Germany. Given the scope of the article, the aim is not to present an exhaustive analysis of German and French energy policy from a historical perspective, but rather to assess the recent public debates and their outputs via a comparative and exploratory approach in order to identify the respective lessons for policy making from these deliberative processes.

The German Energy Debate
in the Context of the Nuclear Issue

German energy policy has been crucially shaped by the conflicting debate on the use of nuclear power, qualified by sociologist Jochen Roose (2010) as one of the greatest techno-political conflicts within Germany in the last 40 years. As a direct consequence, the main framing of the public debate on energy policy has been shaped by conflicting assessments and political polarization regarding the reality and accept-ability of risks linked to nuclear power (Mez et al. 2010). Based on this initial fram-ing, other environmental and political issues (acid rain, nuclear proliferation, climate change) have been connected to reinforce this core rather than replacing it, as was observed in other countries, considering in particular the climate change / nuclear nexus (Bickerstaff et al. 2008). Furthermore, it is interesting to note that the con-cept of the Energiewende (Energy Transition) itself—generally attributed to the 2011 post-Fukushima decisions, is almost as old as the nuclear debate: the first study on the *"Energiewende—growth and prosperity without oil and nuclear power"* was published by the Öko-Institut as early as 1980.

Another particularity of the German debate relates to how economic actors have been included in policy-making processes. For example, the agreement reached between power utilities and unions in 2000 was critical to the success of the 2002 reform of the Nuclear Energy Act, and more broadly to the emergence of a positive discourse relating to the economic opportunities of the energy transition. It can thus be seen that Germany had an established practice of deliberative policy making, and that the nuclear issue crystalized stakeholder engagement in energy policy from quite an early stage.

The Ethics Commission:
A Novelty in the German Energy Debate

With the adoption of the 'Energiekonzept' in September 2010, the 2009-elected CDU–FDP coalition also pushed forward its new reform of the Nuclear Act, aim-ing for a general prolongation (8 to 14 years) of the lifetimes of existing reactors. The main rationale was to use nuclear power as a 'bridging technology,' to achieve climate targets and the expansion of renewables at the lowest costs possible but without put-ting into question the objective of a definitive phase-out (and the energy transition per se). Although the reform had already been adopted by Parliament, the news of the Fukushima accident brought a rapid policy change. While the political reaction to the Chernobyl accident resulted in significant policy adjustments (most notably with the creation of the Federal Ministry for Environment headed by Klaus Töpfer), the political turnaround in 2011 was unprecedented in its pace and the political consensus it generated on the implementation of the Energiewende.

Within this process, the Ethics Commission, established on 22 March 2011 by Chancellor Merkel and headed by former Environment Minister and UNEP Director Klaus Töpfer, represents an important innovation within the German energy policy debate, both in its configuration and the new framing it gave to the issue of energy transition. Regarding its composition, the Ethics Commission gathered former min-isters from different parties, academics, industrial actors, and representatives of the

Church within a novel structure that respected the breadth of attitudes to nuclear power. The framing was innovative in the sense that the mandate included not only a techno-political assessment (on the feasibility and possible risks regarding other policy objectives), but also the ethical and societal aspects of possible decisions.

Qualifying the German Debate in its Historical and Current Dimension

Based on this short assessment, it appears that the German energy transition debate benefitted from its early and rather broad foothold within civil society, leading to a strong politicization of the nuclear issue and of energy policy more generally. While this debate rapidly became an electoral issue, it is remarkable that there was no stakeholder consultation process involving all actors, but rather a strategic dialogue between specific stakeholders and the government through existing channels of communication. In this process, the Ethics Commission represented a novelty—a dedicated structure for deliberative policy making, and was innovative in terms of its composition and its framing of the energy issue, taking into account both technical considerations and the ethical question of risk perception and acceptability.

In terms of substance, this evolution might explain why the German energy transition debate remains largely focused on transformation of the power sector in general and the nuclear/renewables trade-off in particular, as evidenced by the recent public debates on the costs and possible reforms of the support mechanisms for renewable energies. Despite a large consensus on the importance of climate change, and the fact that Germany adopted one of the most ambitious long-term climate change strategies, it is striking how little such issues as transport decarbonization and the phase-out of coal have been politicized and debated. This is all the more significant since both coal and the automobile industry count among the main industrial anchors of the German economy, and since both factors are key to the German energy transition strategy.

The General Context of French Energy Policy

The historical organization of French energy policy has been influenced by the centralized structure of the state. This can be traced back to the reform of the energy sector in 1946, establishing national public monopolies and utilities in all energy sectors. This architecture was further reinforced with the rapid expansion of nuclear power since the 1970s, which presently represents up to 75 % of power generation. In the context of the public organization of the energy sector and the relatively low politicization of energy issues, wider stakeholder debates on energy policy have a relatively recent history, partly linked to the European policy framework around the integration and liberalization of energy markets, and considerations linked to climate and environmental policy. In 2007 a first broad stakeholder consultation process was initiated (the Grenelle Summit) to define concrete sectoral targets related to energy and environmental policy. However, the segmentation of topics, the fact that some issues were not included (nuclear energy in particular), and the medium-term horizon (up to 2020) hindered a broader and more integrated debate on the energy transition as a long-term process.

The 2012–2013 National Debate on the Energy Transition

Based on this legacy, a comprehensive debate on the energy transition in France was announced by the recently elected President François Hollande. Formally launched at the Environmental Conference of September 2012, the debate integrated several important innovations, both in its configuration and substance.

The Institutional Set-up of the Debate

To reinforce the legitimacy of this debate, a comprehensive institutional structure was created ad hoc, as shown in Figure 1. As the centerpiece, the National Council gathered a total of 112 participants from seven stakeholder groups: employers, labor

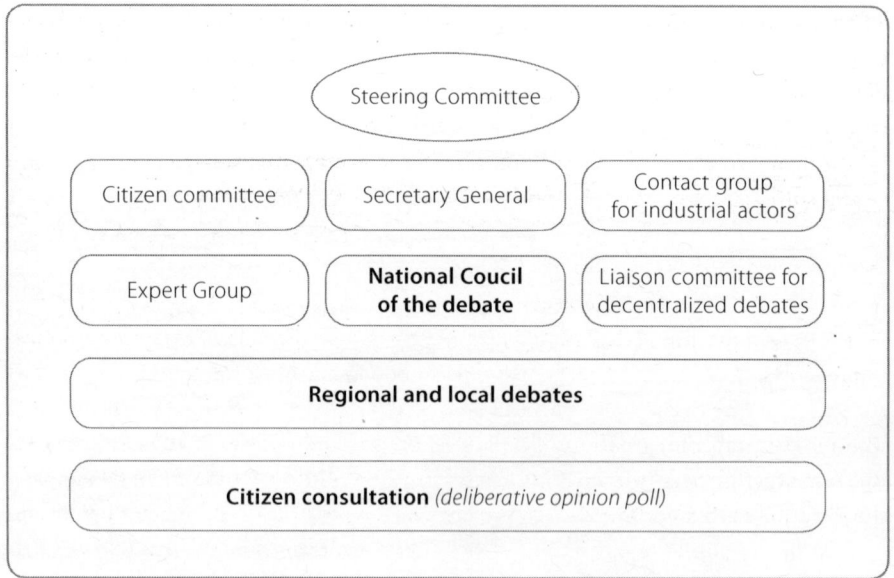

Figure 1: *The institutional framework of the French debate on the energy transition.*

Laurence Tubiana, Andreas Rüdinger, Thomas Spencer

unions, environmental NGOs, local representatives, national and European MPs, state institutions, and a college regrouping several other federations.[2] The steering committee, chaired by the Environment Minister and composed of six other members (including the main facilitator of the debate) was charged with the supervision of the debate and coordination between different institutions. A Secretary General was appointed to lead the operational management of the debate. An interdisciplinary and pluralist expert group (academics, industrial actors, high-level administration) was established to support the work of the National Council, whereas the Citizen Committee (composed of 21 citizens without particular expertise on energy issues) was mandated to give feedback on the clarity and intelligibility of the debate for the wider public. Specific contact groups were organized to facilitate mediation with industrial actors and the organization of decentralized debates. In parallel to the national debate, which lasted from November 2012 to July 2013, a total of 850 local and regional debates were organized across France. Furthermore, a deliberative opinion poll of 1100 citizens (applying the method of the World Wide Views project used for the Copenhagen Climate Summit of 2009) was organized on 25 May 2013 in collaboration with the Danish Board of Technology, to develop a better understanding of the public perceptions and expectations linked to the energy transition.

The Framing of the French Energy Transition Debate

Similar to the diversity of its participants, the substantial framing was established in an equally broad manner, seeking to: Define a common vision on the energy transition, and specific recommendations for the subsequent general law establishing the French policy for the energy transition. Based on this framing, the approach used to structure the debate focused on four issues:

- The demand-side perspective around energy consumption, energy needs, efficiency, and sufficiency as a main entry point to the debate;
- The definition and analysis of long-term energy trajectories and their implications until 2025, 2030, and 2050;
- Strategic and industrial choices on renewable energies and energy technologies;
- The economic impact of the energy transition: financing instruments, benefits, and costs.

The main innovation clearly derived from the fact that the demand-side perspective was established at the heart of the debate in order to avoid the risk of blocking the debate due to a confrontation between conflicting visions on nuclear power and

---

2   The last college included consumer associations, smaller business federations, and NGOs from the social sector.

renewables. This approach was also meant to enable a wider reflection on the evolution of energy demand, including not only the technical and economic potential for energy efficiency but also a broader reflection on energy sufficiency, lifestyles, and the evolution of our society as a whole.

Besides these structural questions, existing French policy objectives and commitments provided a quite precise framing for the definition of long-term visions, including:

* The previous orientation law on energy policy (2005), which adopted the objective of a 75% reduction of greenhouse gas (GHG) emissions by 2050 and a target for the reduction of energy intensity by a rate of 2% (2.5% after 2015) per year;
* French objectives within the European 2020 energy and climate package, including the national target for renewables (23% of final consumption), energy efficiency (20% reduction in final consumption), and GHG emissions (20% reduction);
* Presidential commitment to reduce the share of nuclear energy from 75% to 50% of total power generation.

Process and Outcome of the French Debate

While it is certainly too early to qualify the success or failure of this debate from the political and environmental perspectives (given that the adoption of the orientation law is expected in 2014), some initial conclusions can be drawn at this point.

In terms of participative methods, this debate represents an innovative approach within the French context. The inclusion of both stakeholders and the wider public within a comprehensive dialogue represents a challenge that has been tackled rather successfully. The political momentum generated by the combination of several participative approaches, including stakeholder dialogues, the citizen committee, and deliberative opinion polls may not be directly apparent in the final report, but will certainly have an impact on the political debate in the longer term.

In terms of substance, the economic dimension clearly dominated the debate as a main discursive framing, both in relation to the current economic and budgetary crisis and its impact on French politics. Similarly to the German debate, this led to a structural tension regarding the economic risks associated with the transformation of the existing power system and the general level of ambition regarding the energy transition in the short term. Unlike the German debate, however, this economic framing was not complemented by a structural assessment of technological and environmental risks. More interestingly, despite the tension over possible evolutions of the energy mix and the issue of nuclear power, the debate helped establish demand-side policies as the main lever of the energy transition towards a low-carbon economy. Although starting from a technical perspective on the economic and technical potentials of energy efficiency, this reflection also included the dimension of energy sufficiency from the individual and collective perspectives, leading to a broader discussion on the linkages between energy, economic growth, and prosperity.

Surprisingly—and similarly to the German debate—the issue of mobility and transport was rather neglected within the debate, despite its structural impact on energy consumption, greenhouse gas emissions, urban planning, and citizen's lifestyles.

The French and German Energy Debates in Perspective

While different in their configuration and framing of the issue, both the German and French debates provide interesting examples of the social process of policy making regarding the energy transition. The German debate on the Energiewende built on a long history of intense social and political debate on the role of nuclear energy, and on well-established channels of stakeholder engagement in policy. Traditionally, unions and economic actors such as energy companies have been closely involved in policy making, for example in the reform of the 2002 Nuclear Energy Act. In this context, the Ethics Committee was an interesting innovation: it exemplified an approach that sees the energy transition not as a technocratic policy issue but rather as a wider societal project involving collective approaches to ethical questions and risk perception.

By contrast, France has much less history of social debate on energy issues. This led to the need to develop comprehensive social engagement around existing and new policy objectives, such as the reduction in the share of nuclear energy and the long-term decarbonization of the French energy system. The French debate was impressive, therefore, in its level of institutionalization and its attempt to generate a prolonged and comprehensive participative process on a very complex subject. It is clear that the debate pushed the limits of consultative policy making. There were—and remain—large divergences of interests on key issues such as the future of nuclear, the development of shale gas, and the decentralization of administrative competencies in energy and urban planning. It would have been unrealistic to expect that the initial debate could resolve these divisions: doing so will require a long-term process of consultative policy making as well as political arbitrage. This underscores that while public engagement seems a sine qua non of durable policy, there is also a need for engaged political leadership.

Nonetheless, hindsight will probably conclude that the debate had an important impact on French energy policy. In particular, it developed a reasonably broad consensus on the importance and potential of energy efficiency and energy savings as key levers for the energy transition; and brought certain issues, such as the transport sector and the social aspects of the energy transition, more significantly to the fore.

Implications for
European Energy and Climate Policy

Europe has developed far reaching energy and climate policies dating back at least several decades. It is clear that these have had a significant impact on the policies of EU member states, in particular the 2020 package on greenhouse gas reductions, energy efficiency, and renewable energy. It is also clear that individual European member states cannot undertake the energy transition alone. Cooperation is needed to ensure European economies of scale on technology, markets, and infrastructure; and to reduce the risks of distortions to competition resulting from unilateral action by member states. The key question is how the policy-making process is to be managed across the two tiers: national and EU. This section assesses how deliberative policy making has previously been managed between the EU and member state levels.

Since the 1997 Kyoto Protocol, European energy and climate change policy has undergone a rather rapid process of centralization and harmonization. Under the negotiations on the Kyoto Protocol, EU member states were required to adopt national emissions reduction commitments as well as an EU aggregate commitment.

These individual and joint commitments were developed via a deliberative process of proposal, assessment, and negotiation between member states, guided by the Commission and analysis by external experts organized by the Presidency of the European Council (see Spencer & Fazekas 2012). As a result of this intense negotiation process, each member state emerged with an individual emissions target, which summed to the collective European target under the Kyoto Protocol. This process involved intense exchanges on national assumptions regarding emissions, economic and energy sector trends and policies, and arguably helped to deepen the legitimacy of the targets adopted.

Nonetheless, it is interesting to note that several European member states seem likely to exceed their Kyoto targets by a wide margin. Therefore, while the deliberative process of target development did succeed in negotiating a joint EU Kyoto objective, it did not by itself induce the necessary European and national policies required to always meet those objectives.

Subsequent to Kyoto, EU climate policy has gone through a significant harmonization process, which has progressively reduced the scope for deliberative or negotiated policy making between the European and member state levels. Examples of the harmonization process include the adoption of the European Emissions Trading Scheme (EU ETS) in 2003 and then its reform to a single EU-wide emissions cap under the 2008 climate and energy package; the adoption of harmonized product standards under the Ecodesign Directive (2009); and renewables objectives for each member state.

Laurence Tubiana, Andreas Rüdinger, Thomas Spencer

In contrast to the deliberative process of developing the EU Kyoto objective, the 2008 climate and energy package was adopted in a rather top-down manner. The March 2007 Council agreed to the headline targets, namely a 20% reduction in GHGs, a 20% increase in the use of renewables, and a non-binding objective of 20% energy savings, all by 2020. This occurred after relatively little debate and without assessment of the implications of these EU objectives for individual member states. Subsequently, the Commission came forward in early 2008 with a policy package and impact assessment. This laid out a detailed division of objectives between member states, and the mechanisms used to reach the objectives. These were subsequently adopted, with relatively few adjustments, in the 2008 Climate and Energy Package. This process was therefore significantly more top-down and prescriptive than previous policy approaches. This was based, in part, on the need to provide for harmonization of policies that impact the highly integrated, heavily traded industrial sectors; It reflected the role of the Commission as a technocratic and 'disinterested' arbiter of negotiations between member states; and was also due to the significant political capital associated with climate change at the time, and the willingness of member states to delegate significant sovereignty to the Commission, notably in the definition of national objectives for renewables.

This approach has both strengths and weaknesses. Regarding its strengths, it allowed the Commission to significantly reduce the bargaining space between member states, based on its centralized and broadly recognized capacity in modeling and analysis. It also promoted the adoption of harmonized objectives and policies, which were likely more ambitious and effective than those proposed solely by member states. In terms of the weaknesses of the approach, it tends to be reductivist with regard to the diversity of member state circumstances and policy preferences. This can lead to an absence of national 'buy-in' for EU policy, as evidenced by the UK reticence towards EU renewables objectives.

It should also be noted that a deliberative, negotiated policy approach may be more appropriate to certain policy areas than others. Where there are EU economies of scale or risks of distortions from unharmonized policy, then harmonized EU policies and objectives may make a lot of sense. This would be the case in highly traded product markets (standards for cars) or the highly traded industrial sector (a harmonized carbon price). However, there are sectors with high transaction costs, information asymmetries, and national or local competences, where EU objectives may not be effective. This would be the case for EU electricity infrastructure planning, where the EU approach has been to combine facilitative regulations with deliberative policy-making institutions (European networks of national infrastructure regulators) to drive forward the political agenda of EU energy market integration.

A key question is therefore how the EU can combine the best elements of deliberative and centralized policy making. This question is all the more pressing, given the rise in 'energy nationalism,' i.e., a prioritization of national objectives and increased reticence to cede competence to the EU. Furthermore, it is clear that EU member states have very different visions of the energy transition, and that EU policy will have to take into account these different visions.

Conclusions

The energy transition is a wide-reaching societal project that will profoundly affect the foundations of the economy and the lifestyles of European citizens. There is an inherent complexity and uncertainty associated with such large-scale, long-term technological and social transformation. Social preferences are also dynamic and diverse, and hence building support for the energy transition is necessarily an iterative political and social process.

Deliberative approaches to policy making involve the close integration of stakeholders within the policy-making process and attempts to build social consent and understanding around policy choices. Deliberative policy making has long been a part of German energy policy, which has been strongly characterized by politicization and social engagement on the nuclear issue. In the wake of the Fukushima disaster, this approach was further developed through the establishment of the Ethics Commission. The Commission expanded the sphere of energy policy development to include explicit judgments on risk perception and acceptability. The widespread social and political consensus that was rapidly forged around the nuclear phase-out can be explained by the long history of social and political engagement on this issue, and the use of deliberative policy-making approaches.

In contrast, France faces a long history of centralized, technocratic energy policy. The state and the nuclear industry play strong roles in both energy and economic policy. Any discussion of the energy transition that includes nuclear in its mandate therefore deals with core issues concerning the role of the state in the society. Against this background, the 2012–2013 French energy debate was clearly a difficult exercise, but one that has contributed to long-term policy making on energy in France. In particular, it created a robust consensus on the importance of addressing the demand side, which is a significant development for French energy policy. It also demonstrates, however, the limits of deliberative policy: the ability of highly organized, vocal actors such as the business sector to impose their preferences; and the difficulty of achieving consensus around issues characterized by highly divergent perceptions, preferences, and interests. This was the case with French nuclear policy within the debate.

Ultimately, it underscores the importance of traditional democratic processes of governance as the most effective aggregator of public preferences. Deliberation can

Laurence Tubiana, Andreas Rüdinger, Thomas Spencer

138

support policy making, but it cannot make policy: political decisions are still needed, and often they will involve trade-offs between conflicting views.

Europe can also learn from these deliberative processes. It faces the challenges of reconciling highly divergent visions between member states, and increasing reticence to cede competence to the European tier. In this context, deliberative policy making is needed in order to bridge the national and supranational levels, and to forge a new consensus and legitimacy for EU policy. This coordinated European policy approach is essential to the success of domestic energy transitions. EU policy making needs to strengthen this two-way interaction between the European and member state levels in order to produce a common policy framework that is consistent with national diversity but more than simply the sum of its parts.

LITERATURE CITED

Bäckstrand, K. (2003): Civic science for sustainability: Reframing the role of experts, policy-makers and citizens in environmental governance. In: Global Environmental Politics 3/4: 24–41.

Bickerstaff, K., Lorenzoni, I., Pidgeon, N.F., Poortinga, W., Simmons P. (2008): Reframing nuclear power in the UK energy debate: Nuclear power, climate change mitigation and radioactive waste. In: Public Understanding of Science 17/2: 145–169.

European Commission (2010): Energy 2020. A Strategy for Competitive, Sustainable and Secure Energy. Com(2010) 639 Final: Communication from the Commission to the European Parliament, the Council, the European Economic and Social Committee and the Committee of the Regions.

Fach, W., Simonis, G. (1987): Die Stärke des Staates im Atomkonflikt: Frankreich und die Bundesrepublik im Vergleich. Frankfurt am Main: Campus Verlag.

Kitschelt, H.P. (1986): Political opportunity structures and political protest: Anti-nuclear movements in four democracies. In: British Journal of Political Science 16/1: 57–85.

Mez, L., Gerhold, L., de Haan, G. (Eds.) (2010): Atomkraft als Risiko. Analysen und Konsequenzen nach Tschernobyl. Frankfurt am Main: Peter Lang.

PBL Netherlands Environmental Assessment Agency (2012): Climate and Energy Roadmaps towards 2050 in north-western Europe. A concise overview of long-term climate and energy policies in Belgium, Denmark, France, Germany, the Netherlands, and the United Kingdom. Policy Studies, The Hague/Bilthoven: Planbureau voor de Leefomgeving.

Renn, O. (2008): Risk Governance: Coping with Uncertainty in a Complex World. London: Earthscan.

Roose, J. (2010): Der endlose Streit um die Atomenergie. Konfliktsoziologische Untersuchung einer dauerhaften Auseinandersetzung. In: Feindt, P.H., Saretzki, T. (Hrsg.). Umwelt- und Technikkonflikte. Wiesbaden: VS Verlag für Sozialwissenschaften, pp. 79–103.

Rüdig, W. (2000): Phasing out nuclear energy in Germany. In: German Politics 9/3: 43–80.

Spencer, T., Fazekas D. (2012): Distributional choices in EU climate policy: 20 years of policy practice. In: Climate Policy 13/2: 240–258.

Vasileiadou, E. (2012): Consulting stakeholders? Assessing Stakeholder Consultations in the European Energy Policy. In: Tortora, M. (Ed.). Sustainable Systems and Energy Management at the Regional Level: Comparative Approaches. Hershey: IGI Global, pp. 328–347.

Pekka Haavisto

Global Contract for Sustainability

Green Economy:
What is there for Us?

It is not difficult to be a pessimist these days. When the 1992 Rio Earth Summit adopted Agenda 21 to great fanfare, there was no reason to be a pessimist: even if the agenda for implementing sustainable development was non-binding and voluntary for governments, there was finally a road map for the 21st century. The idea of Local Agenda 21 also gave good reason for optimism: while governments might be slow in their action, local communities and regions might speed the process with the support of active citizens and non-governmental organizations (NGOs). Sustainable business was also already emerging. Now, more than twenty years later, is a good moment for reflection.

Step by step, the image of sustainability became increasingly blurred. In the beginning, we spoke about three important pillars of sustainability: environmental, economic, and sociopolitical. However, whether we have reasons for optimism or pessimism remains to be seen. We need to retain an open mind in order to understand partially contradicting developments which seem to represent both a step in the right direction and a step away from it at the same time.

Then began a debate on what economic sustainability really means. Reference was made to 'sustainable growth' or 'stable growth.' The idea of economic sustainability started to lose its intended meaning and to concentrate on the traditional gross national product (GNP) index. From time to time this was challenged by some other approach, like Bhutan's initiative for an index of 'gross national happiness.' Measuring welfare and sustainability requires criteria other than solely GNP.

Whenever there was a feeling that sustainable development had been hijacked from its original purposes, it was time to return to its roots. For me, these roots are the Club of Rome report in 1972 and the Brundtland report in 1987. We might say that the Club of Rome report 'Limits to Growth' had many flaws: Humankind repeatedly found new ways to exploit natural resources; technology is advancing, and it has become profitable to extract lower-grade mineral sources from the ground or to drill offshore oil and gas reserves; shale oil and gas are now the focus of the latest fossil revolution; with the gas economy, the US might meet its original Kyoto targets for carbon reduction, notwithstanding the many environmental problems of the fossil economy. But 'Limits to Growth' presented a clear picture that endless economic growth in the circumstances of growing world population and limited natural resources is not possible. Now, when the greening of economies is more topical than ever, we have to recognize the value of the analysis made by the Club of Rome at that very early stage.

The Brundtland Commission of 1987 produced the most often-quoted definition of sustainable development: "Development that meets the needs of the present without compromising the ability of future generations to meet their own needs." The great value of the Brundtland report lies also in its global approach, when it recognizes that poverty, individual inequality of opportunity, and international inequality have to be addressed if we want to develop sustainable societies and a sustainable world. Poverty and inequality very often prevent us making the smart decisions for the future.

From Sustainable Development
to Eco-efficiency

While the sustainability debate in the national context very often stagnated to the *"sustainable development versus sustainable growth"* positions, within the international arena it became very much the issue of new, additional resources and the transfer of new technologies. In reality, while many of the industrial countries are maintaining their previous levels of development assistance, the new money promised for sustainable development is missing. This is creating much international frustration and criticism of unfulfilled promises. One can also ask: what is the basis of denying globally equal per-capita emission rights for all individuals, which was the radical demand of many NGOs and some governments in the Kyoto and post-Kyoto climate process? Nevertheless, there is a risk that emerging economies will anyway move towards Western emission levels as a result of rapid economic growth. The whole world order is changing: Asia is emerging from poverty, some economies in Latin America are flourishing, and in Africa there are countries with double-digit growth numbers.

For greening of economies, the concept of eco-efficiency has become a valuable tool. First we had 'Factor-4,' the concept of reducing resource and energy use by 75 percent by doubling output and halving production (see also the chapter by Ernst von Weizsäcker in this volume). Factor-10 was developed from Factor-4, and is the more radical concept for changing societies and dematerialization. It is based on the thinking that 80 percent of the world's resources are distributed among First World nations, which comprise only 20 percent of the global population. This means that developed nations are prompting an unsustainable system of development. The goal of Factor-10 is to ensure that nations do not exceed the planet's carrying capacity, and that they leave sufficient resources for future generations. Based on the predicted increases in population and economic growth, in order to maintain the level of pollution we have today, we need to be able to produce the same output for 10 percent of the impact.

From Eco-efficiency to Green Economies

Eco-efficiency has been growing towards a totally new phase—that of green economies. Whereas during the 1990s we spoke about green taxes steering the economy towards lower consumption of energy and raw materials with correspondingly less pollution, we now have a full set of entrepreneurs, companies, and nations who have found ecological thinking to be at the core of economic development. We Europeans can only regret our progress is outpaced by the rapid changes occurring in countries like South Korea and China—or even in the United States. Europe, once a frontrunner in Rio and Kyoto processes and many global environmental initiatives, is now a back-seater. This is partly due to the economic difficulties and high unemployment rates we currently have in Europe; and yet one might ask, wouldn't the green economy be exactly the right medicine to cure the current economic problems of Europe? In Europe there is one frontrunner left: It is Germany, with its Energiewende (Energy Transition), the concept of closing all nuclear power plants by 2022 in parallel with a shift towards a low-carbon society. The Fukushima nuclear accident in Japan triggered the decision, which the previous government already had on its desk. If sustainable development should be achieved via eco-efficiency or green economy, it needs to pursue transformational changes such as the Energiewende. Otherwise, it runs the risk of downgrading the original intention of the three-pillar concept and will become business as usual or just another form of economic growth. Will Germany be successful in this? We do not know yet. Many observers seem to think that the task is magnificent, almost impossible. But if anybody can do it, it is Germany, the strongest economy in Europe.

What is there for Me?

As in any major development processes and decisions in societies, the people are asking the very justified questions: What is in this change for me? What will it take, what it will give? There is a new future, but is there place for me and my family in that future? These are all extremely relevant questions. We might need to achieve Factor-4 or even Factor-10, but life is not only about producing and consuming: the economy has to be based on values and human dignity. The new green economy might bring many changes: Locally produced organic food; improved public transportation; car-sharing schemes to fill empty seats on journeys; car clubs offering members flexible access to vehicles as an alternative to ownership; greater energy efficiency; but also producing energy within the household and then selling it to the central grid. All of these technological changes also involve big social changes and changes to our lifestyles. This social and cultural development is an increasingly important part of sustainability.

New Levels of Participation

Democracy is evolving new layers. The Internet, mobile text-messaging and com-munication networks, Twitter, and other social media are giving huge potential to citizens and citizens' organizations to participate, to plan initiatives, and to hold to account those in power. In the Arab Spring, in the rise of environmental movements in China, or in citizens' monitoring of elections in Kenya and Russia, we have already seen the power of new media and the new layer of democracy. It is evident that citizen participation and the new channels that facilitate it will be an important new element in the development towards new green and democratic societies.

Poverty and Environment

Within wealthy societies we do not always realize the linkages between poverty and environment. In the Finnish parliament I have, from time to time, faced a discussion that good environment is some kind of "luxury item" that the poor people of the world do not have the understanding to seek, or else cannot afford. Unfortunately, this perspective can be observed throughout Europe and appears to be more prevalent than in the past.

I worked for six years in UNEP under the guidance of Dr. Klaus Töpfer, con-ducting post-conflict environmental evaluations in real theatres of war, in places like

Kosovo, Afghanistan, Iraq, Palestine, Liberia, and Sudan. It was a very good school for understanding how poverty and environmental sustainability are connected. These troubled areas are home to some of the poorest people in the world, many of whom are refugees from conflict. Environmental changes due to war or climate change, for example, represent an additional burden to these people. Wherever we travelled, questions of the environment and safe livelihoods were raised in parallel—Endless, very concrete environmental questions:

Can I cultivate this field, or is it chemically polluted due to the war? Can I use the drinking water from my well? What I should do with all hazardous substances? Where do I live now, after warlords felled the trees around my village and sand took over? Desertification has ruined my grazing areas, where can I take my cattle?

For these people there are not too many options: if livelihoods are destroyed, they will become environmental refugees. When we are heading towards green economies, let us be sure that we also have answers for the poorest people in war-stricken societies. A green economy that fails to provide viable solutions for these people but instead focuses only on rich countries with mature economies may provide a useful complement to current economic systems—but it will fail to foster sociopolitical and environmental stability, and so cannot be a replacement for the idea of sustainable development put forward in Rio 1992.

Klaus Milke and Christoph Bals

Acting–Negotiations–Alliances: The 'Energiewende' in Germany and its Relevance to the Great Transformation and a Global Contract

Civil Society Faces Massive Challenges World-wide

Introduction

Acting–Negotiations–Alliances: International progress to limit climate change rests on those three pillars. The German developmental and environmental organization Germanwatch gained extensive experience in advocacy and campaign work, especially during UNFCCC negotiations. It has built alliances with other political, economic, and civil society actors and, for many years has advocated policies for energy transition, transportation, and agriculture. Since its foundation, Germanwatch repeatedly met with Klaus Töpfer, who promoted—as a visionary pragmatist in different roles—action, negotiation, and innovative alliances. Klaus Töpfer is an honorary member of Germanwatch, a member of the Advisory Board of the Foundation for Sustainability, and patron of atmosfair (jointly initiated by the Federal Ministry of Environment and Germanwatch). We offer him our warmest congratulations on his birthday!

The Environment Minister in the Lion's Den

The Environment Minister is sweating. He has stepped into the lion's den. Peter Altmaier is guest speaker at the 2013 summer party of Greenpeace Germany. Before he can speak, he is challenged by the Greenpeace campaign leader Roland Hipp, who points out mistakes, failures, and inconsistencies of the federal government, particularly regarding the promotion of renewable energy. Altmaier responds to the challenge by firing back questions and pointing to mistakes that were made when the previous administration was in power, and that now need to be fixed.

The event is a good example of an exceptional civil society-oriented culture in Germany. This is expressed by Altmaier's closing remark: *"Please, continue to protest, but please let us talk with each other, because we are working in the same direction!"* Klaus Töpfer said a similar thing when we criticized him in the run-up to the Rio Conference in 1992. A respectful dialogue between politicians and civil society is crucial. Nevertheless, it is also undoubted that, without the decades-long protests against the transportation and storage of nuclear waste, e.g., in the Wendland region, Germany's subsequent nuclear exit and the initiation of the Energiewende (energy transition) would never have succeeded—even after Fukushima.

It is notable that the Greenpeace event that challenged minister Altmaier is dedicated to Poland; the Polish deputy ambassador and other Polish guests are present. Meanwhile, the German Ministry for Environment—frequently thwarted by the Ministry for Economy—is seeking to get the Polish Government on-board to press for greater ambition in European climate policy, which is important considering that the next UN climate summit will take place in Poland at the end of 2013. Poland is an EU partner that is not always easy to handle, and which might present a fundamental hurdle for decisions regarding the future of an ambitious European energy and climate policy.

In contrast to the long German experience of civic engagement, Greenpeace Poland is just nine years old. It faces great challenges, given the country's weak civil society in the field of energy and climate policy. How can Polish civil society be strengthened and evolve in light of Poland's strong fossil fuel-related interests and barely acknowledged climate challenges throughout the population? How can German NGOs support their colleagues in Poland? Especially after adoption of the 'Energiewende,' German civil society also needs to ask itself: Are we well positioned for the future challenges in Germany, but particularly in the context of the EU? What does it mean to actually support a transformation rather than only backing protest?

Klaus Milke and Christoph Bals

Copenhagen: An Exceptional Lesson

Angela Merkel was previously German Environment Minister and the chief German negotiator for the Kyoto Protocol. She learned a lot in the run-up to Kyoto, and with a background in physical sciences she has a clear understanding of the climate challenge. Later, as Chancellor, during the 2008 peak of the climate question, she first ambitiously advanced the European climate and energy policy and then used the G8 venue to win the 'heavyweights' of the global economy over to the idea of a more ambitious climate policy. Sitting in a beach chair in Heiligendamm, she explained the value of a 2°C-limit to George W. Bush, at that time US president and a confirmed skeptic of anthropogenic climate change … suddenly, a global shift seemed to be possible. At least since the third and fourth IPCC reports of 2001 and 2007[1] respectively, no-one can claim to be unaware of the climate challenge—this major experiment of humans with humankind. Chancellor Merkel was a driving force towards a successful climate summit in Copenhagen at the end of 2009.

Copenhagen was—no doubt—an important step forward in global learning. It put the 2°C-limit on the global agenda: This means to limit global temperature increase to 2°C compared to the pre-industrial age; otherwise the effects of climate change might become unmanageable in many parts of the world. However, the Copenhagen summit clearly failed to meet the high expectations to agree a turnaround on fossil fuel emissions. In the months before the finance crisis shifted the focus of political leaders, Copenhagen demonstrated that the rapid shift in geopolitical power no longer allowed successful negotiations via the old negotiating boxes of 'developed' and 'developing' countries. The Danish Premier was not up to the challenge of leading such a complex conference of worldwide negotiators and, in the end, of world leaders. After the negotiations, Chancellor Merkel had the impression that neither China nor the US were ready for the necessary transformation, and she has since dramatically reduced her visibility in the climate context. Copenhagen was also a shock for international climate diplomacy. Some commentators claimed the summit's failure already signaled the death of multilateral climate negotiations. Decision makers and civil society were thus confronted with many questions: Why did Copenhagen largely fail? How can the UN consensus-trap be avoided, be it through new rules or frontrunner alliances? How can a pioneering role be justified even in the absence of consensus?

Ever since, the negotiations have continued and a collapse has been prevented; the nineteenth UN Climate Summit will take place in Poland in late 2013 (the second

---

1 Third and Fourth Assessment Reports (TAR3 and TAR4) of the Intergovernmental Panel on Climate Change (IPCC) of the United Nations.

summit hosted by Poland, following COP14 in 2008), as part of a plan to achieve a worldwide agreement in 2015 in Paris. All states with high emissions should have binding commitments not later than 2020. Countries with higher emissions and greater capability should support transformative climate and resilience strategies in poor countries. However, it is a huge challenge to realize these plans.

Politicians Should Talk to Each Other, Create a Common Understanding—and Finally Act

Some still remember how in 2008 Barack Obama, then the Democratic presidential candidate, spoke at the Victory Column in Berlin, in front of hundreds of thousands of people—full of expectations. Many felt that something could happen then, and that greater rationality and foresight could be brought to the White House. However, not least through the example of climate protection, it became clear that there was a lack of prioritization by Democrats to overcome the legislative blockade by Republicans; driven forward by the Tea Party (with the Koch Brothers as its biggest financial supporter) as well as a fossil lobby employing dubious working methods, there occurred a polarization of society and far-reaching steps failed.

On 19 June 2013, Obama again spoke in front of the Brandenburg Gate in Berlin, this time as US president. Whereas the German chancellor unfortunately missed the chance to at least mention the words 'sustainability' or 'climate protection,' President Obama pressed for a global climate compact and implied that he would announce far-reaching regulations for the American coal industry in the following days: "We will do more. This is our task and we HAVE to get to work."

It is of the utmost importance that these words be followed by actions this time. Within the EU, important parts of the industrial and energy sectors are organizing a roll-back to prevent an ambitious EU climate policy. Instead of initiating investment in a transformation, which could also help combat high unemployment and the economic crisis in the EU, a roll-back would represent a call for stagnation that could undermine the Energiewende; the former minister of economy (Rössler) tested a strong anti-climate profile of the center-right FDP (Free Democratic Party). In close coalition with the Federation of German Industry (BDI)—mainly driven by lobbyists for the BASF industrial group and some other energy-intensive industries—he tested some of the climate strategies of the American Tea Party in Europe. They were, e.g., wrecking the EU Emissions Trading Scheme, which the Americans recommended to the EU prior to Kyoto. This strategy did not pay out. The FDP lost dramatically in the parliamentary elections of September 2013, and for the first time since 1949 are no longer represented in the German Parliament. Such a strategy appears absurd at a time when regions in the US and China are starting to build up their own emissions trading systems and want to work together with Europe. The EU, former pioneer in climate protection, is increasingly brushed off by the two global players. Following the 2013 German elections, the new federal government must find bold and progressive answers to the questions involved with the climate change problem.

In April 2013, the fourth Petersberg Climate Dialogue talks took place in Berlin. Via a live Internet stream, the world public could follow the content and style of the negotiations among the 35 states represented there. The goal of the talks was to create momentum for the next UN Climate Summit. Chancellor Merkel gave the opening speech and requested that action finally be taken. On the one hand, this showed that the climate issue has not disappeared from the German political agenda. It is indeed no longer as high a priority as it was during 2008, and other topics such as the economic and debt crises have become more prominent. Nevertheless, most believe that there is an urgent need to act and that we must achieve internationally binding commitments. On the other hand, the causes and consequences of the global temperature rise are no longer discussed only among a small circle of convinced actors, but on a medial stage in front of the eyes of the world public—even if there are still open attacks against an ambitious climate policy as well as campaigns of ideologically or financially motivated climate change-deniers that go beyond the necessary debates.

After more than 20 years of climate diplomacy we do not have much more time to lose. The concentration of carbon dioxide in the atmosphere has now exceeded the threshold of 400 parts per million for the first time in human history; this is the highest level in at least 2.5 million years. Global emissions have increased faster since the year 2000 than before. We should end a culture of blame and finger-pointing towards others: while we point with one finger at others, three other will point at us. Every year we lose makes the challenge bigger and a responsible solution more expensive.

The Discovery of Civil Society

The beginning of the 1990s was marked by the awakening of the international community, highlighted by many UN conferences that were loaded with high expectations. These great summits reflect the awareness that socioeconomic, ecological, and humanitarian problems, which worsened in many parts of the world during this period, cannot be solved by unilateral action alone.[2] Many actors started to realize that environment and development are two sides of the same coin, particularly

---

2 For example, the fourth UN World Conference on Women in Beijing, the UN World Summit for Social Development in Copenhagen (both in 1995), the UN Conference on Population and Development in Cairo (1994), and of course in 1992 UNCED, the UN Conference on Environment and Development in Rio de Janeiro that produced Agenda 21, important conventions on climate and biodiversity as well as official declarations on sustainable development.

after the Rio Conference in 1992 and the intensive dealing with Agenda 21 that was adopted there. It was a time of high ambitions after the end of the long-running East–West conflict that had absorbed all relevant actors.[3] However, soon afterwards, disillusionment kicked in—regarding the ability to act in the highly complex context of economic globalization and confronted with extremely well-organized self-interests.

Civil society and NGOs assumed an increasingly important role, especially in the climate arena. To a large extent, this was due to their engagement, tenacity, and considerable competence. Farsighted politicians, such as then Environment Minister and Rio preparer Klaus Töpfer, were quick to emphasize that NGOs must be involved in the negotiation processes. This is because they are oriented to the common good, feed ethical and scientific results into the process, and are not bound to quarterly financial results or legislative periods.

The network of regionally and internationally interconnected NGOs is an essential part of civil society and a critical driver of the processes of mutual learning and change.[4] In this context, the Climate Action Network (CAN) is highly relevant in terms of global climate cooperation, as it uses its continental and regional networks (such as CAN Europe) to ensure important continuity and expertise while always considering the perspective of our society's most vulnerable. It also provides a platform to discuss and debate the contents of, and strategies for, climate change-related activities.

The Global Call for Climate Action (GCCA) and its global campaign TckTckTck complement this cooperation through campaign work and media-effective lobbying and public relations activities. International Internet campaign organizations such as Campact and Avaaz also play an increasingly important role, as does the work of Climate Alliance (Klima-Allianz) in Germany. Through the Alliance, more than 110 civil society organizations including churches, trade unions, and social organizations ensure visibility for the broad support throughout society, and build pressure for the necessary changes.[5]

---

3 During this time of shifting paradigms and German reunification, the North–South political initiative Germanwatch was founded in 1991, with the aim of closely monitoring (thus the name) how the newly enlarged Germany handled its new global responsibilities.

4 Germanwatch considers it its task to cooperate as much as possible within these networks, but also to test underlying assumptions and to consistently present innovative approaches. In this regard, the organization particularly utilizes opportunities to cooperate with influential actors representing various foundations. In order to review and adjust the civil society strategy towards pressing global challenges within an international learning process, Germanwatch initiated a strategic NGO dialogue on energy and climate, agriculture, and food security in 2012, and is currently working on its continuance.

5 www.klima-allianz.de

Klaus Milke and Christoph Bals

Developing Countries form the Majority

At first, the climate area was an arena for *environmental* politicians and NGOs. However, some actors realized early on that climate change-related droughts, floods, or increasing storms first and foremost endanger people in developing countries, particularly the most vulnerable.[6] At the same time, the majority of United Nations member states, which also comprises the Framework Convention on Climate Change, were emerging economies or developing countries. However, it still took some time until the developmental perspective (how to integrate the massive reduction of greenhouse gases necessary for sustainable development in combination with adaptation to climate change) became established as equally important within the negotiations.

In the context of North–South and East–West globalization discourses, yet another issue has taken shape. In the past two decades, the confidence and growth of the emerging economies has fundamentally changed the power structure between developed and developing countries. It is therefore important—including from a greenhouse emissions perspective—to create a new common understanding. In light of increasing foreign trade, massive production increases, and rapidly increasing consumption, it is no longer enough to discuss only the CO_2 debts of the rich countries: the development model of emerging economies and their increasingly important part in the solution need also to be scrutinized. The old *fossil-based* pathways that brought industrialization and prosperity to developed nations are still regarded by many as the only promising path to economic development ... from this perspective, climate protection is still regarded as a brake on development, and the solar energy system as leading to second-class status. At this point, it is encouraging that civil society in Europe is discussing with colleagues in China, India, and Brazil how to transform the model of the global middle class in line with the necessary emission limitations.[7]

Politics Rather than the Economy may Decide

Who is in charge when the recognition of planetary boundaries (e.g., of the climate system) is at stake? In this regard, international climate negotiations are an important test case.

The 1992 UN Framework Convention on Climate Change (UNFCCC), which was actually signed and ratified by the United States, provided a framework to nego-

---

6 Immediately after its foundation as a North–South and developmental organization in 1991, Germanwatch decided to address climate change alongside developmental issues. It consequently evolved as a developmental AND environmental organization, particularly in dealing with the respective outcomes of Rio 1992.

7 Germanwatch seeks to achieve this, e.g., through concrete activities with actors in China and India.

tiate international instruments to prevent dangerous climate change. But even before the first United Nations Climate Change Conference (COP1) took place in 1995 in Berlin, it became evident that private sector interests were already well organized. Many economic actors wanted to prevent the adoption of binding targets for emission reduction. The US coal, oil, and automotive industries acted as the so-called Global Climate Coalition (GCC), which presented itself as *the voice* of the economy, and organized naysayers to lobby in its interests. Their strategy was to lock the international community into a prisoner dilemma: Undermine the ability of the US Government to act internationally — this makes it difficult for all others to act with ambition. First, the GCC and its allies fundamentally called into question the scientific evidence that humans are responsible for increasing climate change. As long as science seems uncertain, politicians find it difficult to act. Second, its corporate lawyers lobbied the negotiators representing emerging countries, alleging that climate protection would hinder their own development. They pressed for the exclusion of developing countries and emerging economies from the Berlin Mandate (1995). As a third step they used exactly this exclusion as their key argument for why the US should not ratify Kyoto for reasons of competition and the relevance of the emissions of emerging countries. Together with Saudi Arabia, the GCC developed a strategy — which continues to be pursued by destructive forces today — to block the adoption of negotiation rules that would have enabled a way out of the consensus trap. The hard economic and short-term profit interests of the fossil industry determined this line of action. Thus, the UN climate conferences were already then portrayed by the GCC as presenting a mutually exclusive choice between either ecological or economic progress.

How to change this? In the following years, the Worldwatch Institute; the beginnings of the renewable energy, energy efficiency and co-generation industry; the US Business for Sustainable Energy; and a European counterpart called 'e5,' which was essentially initiated by Germanwatch, became involved in the negotiation process for the first climate protocol. Prior to the foundation of e5, then Environment Minister Merkel called on the companies on the margins of COP1 in Berlin: "Launch quickly, we need you!" With this background, a positive business lobby supported the first modest reduction commitments for industrialized countries in terms of the Kyoto Protocol. However, the Protocol did not enter into force until 2005, following massive efforts surrounding the climate summit in Bonn 2001 (COP6b). To achieve this, a great campaign WITH companies worldwide was extremely helpful: e-mission 55 — Business for Climate. Shortly after, the GCC gave way.

The lesson for politics was: there is no such a thing as the 'one economy.' In the economic sphere, too, the past is mostly better organized than the future. Economic interests should be considered, but politicians — who are legitimized by elections, should always look for solutions to transform the economic sector in ways that fit

Klaus Milke and Christoph Bals

the *public interest* of today and tomorrow. They must steer the climate discourse and should reject the myth that there is only one economy with one interest.

Today, there is a variety of different voices on potential economic pathways. Some still clearly represent the defensively backwards-directed fossil interests, and have gained new strength in Europe due to the economic crisis. But a growing number rely on the innovation potential of the necessary transformation, and stand for renewable energy, energy efficiency, a circular economy, and a comprehensive transformation in the areas of energy, transport, and nutrition.[8]

It is also important to keep in mind that we have a new international human rights framework, in which the protection obligation of states and corporate responsibilities need to be discussed and negotiated. In this regard, the three pillars of the UN Guiding Principles on Business and Human Rights, adopted by the UN Human Rights Council in 2011, are fundamental:

1. *States* should protect their people from violation of human rights by companies (Protect);
2. *Companies* should respect human rights and cease violations (Respect);
3. Both states and companies must grant *affected people* access to complaint and compensation mechanisms (Remedy).

An intelligent mix of voluntary and binding action is needed. This is a dynamic topic which should receive more attention, including from sustainable development politicians![9] As climate change increasingly challenges human rights, this context will gain relevance in the climate debate.

Energiewende in Germany: Laboratory for the world!

In 2011, following Fukushima, Germany decided upon the Energiewende in a comprehensive societal and cross-party agreement. This is the first time that a leading industrialized country has made an ambitious effort to build their prosperity on energy efficiency and renewable energies — not on the high-risk nuclear and fossil technologies. Again, the personal handwriting of Klaus Töpfer is apparent in the report of the Ethics Commission, which laid the foundation[10] for an unprecedented transformation and learning process in this respect. This can be seen as the acceptance that within the paradigm of sustainability not only developing but also so-called

---

8   For example the 2-Degrees Initiative with leading German economic actors, in which business personalities such as Michael Otto play an important role.

9   Cf. http://germanwatch.org/de/6837

10 Klaus Töpfer and his fellow committee members set important impulses for this which, however, were not fully accepted by the federal government.

developed countries need to develop. The directly related unconditional climate goals for 2020 and 2050 demonstrate a clear commitment to the dimension of 'acting' and, so far, no other industrialized country in the world has committed itself to such a comprehensive transformation of its energy system.

However, for emerging economies and developing countries too, a successful Energiewende in Germany—and if possible the entire EU—would represent an important signal. Such countries have good arguments to expect industrialized countries to first demonstrate that low-carbon economic development and economic wealth are compatible. This means, that a successful Energiewende is crucial to building confidence and thus enabling greater dynamics in the negotiations. Many actors around the world are therefore looking to Germany, the leading economic force of the EU, and asking whether the Germans will make it. At the same time, many think: if someone can make it, it's them! Failure would also be devastating for the reputation of German technology around the world.

Against this background, a success story needs to be written. It will most certainly have many repercussions for the international process and—together with cooperation partners—for motivating other countries to follow. German civil society, too, holds a great responsibility in meeting this challenge. The Energiewende is already—and should to a large extent be—a project of citizens and cooperatives. It is fascinating to see how in many parts of Germany, various initiatives, scientists, and innovative business actors are cooperating to make it a success. Others come together to present answers to social questions around the Energiewende.[11] The Energiewende will be a key project for German civil society and a starting point for a strong European dialogue.

There is no time to lose, but at the same time learning curves take their time…

Global Contract:
Acting–Negotiating–Alliances

With all this being said, a 'Global Contract for Sustainability'—as the research cluster led by Klaus Töpfer at the IASS is also called—does not consist of one single regulatory framework but a manifold mix of simultaneous and different approaches.

The lessons of the slow UN climate negotiation process led to the strategic triad and creative mix of **Acting–Negotiating–Alliances**.

 ◆ Everyone (individual, company, nation) should do whatever they identify as useful and what is possible to implement by acting unilaterally (Acting).

---

[11] For example, the Klima-Allianz developed different activities surrounding the "social costs of the Energiewende" together with Klaus Töpfer.

+ We need strong UN climate negotiations with the goal of a global and legally binding agreement (Negotiating). The UNFCCC is also the landing place for many initiatives of other fora and alliances.
+ Those who are ready to move forward should build frontrunner coalitions that are oriented to support action and negotiations towards the 2 °C limit; relatively progressive developed countries in coalition with the most vulnerable and affected countries should underpin the urgency of action (Alliances).

All three dimensions belong together and need to be realized simultaneously to transform the climate cacophony into a symphony. Single states, cities, and progressive companies should act independently, but should also form alliances. Furthermore, global standards and guidelines should be defined for the ecological and social arenas. This is the only way to force free-riders to act and to encourage pioneer alliances.

It is extremely disappointing that the Federal Government of Germany was aligned to the anti-progressive forces in the field of EU climate policy during the last two years, and also that it was unable even to name a ministry that would have been responsible for a national plan to implement the UN Guiding Principles on Business and Human Rights. We expect Germany to take a stronger role in supporting climate protection and human rights. Since Rio (1992), Klaus Töpfer has been an important architect of UN politics (negotiating), of the Energiewende (acting), and an inspiration to diverse alliances, and has thereby shown how climate policy can succeed; and he always ensured that this was managed in ways that did not undermine personal freedom.

The debate on freedom and sustainability is necessary. It is impermissible that those who seek to prevent change—and thereby massively restrict the freedom of current and future generations through the consequences of their actions—insist on the *privilege* of a lifestyle which does not fit within the planetary boundaries. On the other hand, where possible, there should be a focus on incentive-setting and frameworks, not on narrow regulation. This debate needs a positive narrative. Only the protection of common goods can ensure that the individual can develop freely.

In conclusion, there is a lot more to be done by both German and international civil society, for politics, and for visionary pragmatics such as Klaus Töpfer.

Karsten Sach

IRENA
A Story of Conviction, Perseverance, and Transformation

*Contribution
to the IASS Anniversary Volume
on the Occasion of Klaus Töpfer's 75th Birthday*

It was the very day of the Fukushima accident when Klaus Töpfer hosted a workshop on how to strengthen the course of the International Renewable Energy Agency (IRENA), a day that was a prism of the past and the future center of the world's energy system. In his letter of invitation to the workshop participants, Klaus Töpfer spoke of seemingly insurmountable challenges that the world is facing: accelerating trends of climate change and the prospects of irreversible impacts; fossil fuel price volatility and its impact on economies; and growing energy needs and energy poverty of over one billion people on the planet. At the same time, he offered a way forward: a search for practical, economically viable measures to change this bleak picture, and the premise that, with renewable energy, we already possess the knowledge and technology to act.

It is not a coincidence that Klaus Töpfer offered the Institute for Advanced Sustainability Studies (IASS)—a center for transdisciplinary, action-oriented and transformative research and thought—as a venue for this discussion; it was another confirmation of his remarkable ability to combine a visionary idea with a pragmatic approach, in a quest for transformative paths to sustainable solutions.

Fukushima triggered world-wide debates and significant changes in energy policies in a number of countries. A few days after the accident, Klaus Töpfer was appointed to chair the 'Ethics Commission for a Safe Energy Supply,' tasked by the German Chancellor Angela Merkel to identify a societal consensus on how to transform a modern energy system without nuclear energy, with renewables being central to the energy mix. In its final report, the Ethics Commission recommended withdrawal from nuclear energy within a decade, and clearly stated that Germany has alternatives available, including, "electricity production from wind, the Sun, water, geothermal energy, biomass, the more efficient use and increased productivity of energy, as well as the climate-compatible use of fossil fuels." The Commission also stated that realization of a nuclear-free energy system will require, "a collective effort spanning all levels of politics, business, and society."[1]

Today, some two years later, renewable energy is a mainstream option in consideration of the transformation of countries' energy systems. A growing list of examples around the world shows different renewable energy technologies increasingly reaching grid parity with their more conventional counterparts. The improved competitiveness of renewables is being driven by a virtuous circle whereby the deployment of renewables, encouraged by support policies to overcome the barriers, is leading to significant cost reductions. More than 120 countries have some form of national target or renewable energy support policy in place. The price of solar photovoltaic modules declined by 65 % in the last two years, and the global installed PV capacity surpassed 101 GW in 2012. China has set solar targets of 35 GW by 2015 and 75 GW by 2020. Even oil-based economies are joining the renewables race—Saudi Arabia has set goals of generating some 24 GW by 2020 and 54 GW by 2032. In the first quarter of 2013, renewables represented 82 % of the new generation capacity added in the United States.

The Case for Renewable Energy

The increasing global interest in renewables is driven by a defining challenge of our times: the search for affordable, clean, and secure energy. The world will be home to 8 billion people by 2030, 60 % of whom will live in cities—with higher standards of living and more energy-intensive lives. Markets are increasingly emerging outside of developed economies; they are now found in both geographically and economically diverse areas; and the year 2010 was the first year when investment in developing countries surpassed that in developed countries. The world economy is set to grow four-fold by 2050 and, in the absence of transformational changes, both energy demand and energy-related emissions will increase in unmanageable ways.

Still, more than 1.3 billion people lack access to modern energy services—a key impediment to social and economic prosperity. Klaus Töpfer once said, "The main quest for overcoming poverty and a secure future is to make energy available, because we cannot cut poverty if we cannot bring affordable energy to the people." Indeed,

---

1 Final Report of the Ethics Commission for a safe Energy Supply, Germany's energy transition—A collective project for the future, 30 May 2011.

a vast un-met and growing demand places energy on the central stage of policy making at the national, regional, and global levels.

Inseparable from this debate is the issue of sustainability and the alarming state of the climate system. The critical issue of climate change means that fossil fuels cannot be considered a complete or long-term solution to the expansion of energy access that is required to combat poverty. Renewable energy based on indigenous energy resources offers the potential to address at least part of this problem. This is particularly pertinent in rural areas far from the likely reach of the electricity grid, where decentralized renewables have already become a cost-effective solution.

Today, we find ourselves in a world that has changed dramatically since the discussions of the 1990s. Sustainable development is no longer only an environmental concept, and Klaus Töpfer's words, "Sustainable development is the peace policy of the future" ring true more than ever before. The Rio+20 conference in 2012 reflected the fact that countries around the world are balancing energy issues such as growing demand, security, and access with the reality that the impacts of climate change are being felt with greater frequency and severity.

New geopolitical dynamics of the 21st century have profound implications on the energy sector and, conversely, an emerging energy landscape is shaping new geopolitical dynamics. Countries that once were not major energy consumers are now energy hungry, and those that previously depended on others for their energy are now producers. These issues are charting a new global dynamic, and their effects on the climate, people's economic conditions, and social wellbeing is still unknown. There is, however, a widespread conviction that renewable energy will play a major role in determining the outcome. The political and policy traction created by these issues, coupled with the rapid development of renewable energy technologies and their falling costs, are transforming the menu of energy choices for countries, industry, and society as a whole.

The creation of the International Renewable Energy Agency (IRENA) is a reflection of this transformation. In April 2011, the inaugural Assembly of the IRENA took place in Abu Dhabi, United Arab Emirates. Some 1000 people gathered to celebrate the establishment of the organization, mandated to promote the widespread and increased adoption and use of renewable energy, with a view to sustainable development and the alleviation of problems of energy security and climate change. This momentous occasion was the pinnacle of a long process that, over the course of some 20 years, evolved from an idea to reality.

Early Developments

Triggered by oil price shocks and the finite nature of conventional energy sources, an international agency for renewable energy was first proposed in 1981 at the United Nations Conference on New and Renewable Sources of Energy in Nairobi, with no success in advancing the idea. In 1990 Hermann Scheer, late parliamentarian of the German Social Democratic Party and a tireless supporter of renewable energy, called for the establishment of an International Solar Energy Agency (ISEA) within the United Nations. Austria formally proposed the idea to the UN General Assembly, and Javier Pérez de Cuéllar, UN Secretary-General, established the UN Solar Energy Group on Environment and Development (UNSEGED) to develop proposals on promoting renewably energy, including the possible creation of an agency. However, there was reluctance among existing UN organizations and many member states, to the introduction of a new organization into the existing international energy structures. Furthermore, there was little enthusiasm for founding a new international organization. Over time, it became evident that a new organization on renewable energy could not be established within the UN system. In 2000, Herman Scheer proposed the establishment of an International Renewable Energy Agency (IRENA) outside the UN system, starting with those countries interested in and committed to renewable energy.

Since the year 2000, the German Government engaged actively to foster renewables at the international level. This was a reflection of its domestic positions: A coalition of the Social Democratic Party and the Greens governed the country from 1998 to 2005, during which time renewable energy was afforded increased political attention. In 2000, the Renewable Energy Act was enacted as the central political element of the paradigm shift from fossil and nuclear energy to renewable energy sources. In its 2002 Agreement, the coalition underlined the importance of renewable energy targets for the development of renewable energy markets and, ultimately, a substantial increase of the share of renewable energy in the global energy mix. Importantly, it also called for the establishment of IRENA.

The German Government made renewable energy one of its priorities at the 2002 World Summit on Sustainable Development in Johannesburg, South Africa. This agenda included proposals for internationally-agreed targets and timetables for the adoption of renewable energy, the phasing-out of fossil fuel subsidies, and the transfer of clean energy technologies to developing countries. Yet, representatives of many developing countries, along with the US, Australia, Canada and Japan, strongly opposed this proposal. Developing countries feared that the focus on renewable energy would divert attention from the primary goal of ensuring universal access to modern energy services, whereas the US, Australia, Canada, and Japan questioned the one-fits-all approach.

Karsten Sach

As the Summit did not produce the desired outcomes, Germany and other EU member states, in partnership with the Small Island Developing States (SIDS), decided to establish a loose international coalition of like-minded countries—the Johannesburg Renewable Energy Coalition—to engage in more ambitious cooperation on renewable energy. In addition, the then German Chancellor, Gerhard Schröder, announced that Germany would host an international conference on renewable energy.

The 'Renewables 2004' Conference was held in Bonn in June 2004. Some 3600 participants from more than 150 countries discussed how to increase the share of renewable energy in both developing and industrialized countries. Three themes were central to the conference: enabling political frameworks; increasing private and public finance; and enhancing capacity building, research, and development. The conference adopted three outcomes: Policy Recommendations, an International Action Programme, and a Political Declaration. The 'Policy Recommendations for Renewable Energy' document addressed a wide range of issues concerning the uptake of renewable energy, including priorities, enabling policy frameworks, and financing. The International Action Programme included almost 160 voluntary renewables-related commitments by governments and international organizations. The Political Declaration contained a joint vision for a sustainable energy future. The Declaration recognized the contribution of renewable energy to sustainable development, alleviation of poverty, and mitigation of climate change, and urged its increase in the global energy mix. In subsequent years, the text of the Political Declaration was used as a premise for the development of the IRENA Statute. Parallel to the Bonn 'Renewables 2004' Conference, an International Parliamentary Forum for Renewable Energies, chaired by Hermann Scheer, called for the creation of IRENA.

At 'Renewables 2004,' the German Government did not yet wish to raise the issue of creating a dedicated international organization, as it was presumed that many countries would not support such an institutional move. Instead, it focused on mobilizing contributions to the International Action Programme and to creating the multi-stakeholder renewables network, REN21. Largely financed by the German Government, REN21 was established to promote rapid expansion of renewable energy in both developing and industrialized countries. Its Global Status Report has become the point of reference on annual developments on renewable energy.

While REN21 represented welcome progress for the renewables agenda, Germany remained committed to the establishment of an international agency. The Environment Ministry commissioned an extensive assessment of different institutional options. After a thorough analysis of existing initiatives to promote renewable energy, the study presented three options to enhance international cooperation: creating a new international organization; mandating UNEP as a central coordinating institution; or advancing the deployment of renewable energy through existing or new partnerships. Although the study stressed that founding an intergovernmental organization would be the best option for the world-wide promotion of renewable energy, it also expressed serious doubts concerning the political viability of this approach at that time.

Pushing the Paradigm

In autumn 2005, a 'grand coalition' of Christian Democrats and Social Democrats formed the German Government. The commitment to renewables remained on the agenda, including the decision to create an international renewable energy agency. This commitment remained at the forefront of internal discussions, and a decisive political opportunity for international action emerged in 2007, when Germany held the presidency of both the EU Council and the G8. During this period, Germany made significant efforts to make renewable energy an integral part of the EU and global agenda, including through the UN mechanisms and processes. While great progress was made in setting renewables targets within the EU, the UN efforts yielded no results.

Considering the reluctance within the UN framework, the most promising avenue for the establishment of an international agency appeared to be a coalition of like-minded countries. To advance this idea, the Government formed a campaign taskforce, comprising mainly officials from the Ministries of Environment, Development Cooperation, and Foreign Affairs, supported by other ministries, as well as Hermann Scheer as an ex-officio member. I was entrusted with leadership of the taskforce and, in summer 2006, a small team began a three-year journey filled with boundless enthusiasm, sleepless nights, and surprising developments. It was also a journey which proved that innovation and determination can challenge the existing institutional balance and create new models of international cooperation.

The first phase of the campaign was focused on developing the concept internally and ascertaining the wider interest in establishing IRENA. Germany appointed three special ambassadors who consulted a wide range of countries around the world. In parallel, the campaign taskforce also reached out to international organizations, networks, and stakeholders in the field of renewables. The focus of the campaign was two-fold: achieving a critical mass of like-minded countries, and devising a meaningful yet broadly acceptable mandate. After being convinced that there was enough interest, Germany invited Denmark and Spain to join the campaign.

In early 2008, Germany, together with Denmark and Spain, invited countries considered interested in the promotion of renewable energy and/or politically influential to attend the First Preparatory Conference for IRENA, to be held in Berlin in April 2008. More than 50 countries attended the conference and remained engaged throughout the year, including two preparatory workshops in Berlin and the final preparatory conference that took place in Madrid in October 2008.

Karsten Sach

At the outset, a number of discussion papers were prepared by the German Government to help guide the dialogue and to preempt some of the issues already known to be contentious. A proposed objective for the agency was, "… to accelerate and enhance the global application of renewable energy sources among its members and throughout the world. Their deployment will help to promote [an] environmentally sound economic development, to overcome poverty, to conserve natural environment, and help avoid international tensions and conflicts caused by shortages of energy supply. The use of renewable energy sources will lead to the stabilization of the global climate, healthier living conditions, and a secure energy supply for every country in the world. The Agency shall support energy saving and energy efficiency activities." (IRENA-Discussion Paper: Objectives and Activities. The Government of the Federal Republic of Germany 2008, p. 3). It was further noted that, "IRENA will not aim to draw up international regulations or treaties. It will provide its services as and when requested by member states or groups of member states. It will not involve itself in states' energy policies of its own accord or try to enforce policies. All its activities will be decided upon by members." (The Case for International Renewable Energy Agency. The Government of the Federal Republic of Germany 2008, p. 6).

This period was a balance of short-term gains and long-term perspectives for the Agency and, ultimately, for the deployment of renewable energy globally. While the ambition was to create an agency with a meaningful mandate, the framework had to be malleable to allow broad participation and global acceptance. A number of suggestions and proposals contained in the discussion papers were subject to lengthy debates and negotiations. The starting point was finding a common understanding of how to define renewable energy, which in the end included six sources: solar, wind, marine, geothermal, biofuels, and hydro, on the premise that all had to be used in a sustainable way. The work on the development of normative and regulatory standards was confined to the analytical and advisory role, and the focus was placed on supporting countries and fostering cooperation.

While it became evident that an increasing number of countries shared Germany's vision and commitment, it was also apparent that some of the major players were not convinced or—worse still—opposed the idea. Some expressed reservations about the promotion of renewable energy and possible adverse impacts on conventional sources of energy. Mirroring the experiences of the previous decade, the possibility of a new international organization was also met with resistance. The perceived inefficiency of international organizations and the financial burden imposed on member states were important arguments. Several OECD countries were of the view that there was no need for another agency, given the existence of the International Energy Agency. Some others were concerned about possible limitations to national energy policy-making, or undue advantages or disadvantages among different forms of renewable energy.

In spite of this, Germany persisted in its efforts, which proved to be the right decision. In less than one year, agreement was reached on the substantive and institutional framework, as well as the preparatory process for the creation of IRENA. The IRENA Statute, which needed ratification by 25 countries to come into force, defined the Agency's aims and objectives, and a range of institutional matters. IRENA membership was open to all UN member states and to regional intergovernmental organizations constituted by sovereign states committed to renewable energy. The Statute preamble sets the premise for the new Agency: the conviction and desire to promote renewable energy as a major contributor to sustainable development and alleviation of the climate change impacts.

IRENA's objectives reflected this premise. The Agency was entrusted with the widespread and increased adoption, and the sustainable use, of all forms of renewable energy, taking into account two aspects: First, the recognition that each country has individual needs and priorities, in which renewable energy, combined with energy efficiency measures, can play a role. Second, the contribution that renewable energy makes across the pillars of sustainable development: to environmental preservation, climate protection, economic growth, and social cohesion, as well as energy access, regional development, and intergenerational responsibility (IRENA Statute, Article II). To meet these objectives, the Agency was tasked with a range of activities in support of all matters relating to renewable energy, ranging from advisory through facilitating, to catalyzing functions (IRENA Statute, Article IV).

IRENA's organizational structure—encompassing an Assembly, a Council, and a Secretariat—resembles UN structures. Its statutory provisions reflect an effort to create a process that would be democratic and inclusive, but also action-oriented and free of vetoes and possibilities of filibustering. To facilitate this approach, the Statute envisaged that decisions on matters of substance would generally be adopted by consensus. However, the Statute also allows for reaching decisions if no more than two members object, thereby diminishing the veto power of a single member (IRENA Statute, Article IX/F-H). Securing a stable and predictable financial basis was key. Thus, the Agency was to be financed through mandatory, assessed contributions, and additional voluntary contributions. The Statute also allowed for other possible sources of funding, the provisions for which the members could define in the future (IRENA Statute, Article XII/A.3).

At the end of the preparatory process in October 2008, it could not be said with certainty whether sufficient international support existed to found an agency. Nevertheless, the German Government was of the view that the momentum created would be best sustained by a speedy follow-up. The German Government invited all UN member states and a broader renewables community to take part in the IRENA Founding Conference and the first session of the Preparatory Commission in January 2009 in Bonn.

The work undertaken in 2008 enlarged the circle of supporters, and it was evident that a number of EU countries, as well as the SIDS, were committed to the creation of the Agency. In addition, only a few days before the Founding Conference, Barack Obama was inaugurated as the 44th President of the US. The imminent founding of IRENA presented a good opportunity for the new administration to give an early signal that it would take a different approach towards multilateralism and climate protection. The US signing of the Statute prompted a number of its allies in energy policy to also join the Agency.

The Founding Conference exceeded the most optimistic expectations. The small German team which, with its supporters, ran the cause of IRENA for almost two years, watched with amazement and satisfaction the Statute being signed by 75 countries.

A New Beginning

The founding of IRENA on 26 January 2009 in Bonn marked the end of an era of anticipation and uncertainty. But it was also the beginning of a new era of challenges and upheavals. The fact that IRENA was founded at this point in time was a remarkable achievement. Certainly, a good part of this was due to the recognition that renewables are the key for sustainable energy future, for which enhanced international cooperation will be critical. Germany was prepared to take a political risk and, despite the odds, start a process that empowered those who wanted to advance. However, as in other multilateral contexts, there was an array of seemingly unrelated issues that each played a role. In the years to come, some of these issues played a decisive role in the forming of the Agency.

The day after the Founding Conference was also a day of awakening and realization that creating a new agency is a puzzle with many missing pieces. The Conference decided to establish a Preparatory Commission (PrepCom) with a three-fold purpose: to guide the preparation for the establishment of IRENA at its first Assembly, to ensure the Agency's early presence within the renewables landscape, and to commence the implementation of IRENA objectives.

Under my chairmanship, the first PrepCom met on 27 January 2009. The excitement of the success of the Founding Conference was met with the reality of balancing the mundane yet necessary institutional issues, and by increasing pressure to define the Work Programme and deliver substantive outcomes. We started to grapple with issues that are normally taken for granted in other multilateral settings, and soon discovered that the puzzle of creating a new international agency was not only complex but, at times, also unpredictable.

One critical piece—and one commonly found in similar settings—is a Secretariat that would support the intergovernmental process and carry forward the foundational work of building an institution. IRENA did not have that. The first PrepCom there-fore formed the Administrative Committee that, in the absence of the Secretariat, would fulfill its function. The PrepCom also agreed that, "… Germany should continue to keep a facilitative and coordinative role and become Chair of the Administrative Committee." (IRENA/PC.1/SR, 27 January 2009). Austria also offered support by hosting a workshop in April 2009 to further develop the Agency's programmatic activities. In addition, a politically charged process of nominations and selection of the Interim Director-General and interim seat of the Agency accelerated, with the aim of making a decision at the second PrepCom set for June 2009 in Sharm El Sheikh, Egypt. Naturally, Germany's objective was to continue its leading role, so it opted to run for the seat of the Agency.

What unfolded in the months ahead probably would not be so surprising today, considering the ambition of the oil economies to accelerate the deployment of renewables domestically. But in 2009, a campaign by an oil economy—the United Arab Emirates (UAE)—was seen as a novelty that many did not know how to interpret. The campaign premise was the UAE commitment to renewables—already demonstrated through its clean energy project Masdar City, and that IRENA would have been the first international organization headquartered in the Middle East, with significant geopolitical consequences for the region and globally. In its bid, the UAE offered generous support to the Agency and its staff, as well as a dedicated fund for the deployment of renewables in developing countries. The campaign triggered the imagination of political pundits and climate enthusiasts.

As the time of the second PrepCom approached, three countries were in the running: Austria, Germany, and the UAE. The UAE was selected as the interim seat of the Agency, with Germany hosting the IRENA Innovation and Technology Centre in Bonn, and Austria supporting a liaison office in Vienna. The outcome of the conference in Sharm El Sheikh was a political compromise that, in hindsight, was probably one of the most optimal starting points for IRENA. In the coming months, the commitment and financial support from the UAE and Germany became critical not only for the establishment of the Agency, but also for its survival.

The second PrepCom also selected Hélène Pelosse of France as the Interim Director-General (IDG). As the Interim Secretariat was yet to be established, the Administrative Committee continued to perform its role for the months to come. Pelosse took office in October, and Germany and the UAE seconded a small number of staff to support her and her immediate team from the outset. In the coming months, more countries seconded personnel to assist, while the Administrative Committee, together with the fledgling Interim Secretariat, worked on the institutional and programmatic plans and developments.

In January 2010, the third PrepCom adopted the first Work Programme and Budget, which included the organizational structure and formalized the linkages between headquarters in Abu Dhabi, a programmatic division in Bonn, and a liaison office in Vienna. However, it was becoming obvious that the Interim Secretariat was falling short of members' expectations. As time progressed, this situation deteriorated, with some members considering withdrawing their financial support and others wanting to be involved in a very direct manner. The drift between the IDG and the members widened, and the Administrative Committee formed a number of working groups to help navigate through the turbulent waters ahead. Despite these problems, a 25th member state ratified on 8 June 2010 and the IRENA Statute entered into force four weeks later.

With countries increasingly assuming various management functions as a sign of their shaken confidence in the leadership of the Interim Secretariat, Pelosse submitted her resignation to the fourth PrepCom in October 2010. The PrepCom appointed Adnan Amin of Kenya, already selected as Deputy Interim Director-General, to be acting Interim Director-General. Amin, a seasoned diplomat and long-term UN official, had the necessary skillset and personal traits to diffuse the tensions and gradually restore the members' confidence in the Interim Secretariat. Amin brought in a small team with a great deal of experience in the international setting which, coupled with a number of outstanding individuals who already worked for the Secretariat, helped prepare for the transition to a full-fledged international organization.

As Chair of the Administrative Committee who, together with my team and member states-driven working groups, spent much of our time on the management of IRENA, this was a welcome change, especially considering the final stages of preparations for the inaugural Assembly. We were again charting new territory: how to transition from the preparatory phase as seamlessly as possible. The list of unresolved issues seemed to be endless, and the proximity of the Assembly brought added concerns about the number of ratifying members who would be sharing the responsibility for financing the core budget. In parallel, discussions were held on the ambition and focus of the Agency's work programme. Again, old tensions between different priorities and visions came into play, but it was also becoming obvious that IRENA was awaited with high expectations from many stakeholders. This was evident in the strategic workshop hosted by Klaus Töpfer on 11 March 2011, and was further accentuated with the news of the Fukushima accident.

The last stretch of the preparatory marathon took place one week before the inaugural Assembly on 4–5 April 2011. The working groups and the Administrative Committee, which at this point mirrored the membership of the PrepCom, managed to achieve a delicate balance of diverse interests, passions, and priorities that offered an acceptable compromise and sound basis for the transition. The fifth PrepCom adopted the recommendations and, on the eve of 4 April, we were ready for a new beginning. On 4 April 2011, IRENA became a full-fledged international organization with 70 ratifying members and some 80 signatories.

One of the first decisions that the Assembly had to make was on the seat of the Agency. The Assembly confirmed that Abu Dhabi, UAE, would host the Agency, with Adnan Amin as the Director-General. The Work Programme and Budget were adopted, and the Council with UAE as Chair and 20 other countries—including Germany—as members, was elected.

Coming of Age

IRENA is preparing for its fourth Assembly. In just over two years, its membership has grown exponentially and today stands at 117—an additional 47 countries have ratified its Statute since April 2011. Since the concept of IRENA was first conceived, there has been significant worldwide progress on the development and deployment of renewable energy technologies. Consequently, the number of institutions involved in renewables has grown, as has the number of countries who wish to receive assistance and advice from IRENA, share their experiences with peers, or promote best practice and success stories. IRENA has evolved cautiously but rapidly, making partnerships with key international organizations, networks and other stakeholders central to its activities. These positive developments come with added responsibilities and increased expectations of IRENA, and require careful balance to ensure that IRENA is present and heard, while strengthening its substantive competence.

IRENA's medium-term strategy is to be the authoritative global voice for renewable energy by serving as a center of excellence; renewable energy advisory resource for countries; and a network hub of country, regional, and global programs. Indeed, IRENA is making great strides in meeting these ambitions, even against the background of still-limited budgetary and personnel capacities: Its costing analysis and employment studies are authoritative points of reference for countries and other stakeholders; Its Renewable Readiness Assessment methodology is a sought-after tool by countries devising their renewable energy strategies. The Global Atlas, initiated by the Clean Energy Ministerial (CEM), evolved as an example of what can be achieved with an open mind, inclusiveness, and transparency. IRENA created the Global Renewable Energy Island Network (GREIN) as a platform for islands around the world to pool knowledge, share best practices, and seek innovative solutions for renewables-based alternatives to costly fossil fuel imports. Even those who are not members of IRENA see its potential in contributing to the renewables agenda. The UN Secretary-General's initiative Sustainable Energy for All (SE4ALL) has asked— and IRENA members agreed—that the Agency would serve as a hub for renewable energy in a global effort to double the share of renewables by 2030. While we are at the early stage and much remains to be done, all indications are that the Agency is on the right path to become a powerful voice for renewable agency.

Karsten Sach

Germany's recommitment to IRENA is unwavering. We continue to search for ways to strengthen and support the Agency. This year, German Environment Minister Peter Altmaier founded a Renewable Energy Club, comprising 10 countries and the IRENA D-G, to continue to push the boundaries and to innovate in the quest to promote the deployment of renewable energy. In the years to come, the Agency must continue to grow so that it can meet the ever-increasing expectations of its members and the renewables community. For that, IRENA will need the engagement and support of its members and those who believe in and are committed to its mandate.

Transforming the Future

Klaus Töpfer is a friend of IRENA, a sounding board and a go-to source of advice. At the second IRENA Assembly in January 2012, he was invited to attend the ministerial discussion to help shape the Agency's medium-term strategy. He shifted the discussion with ease from local to global, from technical to political, from renewables to sustainable development. He also provided succinct, profound advice: make integration your trademark.

As the current Chair of IRENA's Council, I am again witnessing a milestone in its life. There are now 160 countries as part of IRENA, with China being the latest country to apply for membership. IRENA is indeed making integration its trademark. It is now a melting pot of countries from all over the globe, ranging from the most developed, through the transitional and blossoming emerging economies, to small islands fighting for survival. Having dealt with all the foundational and institutional issues, in the June 2013 Council session we concentrated on substance only—and had an open, inclusive and constructive discussion on our experiences, successes, and challenges in deploying renewable energy.

Even in the few short years since IRENA's founding, the global landscape has shifted profoundly, and in some respects adversely. IRENA gives us a place to step back and reflect on the vision of the founders who long ago recognized the role renewable energy could play in support of sustainable development and the fight against the adverse impacts of climate change. The challenge before us is to stay focused on the vision but remain flexible, so that the Agency can both reflect and influence the spirit of the times.

It is commonly said that the time for renewable energy has come. Indeed, developments across the globe attest to this. But at the heart of this lies the fact that there are few individuals with the foresight to recognize the potential renewable energy presents and the fortitude to act on it. Klaus Töpfer is one of them.

Manfred Konukiewitz

International Climate Finance for Developing Countries: The Green Climate Fund aims for Transformative Ambition

Introduction

Issues of funding climate-related investments in developing countries have played an important role in international climate negotiations from the start—that is, since the 1992 UN Framework Convention on Climate Change. Developing countries were—and still are—concerned that they would have to bear the additional financial burden of mitigating GHG emissions and of adapting to the consequences of climate change to which they have contributed little (if anything at all), and that this would constrain their efforts to emerge from poverty. This concern remains a powerful rationale for developing countries' approaches to international climate efforts.

A financial clause was included in the Convention (Article 4, 3), which defines an obligation of developed countries to provide "new and additional financial resources" to cover costs incurred by developing countries. It remains the only obligation in international law related to development finance.

Over the past years, climate-related international finance has grown remarkably as awareness of the risks for vulnerable countries has increased and the knowledge of GHG emissions originating in developing countries has improved. The OECD and IEA have estimated that climate-related North–South finance flows reached the order of USD 70–120 billion by 2010, depending on the methodology of tracking. Of this total, USD 30–45 billion is from public budgets, while the remainder consists mainly of private flows (OECD/IEA 2012). The Climate Policy Initiative (CPI, 2012), in its report 'The Landscape of Climate Finance 2012,' estimated that development finance institutions (multilateral, bilateral, and national) distributed climate finance of around USD 77 billion (yearly average) in 2010/2011. This corresponds approximately to the estimates produced by OECD/IEA even though numerical values vary: commitments by banks often include funds raised in the commercial sector and amalgamated with public funds.

Recent years have seen a surge in finance flows, because the commitment by developed countries in Copenhagen 2009 to mobilize fast-start funding has actually motivated donors to increase their budgets. The commitment was to provide additional funds of an aggregate USD 30 billion in the period 2010–2012. While there was no clear definition of the base to which the fast-start funds would be additional, it is generally recognized, and confirmed by the Doha COP 2012, that this commitment has been delivered. As an example: Germany increased its climate-related funding to developing countries from a base of Euro 0.9 billion in 2009 to 1.4 billion in 2012.

There is a wide variety of funding channels through which climate finance is being allocated and invested. They range from traditional bilateral cooperation programs to national and regional development banks; further to multilateral development banks, led by the World Bank; and to dedicated global funds like the Global Environment Facility (GEF) or the Climate Investment Funds, managed by the World Bank and regional development banks. The Clean Development Mechanism (CDM) is a unique institution that channels funds via carbon trading. The CPI report plotted all of the funding channels in what has become known as the 'spaghetti diagram.' To most observers, this variety causes confusion, and questions may appropriately be asked whether this multitude of funds and channels really serves the intended purpose.

While this volume of funding and its dynamic growth has been impressive, there was consensus from the Bali COP 2007 onwards that substantially more funding for developing countries was needed to address the challenges of adaptation, building resilience, and mitigation of GHG emissions. In Copenhagen 2009, and later confirmed in Cancun 2010, developed countries committed to mobilize jointly "$100 billion per year by 2020 to address the needs of developing countries […] from a variety of sources, public and private, bilateral and multilateral, including alternative sources" (FCCC/CP 2009, L.7).

On the institutional side, the Green Climate Fund (GCF) was created as a new operational entity of the financial mechanism of the UNFCCC (in addition to the GEF, which the convention designated in 1992 as the 'interim' operational entity). It was agreed in the Cancun decisions "that a significant share of new multilateral funding for adaptation should flow through the Green Climate Fund" (FCCC/CP 2010, 7/Add.1), indicating the widely shared ambition to position the GCF as a major, if not *the* major multilateral player in international climate finance.

Building Ambition for Transformative Action
into the Operation of the GCF

While the GCF was expected to handle a significantly higher level of funds as part of the USD 100 billion, many actors also expected a greater level of ambition in terms of contributing to the transformation to low-carbon development. Too often, key actors in development finance institutions were seen to prefer conventional solutions (particularly in power generation) over low-carbon solutions, which were deemed to carry a higher risk and higher costs.

This perception (correct or otherwise) led to the establishment of this new institution, linked to an ambition to transcend business-as-usual (BAU) approaches in order to focus on transformative investments. While this ambition was not shared universally, and sparked controversial negotiations, it did result in a consensus decision that "in the context of sustainable development, the Fund will promote the paradigm shift towards low-emission and climate-resilient development pathways" (Governing Instrument, para 2). To many negotiators, those two words, "paradigm shift" signaled the added value that GCF should have over the existing funding institutions.

Defining an ambition and getting it agreed in a decision is one thing, and is challenging enough; Translating it into operational criteria and allocation frameworks is another thing, and is at least equally challenging. The GCF Board has undertaken the task as part of its design work, based on the Governing Instrument of the GCF, aiming to create a business model and a resource allocation framework that corresponds with the ambition.

With the purpose of contributing to an informed deliberation of options, the German member of the GCF Board shared a paper with the other board members that proposed key elements of such a resource allocation framework. The following sections are adapted from that paper.[1] According to the GCF Governing Instrument (GI, para 2), the objective of the GCF is to: *"...contribute to the achievement of the ultimate objective of the United Nations Framework Convention on Climate Change (UNFCCC). In the context of sustainable development, the Fund will promote the paradigm shift towards low-emission and climate-resilient development pathways by providing support to developing countries to limit or reduce their greenhouse gas emissions and to adapt to the impacts of climate change, taking into account the needs of those developing countries particularly vulnerable to the adverse effects of climate change."*

Clarification of the concept of "paradigm shift" is an essential element in the development of a resource allocation framework. This concept can be seen to include the following three pillars:

---

1 The paper was based on contributions from several experts outside and within the German government.

Shift of current practice: A new quality or type of action undertaken, suitable to overcome barriers to systemic change. Achieving such transformational change takes time and therefore efforts and support need to be sustained over appropriate periods of time.

Scale: Activities which contribute to sector-wide, regional, or economy-wide activities instead of isolated, project-based approaches.

Learning: Continuous improvements facilitating rapid replication based on lessons learnt and best practices that can only be achieved by transparency.

Despite the expected universal validity of the approach, differences in how the concept can be applied to adaptation and mitigation under the GCF have to be taken into account.

Mitigation Specifics

For mitigation, the agreed objective of the UNFCCC, to limit global average temperature increase to no more than 2°C above pre-industrial levels, provides a framework towards which activities supported by the GCF will have to contribute. Modeling results (Riahi et al. 2012) show that in order to achieve this objective, global emissions need to start decreasing before 2020, mainly through reductions in developed countries.[2] However, in many of the scenarios, developing countries would also need to show reductions in absolute GHG emissions by 2020. Even those developing countries with increasing emissions after 2020 would be required to only show moderate increases until 2020 and to be on a downward trajectory by 2030. The main challenge is to achieve the emission reductions that are needed to reverse the trend of a strong increase of BAU emissions.

It is widely understood that, in order to stay below the 2°C limit, comprehensive changes need to take place in many areas as fast as possible. These changes can be summarized as follows:

♦ A significant change in how we use energy, facilitated by a re-direction of investment away from any emissive and inefficient use of energy, leading to structural changes in all sectors. Often mentioned measures are: a rapid deployment of energy efficiency in the industrial, transportation, and building/construction sectors as well as a significant increase in the use of renewable energy. Scientific find-

---

2 This study includes a comprehensive set of scenarios that were developed by different institutes coordinated by IIASA, Austria, to assess the technological feasibility as well as the economic implications of meeting a range of sustainable development objectives simultaneously. The scenarios not only allow feasibility assessment of different technology choices but are also all designed to: Provide a 50–67% probability of: staying below 2°C; provide almost universal access to affordable clean cooking and electricity for the poor; limit air pollution and health damage from energy use; and improve energy security throughout the world.

ings[3] also show the need to phase-out coal, the use of which can only continue if linked to carbon capture and storage (CCS) or—better—carbon capture and usage (CCU). Currently, CCS is still at the developmental stage, and therefore implementation of CCS is subject to a range of uncertainties which need to be addressed when considering this option.

• An integrated approach to land use planning and management, incorporating the sustainable management of forests, land use change, and sustainable agricultural practices.

Against this background, the GCF has to find an approach for operationalizing the required paradigm shift that allows the Fund to contribute to the agreed 2°C objective, while at the same time leaving sufficient room for countries to propose activities that are in-line with their national priorities. Such an approach for paradigm shift with regard to mitigation could be to adapt existing positive lists of mitigation activities (for example a mitigation typology list used by the International Development Finance Club, IDFC) to the priorities identified against the background of the 2°C objective. However, the positive list by itself would not lead to the identification of activities that can be considered to lead to paradigm shift. The positive list would only work in combination with the investment criteria (see the section *Resource Allocation for Adaptation* for more detail), based on which the most ambitious and thus transformational proposals are selected.

Adaptation Specifics

Despite a growing literature, there remains no agreed definition or description of what would constitute a paradigm shift or transformative change in adaptation actions. Usually, transformational adaptation is contrasted to the current dominant approach of adaptation, where the central aim is to maintain the integrity of existing systems and processes by means of small corrective changes. In contrast, transformational adaptation seeks to change the fundamental attributes of a system in response to experienced and anticipated climate impacts. This may be achieved by adopting policies, measures, institutional constructs, and activities that are new (at least to the location), thus crossing thresholds and creating discontinuity in practices. Transformative change needs to be a deliberately planned activity taking into account the often major impacts on the people involved and the positions of a full range of

---

3 Additional to the GEA scenarios used for the main part of this analysis, this finding is supported by a wide range of assessments, including the IEA's 450 scenario in its World Energy Outlook 2012 and papers modeling the Representative Concentration Pathways (RCP) for the IPCC's upcoming AR5 (see Van Vuuren et al. 2011). Even higher temperature RCP pathways start to reduce conventional coal after 2035 with complete phase-out after 2065 (see Thomson et al. 2011).

stakeholders. However, significant action on the ground may have to await triggering circumstances that allow the new paradigm to be put in place. Therefore, there is a continuum towards transformative adaptation activities, and little agreement exists among either the scientific or policy communities regarding the point at which adaptation becomes transformative.

For adaptation, one would have to rely on a qualitative argumentation explaining how a proposal addresses the three pillars (shift in current practice, scale, and learning) among others. Once the proposal is considered to be transformational, it is assessed based on further criteria, including pre-conditions for implementation of the activity. Such pre-conditions relate to initial planning (e.g., national plans explicitly identify situations where transformative change might be needed and is feasible), the preparation of the decision process (e.g., an inclusive decision process exists to select between the options and to decide on the conditions under which to initiate the transformative process), the preparation for implementation (e.g., a plan exists to identify and/or build capacity in skills related to building shared visions, adaptive management etc.), and the preparation for adaptive learning and sustainability of transformative change (e.g., explicit plans exist to enable institutions to learn and change). Further details on the allocation of resources for adaptation are specified in the section titled *'Resource Allocation for Adaptation.'*

Funding Windows and Resource Allocation

The GI states that, initially, the Fund will have windows for adaptation, mitigation, and a private sector facility (GI, para 37 and 41); and asks the Board to balance the allocation of resources between adaptation and mitigation activities and to ensure appropriate allocation of resources for other activities (GI, para 50). Furthermore, it demands that "the urgent and immediate needs of developing countries that are particularly vulnerable to the adverse effects of climate change, including LDCs, SIDS, and African States, are taken into account, using minimum allocation floors for these countries as appropriate" (GI, para 52).

Since there is no agreed definition of—or a single scientific approach for—how to balance mitigation and adaptation (see Klein et al. 2007), the allocation of resources to the mitigation and adaptation windows as well as to other areas will have to be based on a pragmatic and flexible approach. In order to define the appropriate balance while at the same time leaving flexibility to adapt the allocation between windows, corridors could be defined for the allocation of resources to windows over the lifetime of the GCF (e.g., 10–15% for the Private Sector Facility[4], 30–45% each for

---

4   The PSF can support mitigation and adaptation.

the public adaptation and mitigation window). Since the GCF should be a learning institution (GI, para 3), the resource allocation for each replenishment period could be evaluated against the actual disbursement and revised at regular intervals based on the lessons learnt.

In accordance with the GI (para 50), resources available in each replenishment period are allocated to adaptation window, mitigation window, and other areas (After subtracting costs for administration of the fund, assumed to be 5 % of available resources). Assuming that, for example, 12 % of resources are made available to the Private Sector Facility (PSF), the remaining resources could be allocated evenly between the adaptation and mitigation window. A set-aside (e.g., 3 % of overall resources) could be used to provide some flexibility for resource allocation to mitigation and/or adaptation (e.g., for integrated projects) in each replenishment period.

An impact-based resource allocation framework would be used for all resources in the mitigation window (including REDD+) and part of the resources in the adaptation window. The other resources available to the adaptation window would be allocated ex-ante to the urgent and immediate needs of developing countries that are particularly vulnerable to the adverse effects of climate change, including LDCs, SIDS, and African States. The ambition of mitigation proposals and adaptation proposal in the impact-based allocation tranche is evaluated based on investment criteria. A certain percentage of the resources in the mitigation and adaptation windows (e.g., 1–3 % of overall funding volumes) would be reserved for readiness and preparatory support linked to concrete proposals.

In line with the GI (para 54), financing will be in the form of grants and concessional lending, and other modalities, instruments and facilities if approved by the Board, and will cover the identifiable investment necessary to make the project economically viable.

Basic Elements of the Allocation Process

The GCF will mobilize resources for each replenishment period, which could last 3–5 years. Once resources for a replenishment period are known, ex-ante country allocations for the adaptation window would be determined and the GCF would publish calls for proposals for all windows (e.g., once a year).

Proposals for adaptation and mitigation could be submitted either in a one- or two-step process. In a two-step process, a detailed proposal would only be prepared if an outline of the proposed activity had previously been approved by the Board. In a one-step process, the detailed proposal would be elaborated and directly submitted to the GCF. A two-step process might be more appropriate at the beginning of fund operations, while a one-step process could be desirable—with growing experience and numbers of proposals—against the background of the workload for the Secretariat, the Board and respective expert panels.

After a check for eligibility and completeness, the Secretariat would prepare the evaluation of the proposals. While criteria would differ between the various windows and tranches,[5] in all cases the evaluation would need to draw upon considerable expert knowledge. This is also reflected in the decision of the Board[6] to consider the establishment of mechanisms to draw on appropriate expert and technical advice, including independent scientific and technical advice and from the other relevant thematic bodies. Proposals would therefore need to be evaluated according to the respective criteria and indicators by an independent technical expert panel, and the results of this evaluation would be published on the GCF website. For each call, based on the expert input, the Secretariat would elaborate to the Board its recommendations for distribution of the available resources in each window and tranche. The Board could then decide to approve or reject the proposal.

Resource Allocation for Mitigation

For mitigation, all resources are allocated to transformative proposals based on ambition only. After the Secretariat has checked proposals for completeness and eligibility (e.g., based on a positive list), a technical expert panel would evaluate the proposal according to a list of investment criteria (summarized in Table 1).[7] Investment criteria include not only the evaluation of the proposal itself, but also criteria that relate to the framework conditions for the proposal within the country. The result of this evaluation would be a score, including a report summarizing the reasoning for the scoring. Using a scoring system also means that not all investment criteria would have to be fulfilled by all proposals, but the score would depend on the weighting of indicators and criteria, which still needs to be developed. Some of these indicators are quantitative, and proposals would therefore need to specify the values and calculation methods used to derive them. Others are qualitative, and need to be explained based on guiding questions provided in the proposal templates.

A set of indicators measure how the proposal contributes to the investment criteria **paradigm shift**. A first indicator of the investment criteria looks at the *existence as well as ambition of a low-carbon strategy*, considering the scale of the strategy (national, regional, sectoral, etc.) in addition to the relative emission reductions as compared to BAU. Further aspects included within the ambition of the low-carbon strategy

5 Cf. later sections for details on minimum requirements and criteria for proposal evaluation.
6 See GCF/B.04/17, Decision B.04/09 c) and d).
7 For REDD+ proposals additional criteria will have to be considered. Detailed criteria for REDD+ still need to be developed.

Table 1: *Possible Investment Criteria for the Evaluation of Mitigation Proposals*

Criteria	Unit/value
Contribution to paradigm shift	
Ambition of low-carbon strategy	National, regional/sectoral, sub-national/technology, % deviation of BAU
Proposal is embedded in overall strategy	Fully, partly, no
Ambition of the proposal	Absolute and relative emission reductions (t CO_2e and % deviation from BAU), shift in current practice
Learning and replicability	High, medium, low
Avoidance of lock-in	Preventing long-term, medium-term, none, enabling long-term, medium-term
Second-level critera	
Private sector leverage	$USD_{private}/USD_{public}$
Sustainable development co-benefits	High, medium, low
Co-funding	$USD_{GCF}/USD_{Other\ public\ funding}$
GNI/capita	USD/capita
Cost per unit of emission reduction	USD/t CO_2e reduced
Implementation potential	
Ambition of national policies	% deviation from BAU or high, medium, low
Business environment	(Will depend on activity)
Implementation risks are taken into account in project planning	Yes, no

relate to the commitment to sustainable development within the general development framework of the country (coherence of policies).

Where low-carbon strategies or similar plans exist, it is essential that the proposed activity *is embedded in the strategy*, contributes to its implementation, and is not contradictory.

The *ambition of the proposal* aims to assess the relative as well as absolute emission reductions of the activity compared to BAU development. For all sectors, a significant change from BAU is required to allow a pathway compatible with the objective of the fund. For smaller countries and sectors this could be a way to demonstrate that large-scale paradigm shift is feasible, even though total reductions may not be large. Estimated absolute emission reductions would be assessed based on the total

GHG emissions avoided by implementing a measure compared to BAU in the short, medium, and long term. Quantification beyond 2050 would be technically difficult and would entail growing uncertainties. Therefore, a pathway that covers 2020, 2030, and 2050 should be provided. Part of the ambition of the proposal also includes the extent to which the proposal implies a shift of current practice.

Learning and replicability aims to assess how well the activity is suited to replication in other countries and contexts based on lessons learnt. This can only be a qualitative assessment based on the design of the activity and the extent to which learning is integrated as an element. Measures that are, for example, designed to remove a very specific, country-related barrier will not be as readily applicable to a barrier that is widely found in different countries.

The *avoidance of lock-in* is an essential element for the assessment of proposals. Given the speed of the required transformation, any funding needs to be targeted towards generating the framework conditions that avoid the lock-in of high-emission technologies.

A further set of **second-level criteria** are considered:

- An important criterion is the extent to which a proposal *leverages private sector investment* to supplement public funding.
- A wide range of *sustainable development co-benefits* could potentially be connected to proposed activities, ranging from health benefits to economic impacts or other environmental services. The last Board meeting decided to focus on climate-related activities, but nevertheless co-benefits will play an important role for the implementing countries.
- *Co-funding by other public funds* (e.g., domestic, bilateral, etc.) is desired and can increase the ownership and impact of activities.
- The *income per capita* indicator of the country receiving funding takes into account the capacity of the country to finance the activity from domestic resources.
- Including *cost per unit of emission reduction* in the scoring system recognizes that the GCF mechanism does not aim to finance 'low-hanging fruits' that could be implemented by the countries without GCF support.
- The criterion *'implementation potential'* aims to measure the likelihood of the proposal being implemented and leading to the estimated emission reductions:
- The indicator *ambition of national policies* measures the progress already achieved in implementing mitigation actions in the past.
- For certain projects, the respective *business environment* (e.g., for renewable energy projects) is relevant to the implementation potential of the proposal.
- Furthermore, the quality of project planning and the way *project risks are taken into account* and addressed in the proposal are relevant to the project's implementation potential.

Manfred Konukiewitz

Resource Allocation for Adaptation

For adaptation, resource allocation would also be impact-based. However, part of the resources would be allocated ex-ante to special-consideration countries.

Impact-based Allocation for Transformative Proposals

All developing countries are eligible to seek funding for transformational adaptation proposals. While there is no clear threshold for when a proposal is transformative or contributes to paradigm shift, a technical expert panel would evaluate whether a proposal was eligible, guided by a subset of criteria (see Table 2) covering, among others, the three basic questions for paradigm shift mentioned above.

Once a proposal has been identified as transformative in nature, the expert panel would then assess further investment criteria, including a range of pre-conditions for transformative change that aim to evaluate whether the concept can actually be turned into action on the ground. Scores resulting from this evaluation are then published, from which the Secretariat submits recommendations for resource allocation to the Board.

Table 2: *Possible Investment Criteria for Adaptation Proposals*

Criteria	Unit/value
Contribution to paradigm shift	
Proposal is embedded in overall strategy	Fully, partly, no
Ambition of the proposal	Shift in current practice, scale
Learning and replicability	High, medium, low
Avoidance of mal-adaptation	Preventing long-term, medium-term, none, enabling long-term, medium-term
Second-level critera	
Private sector leverage	$USD_{private}/USD_{public}$
Sustainable development co-benefits	High, medium, low
Co-funding	$USD_{GCF}/USD_{Other\ public\ funding}$
Pre-conditions for implementation fulfilled	
Initial planning, preparation of decision process, of implementation as well as adaptive learning and sustainability of transformative change	Based on a list of questions/checklist

For adaptation, currently it is more difficult to define universally applicable investment criteria that allow selection of the most ambitious proposals for funding (A common metric such as tCO_2e reduced for mitigation does not (yet) exist for adaptation and resilience). However, in the initial allocation cycle there are unlikely to be a sufficiently large number of proposals to lead to significant competition. Many proposals would have substantial scale-up periods, and it is therefore likely that the transformative requirement would be the main decision criteria for adaptation proposals. Building on experience gained with criteria, indicators, and reporting on activities funded in Category 2 countries, the GCF could continuously develop and refine the methodology to evaluate and select adaptation proposals in future replenishment periods.

Table 3: *Overview: Impact-based Allocation for Adaptation*

Eligible countries	All
Proposal meeting definition of transformational change	Yes
Impact-based allocation	Yes, proposals will be evaluated based on specified investment criteria and the most ambitious proposals are funded
Minimum requirements	◆ Meeting definition of transformational change ◆ Detailed demonstration of integration of adaptation funding with national development spending ◆ Well documented analyses of expected benefits, including quantitative measures of vulnerability and losses as well as saved wealth/health

Proposals in this tranche would be subject to high standards of reporting against common indicators, including quantitative measures of vulnerability and losses, as well as measures like saved wealth/health, and would need to take place in the context of substantial plans as well as demonstrate commitment to sustainable development plans.

Special Consideration of the Urgent and Immediate Needs of the Most Vulnerable Developing Countries

A simple categorization of countries may be used to enhance the equity, effectiveness, and efficiency of the allocation process, and to encourage progression towards transformational change. In order to take into account the urgent and immediate needs of the group of countries mentioned in the GI (see para 52), special consideration can be given to such countries by providing simplified access to a fixed amount of financing. Countries belonging to this group would be LDCs and those SIDS, African States,

Country-level Indicators or Indices

Vulnerability:

Various components of vulnerability have been described, and favored definitions keep changing. The most commonly used breakdown is that vulnerability is a function of a country's exposure to climate-related hazards, its sensitivity to them, and its capacity to cope with the impacts that result. A range of indicators exist (e.g., people affected by climate related disasters) and indices (e.g., Wheeler, GAIN, World Risk Index), which show modest correlations in their general agreement about the most vulnerable countries; however, their detailed conclusions are sufficiently different that allocation outcomes would vary according to the choice of index.

Performance:

Two approaches can be used to capture country performance, either separately or in combination: One, such as the World Bank's CPIA (Country Policy and Institutional Assessment) is to assess the broad indicator of governance and effectiveness in the use of resources, while the other is to assess a country's track record in effective project management in the Fund or similar funds. Both dimensions of performance can be found in allocation approaches used by the World Bank and the regional development banks, e.g., the GEF STAR approach as well as IDA country performance ratings (CPR).

and other countries that are classified as low-income countries in agreed classification schemes.

The ex-ante allocation for these countries could be based on a formula taking into account population, vulnerability, and performance (see the text box above for an explanation). A technical expert panel would have to be tasked with elaborating country-level indices and indicators such as vulnerability and performance. Using these indices, the Fund could then determine ex-ante allocations based on an agreed formula. Countries warranting special consideration could submit proposals up to their allocation cap under rules similar to the Adaptation Fund. Such requirements include, e.g., that the principal and explicit aim of the proposal is adaptation and increased climate resilience; adaptation impacts would need to be clearly demonstrated and monitored based on a number of key results indicators. However, proposals do not need to demonstrate transformative impact. Funding in this tranche would be approved by the Board if proposals meet the specified minimum requirements. The main characteristics of ex-ante allocation and proposals submitted by special-consideration countries are summarized in Table 4.

Table 4: *Overview: Resource Allocation for Special-Consideration Countries*

Categorization of countries	LDCs and those SIDS, African States, and other countries which are classified as low-income countries according to the UNDP classification for TRAC resource allocation
Determination of ex-ante allocation	Formula based on population, vulnerability, and performance
Proposal meeting definition of transformational change	No
Impact-based allocation	No, ex-ante allocation is disbursed if proposal(s) fulfill(s) defined minimum requirements
Minimum requirements	Similar to those of the Adaptation Fund, e.g., adaptation is main focus of the proposals; expected adaptation impacts are clearly demonstrated and monitored based on indicators

Final Remarks

This proposal outlines a possible approach for resource allocation within the GCF, taking into account the guidance of the Governing Instrument. Its primary purpose is to operationalize transformative ambition into criteria, rules, and procedures that can be applied by a global fund, its bodies, and its secretariat. In essence, it suggests mechanisms for an evidence-based assessment of transformative potential among competing proposals. Ex-ante assessments of impacts and results are not new in the operation of such funds, yet are rarely utilized in allocation decisions that include comparative—and thus competitive—selection steps.

The proposal has a high level of detail, which allows visualization of the management challenges associated with such an approach. Few of these details, however, are crucial or indispensable: they have been proposed for discussion and critical review, and they can be changed. What counts is to implant transformative ambition into criteria and procedures for decision making.

With its focus on impact and achieving results, the proposal is in-line with a broader move to measure results and to improve development effectiveness. Delivering results towards shared objectives: this has been a key motive of the Busan Partnership for Effective Development Cooperation, forged in 2011 to also enhance effectiveness and country ownership. Yet the methods and instruments remain a work in progress. Designing the operation of the Green Climate Fund to incorporate transformative ambition will not only ensure that finance will deliver better towards GHG mitigation and resilience, but will also catalyze other partnerships in sustainable development.

Manfred Konukiewitz

LITERATURE CITED

CPI (2012): The Landscape of Climate Finance. Climate Policy Initiative. November 2012.

FCCC/CP (2009): Report of the Conference of the Parties on its Fifteenth Session, L7.

FCCC/CP (2010): Report of the Conference of the Parties on its Sixteenth Session, 7/Add 1.

Klein, R.J.T., Huq, S., Denton, F., Downing, T.E., Richels, R.G., Robinson, J.B., Toth, F.L. (2007): Inter-relationships between adaptation and mitigation. Climate Change 2007: Impacts, Adaptation and Vulnerability. In: Parry, M.L., Canziani, O.F., Palutikof, J.P., van der Linden, P.J., Hanson, C.E. (Eds.). Contribution of Working Group II to the Fourth Assessment Report of the Intergovernmental Panel on Climate Change. Cambridge, UK: Cambridge University Press, pp. 745–777.

OECD/IEA (2012) Tracking Climate Finance: What and How? Paris: OECD.

Riahi, K., Dentener, F., Gielen, D., Grubler, A., Jewell, J., Klimont, Z., Krey, V., McCollum, D., Pachauri, S., Rao, S., van Ruijven, B., van Vuuren, D.P., Wilson, C. (2012): Energy Pathways for Sustainable Development. In: Global Energy Assessment – Toward a Sustainable Future. Cambridge, New York: Cambridge University Press; and Laxenburg, Austria: The International Institute for Applied Systems Analysis, pp. 1203–1306.

Thomson et al. (2011): RCP4.5: A pathway for stabilization of radiative forcing by 2100. In: Climatic Change 109: 77–94.

Van Vuuren et al. (2011): RCP2.6: Exploring the possibility to keep global mean temperature increase below 2°C. Climatic Change 109: 95–116.

Uwe Schneidewind and Mandy Singer-Brodowski

Enabling the Great Transformation: Transdisciplinarity as Individual and Institutional Challenge

Introduction

Realizing a sustainable future in the Anthropocene requires a 'great transformation.' The massive technological, economic, social, and cultural change this implies is based on new forms of literacy and knowledge integration. It depends on a highly transdisciplinary 'transformative science,' i.e., scientific knowledge production that not only focuses on 'system knowledge' but also on 'target' and on 'transformation' knowledge, and thus integrates different disciplines and practical expertise.

The existing science system is actually not fulfilling this new social contract between science and society. Frontrunner institutions like the IASS and 'transdisciplinary personalities' like Klaus Töpfer are important change agents to bring forward the transformative mission of a future Earth science.

The Great Transformation: A New Social Contract for Sustainability

In 2009, Johan Rockström from the Stockholm Resilience Center, together with about 30 co-authors, published a seminal article in *Nature* journal on the 'planetary boundaries' that reframed the sustainability debate. The study demonstrated in an impressive manner the concept of the Anthropocene proposed by Paul Crutzen: humankind is the engine of dramatic developments in global ecosystems. In nine different areas (e.g., climate change or the loss of biodiversity), bio-physical thresholds can be identified; for seven of them, thresholds can even be quantified precisely. If these thresholds are exceeded, then we will face risks in other areas that cannot yet be calculated. A popular and widely discussed area is climate change. The international commitment to limiting global warming to two degrees Celsius is based on the insight that, with greater global warming there will be so-called tipping points. These tipping points initiate non-linear changes of huge dimensions and their consequences will be irreversible (e.g., the massive melting of the polar ice caps).

Science has contributed extensively to the roots of this development. Modern societies are driven by innovations and they follow a path of growth that is purported to be the only possibility to stabilize social systems. The science system, largely financed by the public sector, thereby forces the development of new and innovative technologies. These technologies further contribute to the increasing exploitation of resources and pollution of the environment.

Many of the new technologies influence the surrounding environment in ways that seem to be irreversible, because the consequences have such far-reaching ecological, social, and economic impacts. They cause new and also incalculable side effects; modern societies can thus be characterized as 'side effect societies' or risk-societies (see Beck 1998; Schneidewind & Singer-Brodowski 2013).

The relationship between science and society is out of balance; it can even be argued that an estrangement of science and society has taken place over the past decades. The science system itself abdicates its own responsibility as it calls for the freedom of research and teaching at universities. Helga Nowotny's 'Insatiable Curiosity: Innovation in a Fragile Future' (2008) shows the pressure of innovation, i.e., the urge to continually invent material things in modern societies—and the consequences of it. The current debate about fracking and oil sands is one of the best examples of this disturbed relationship between science and society. Currently, huge investment is being made to improve the technologies for extracting unconventional gas and oil reserves, despite the essential need to prepare alternative pathways towards a post-fossil economy.

To avoid further exceeding planetary boundaries, a great transformation and a new social contract for sustainability are needed (see WBGU 2011). This social contract consists of a new cooperation between different stakeholders. The new social contract forms a bridge between these different stakeholders (see Figure 1), who have changed fundamentally in their own self-concept and their role in society in the 21st century. The strong, proactive, and empowering state plays an important role in the flagship report of the German Advisory Council on Global Change (WBGU). The economy has to be developed towards a more sustainable direction through investments and alternative economic branches. One important stakeholder is science, which has to contribute to the development of sustainable technologies, but also the production of knowledge about transformation processes. Scientific research should focus on the Grand Challenges and produce knowledge for facilitating the transitions needed to

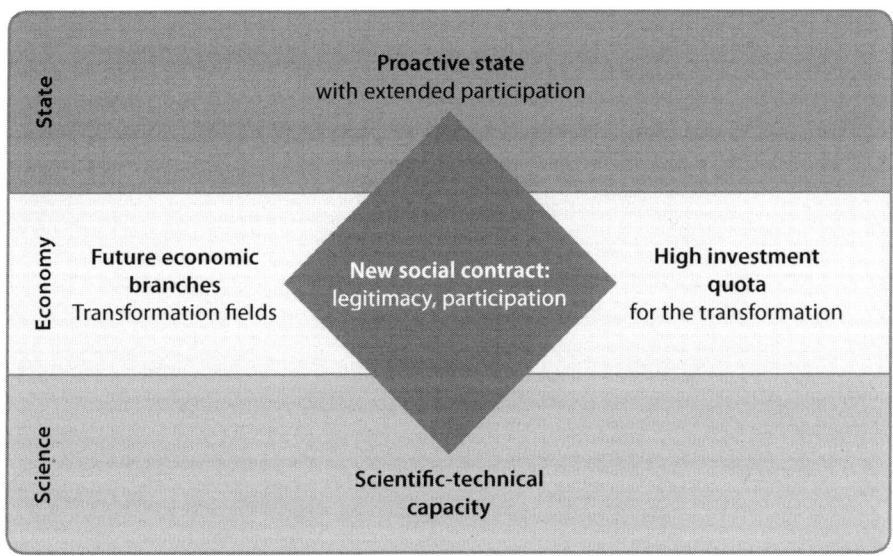

Figure 1: *New social contract (Source: WBGU 2011, p. 275).*

reach a sustainable future. Finally, all these stakeholders are part of a contract with civil society, which appears to become increasingly self-confident, competent, and aware of its role in this relationship.

In the flagship report of the WBGU (2011), several contract theories are described. Now, from the perspective of the WBGU, a revised social contract accompanies huge challenges, because the contract has to be adapted to the reality of a globalized society:

1. "Because of progressive economic and cultural globalisation, the nation state can no longer be considered the sole basis for the contractual relationship. Its inhabitants must responsibly take into account transnational risks and natural dangers, and the legitimate interests of 'third parties,' i.e., other members of the world community.

2. Traditional contract philosophy presupposed the fictitious belief that all members of a society are equal. Considering the disproportionate distribution of resources and capabilities in today's international community of states, we must have effective, fair global compensation mechanisms in place.

3. The natural environment should be given increased consideration when revising the social contract.

4. The contract has to bring two important new protagonists into the equation: the selforganised civil society and the community of scientific experts." (WBGU 2011, p. 277).

Enabling the Great Transformation: Transdisciplinarity as Individual and Institutional Challenge

Citizens consent to expectations of innovations that are connected with the sustainability postulate. They exchange their own spontaneous wishes (for example to consume in an exorbitant way) for the advantages that are expected with the contract (for example a safe operating space within planetary boundaries or the right to participate in a strong state) (see WBGU 2011, p. 277). The strong, proactive, and empowering state guarantees these advantages, and actively involves its citizens in decisions that are made for the future and which aim to achieve sustainability targets. It is important to note that this is not the same as merely calling for citizens' acceptance of decisions after a political decision has actually been made. In Germany, the energy transition—the 'Energiewende'—is a prominent example of a situation where many people agree with the overall aim of developing renewable energy but refuse to accept new technologies within their own environment for esthetic reasons. This is called the "not in my back yard" (NIMBY) mentality, and it seems to be grounded—at least partly—in governments' unrealistic expectation of public acceptance and in a lack of opportunities for citizens to participate in the transition process. "This links a culture of attentiveness (born of a sense of ecological responsibility) with a culture of participation (as democratic responsibility) and a culture of obligation towards future generations (future responsibility). This is no demand for a merely superficial or even resigned acceptance on the part of civil society; rather, it is acknowledged as an actively involved partner with shared responsibility for the success of the transformation process, and mobilised, thereby entering into the contract voluntarily—as assumed by the republican-liberal version of the original social contract. The idea of a powerful state is therefore indelibly linked with the recognition of civil society and the way it has evolved since the 19th century, the innovative powers inherent in the economy, and the proactive and proinnovation forces active in political and administrative elites. Today, all of this always applies in the global arena as well" (WBGU 2011, p. 277).

A New Social Contract between Science and Society

A pivotal part of the new social contract for sustainability is the contract between science and society. It comprises not only the integration of sustainability aspects, but also structural reform of the institutions where scientific knowledge is produced, and the infrastructures that frame the conditions of these institutions.

Helga Nowotny and colleagues (2001) have pleaded for a new cooperative relationship between science and society, and have developed the concept of a Mode-1 and Mode-2 science in reflexive modernity. The conventional mode of knowledge production in the science system is mono-disciplinary and technocratic. Scientists seem to produce findings that are certain and predictive. The production of scientific knowledge takes place in well-insulated areas, for example "large research laboratories and their closed walls." This kind of research is displaced "by Mode-2 research, which is a more open undertaking that is characterized by a transdisciplinary orientation toward social, environmental, industrial, or medical problems" (Nordmann et al. 2011, p. 5).

In the age of reflexive modernity (Beck et al. 1994, Beck in this volume), a new type of research is required that accepts different forms of knowledge, i.e., knowledge of stakeholders and scientific knowledge. In an age of uncertainty we therefore need transdisciplinary research processes and a non-hierarchical structure of research organizations. This is also mentioned in the IASS TransGovernance project, which described the new interdependence and interplay between different societal actors such as the media, representative democracy, and scientists (in 't Veld et al. 2011). Furthermore, in a transdisciplinary research project, the evaluation and quality control of research outcomes should be organized in a participatory way. In our latest book, 'Transformative Wissenschaft' (Transformative Science, Schneidewind & Singer-Brodowski 2013), we develop—based on the idea of a Mode-1 and Mode-2 science—the concept of a Mode-3 science.

This Mode-3 science represents the institutionalization of a permanent self-reflection in the science system. It refers to Niklas Luhmann's idea of an observation of the third order. Luhmann says: "The observer of the first order only reads a text; the observer of the second order asks how the text is to be read and understood and what arguments the text supports; the observer of the third order wonders why the text is written and which function the arguments have." (see Luhmann 1997, p. 1126). A Mode-3 science therefore asks which functions the current science system has, which routines are established, and which dependencies exist between the science system and society. It reflects its own interplay with society and questions its institutional basic conditions (e.g., incentives, structures in the funding of research, career pathways, and the balance between society-oriented and technology-oriented approaches). These basic conditions include individual and institutional matters as well as the scientific infrastructures.

Miller et al. (2011) advocate a different approach to the organization of academic institutions. The production of sustainability knowledge requires a fundamental shift towards an epistemological pluralism and reflexivity: "epistemological pluralism involves promoting the use of all relevant knowledge, perspectives, and viewpoints in a structured, rigorous manner [...] Reflexivity involves the understanding that the institution itself is part of the dynamics of the system that it seeks to change, thus it continually reexamines and reevaluates the foundational assumptions of its work by 'opening up' its boundaries to multiple representations and discourses outside the institution." (Miller et al. 2011, p. 178). They argue that there exist both internal reflexivity and external reflexivity, which emerge in the cooperation with society. Civil society therefore has a very important role to play in this context—it reflects the blind spots of the current scientific mainstream and calls the members, institutions, and infrastructures of the scientific community to transform themselves and their work permanently into the direction of society-based research. In the end, this may lead to a new innovation-capability within the science system, addressing a fundamental paradox that has long existed within the science system: while it is under constant pressure to produce innovations (and quite successfully does so), it is itself characterized by complete inertia as regards changes in its own established institutions, structures, and processes.

What is currently needed seems to be a harmonization between science and society—a re-embedding of the science system in society, creating both awareness for the great societal challenges and a new contract between science and society. This is also the aim of Mode-3 science. To support the co-design and co-production of knowledge together with civil society, new institutional settings are required. The central question is thus: how might the permanent participation of civil society be organized in a science system that normally strives for mono-disciplinary excellence? With regard to research (as one central task of the science system), the answer can be a transdisciplinary approach, which has been developed during the last 10 years in the context of the debate on sustainability science (see Lang et al. 2013). This has been enriched by the call for acceptance of different epistemic cultures in recent years. This new approach is able to cope with different forms of knowledge beside the original scientific knowledge: system knowledge, target knowledge, and transformation knowledge—all these forms of knowledge are required to deal with sustainability challenges.

In the field of education, this new approach would lead to an embedded curriculum that enables education for participation and transformative learning with societal impact. It complements the concept of employability, which is prominent in the EU Bologna Declaration, by also addressing the development of young personalities in the 21st century. For university students, Higher Education for Sustainable Development could frame a 'learning for change' and contribute to sustainable development in fostering three dimensions of learning: 1. individual action and behavioral change; 2. organizational change and social learning; and 3. inter- and transdisciplinary cooperation (see Michelsen & Barth 2013). This kind of learning often appears in project-oriented settings (see Brundiers et al. 2011) and can be explained via social-constructive theories. According to these theories, learning is mainly guided by the activity of the learner; happens with concrete experiences (see Dewey 1925); and takes place with cooperative participation in a community of practice (see Lave & Wenger 1994). Self-organized learning settings therefore offer an ideal context for developing key competencies. As Stephen Sterling argues, "Sustainability is not just another issue to be added to an overcrowded curriculum, but a gateway to a different view of curriculum, of pedagogy, of organizational change, of policy and particularly of ethos." (Sterling 2004, p. 50).

Uwe Schneidewind and Mandy Singer-Brodowski

How Do We Reach the
Great Transformation in the Science System?

Apart from the description of this unwritten social contract for sustainability in its flagship report, the WBGU has created something very interesting, which is extremely important for our debate: the council members introduced the concept of a 'great transformation for sustainability' into the discussion and based it on the description of societal transitions in general. It refers to a heuristic approach to transformations and focuses on a fundamental question: "Do we want to suffer from a transformation by disaster or proactively create a transformation by design?" In its analysis, the WBGU looks for historical transformation processes like the Neolithic (when mankind developed agriculture) or the industrial revolution. In particular, the industrial revolution was (more or less) a planned process where new concepts, infrastructures, and technologies fundamentally changed the lifestyle of humankind in terms of social, cultural, and technological innovations. What can be learned from this? That we are already in the process of the transformation of our world-society, and that we can shape it actively and creatively.

The WBGU refers to a new research approach developed in the Netherlands: the transition approach. Members of the Dutch Research Institute for Transitions (DRIFT) observed and analyzed the diffusion of innovations into the societal mainstream, and through this built up a new theoretical approach. They started with the observation of sectoral transformation processes and then continued to transfer their emerging model to societal transformations in general. The model can be used for different levels of observation (for example an economic sector, a nation, or a single organization). This is its strength, because it can be used to describe different transitions. Uwe Schneidewind and Karoline Augenstein (2012) have applied the transition theory model to the German science system (see Figure 2, which also shows the functional and interdependent levels within a system that are important in order to understand the model). The level of the landscape includes great global and societal trends, like demographic change or the revolution through information and communication technologies. They cannot be influenced by the stakeholders of the other two levels; The level of the regime frames all the rules, routines, and institutional habits that contribute to the stabilization of the current system; Last but not least, there is the level of the niche, wherein change agents develop technological and social innovations. These change agents are trendsetters: they modify and improve their innovations until they have reached readiness for marketing; and through the ongoing process of networking between the different change agents, they contribute intensively to the mainstreaming of innovation, especially through the use of so-called 'windows of opportunity.'

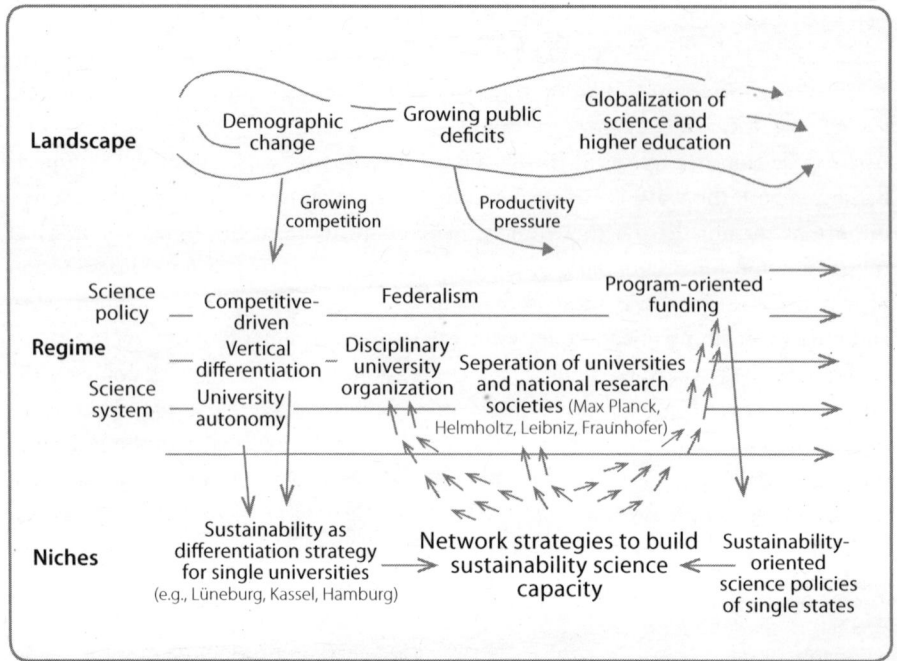

Fig. 2: *How to transform a science system? The example of the German Science System.*
Source: Schneidewind & Augenstein 2012.

A characteristic of the German science system is the existence of many indepen-dent research institutes that are unaffiliated to universities. Many of these institutes for sustainability (like the Öko-Institut in Freiburg) developed out of a protest move-ment against a strong mono-disciplinary bias in universities. They have supported the development of important concepts within the scientific debate on sustainability in Germany. One example is the socio-ecological research program of the German Government, which was developed by an alliance of these sustainability institutes and now receives funding of 12 million euros per year. The funding of this program also introduced institutional innovations into the science system, such as the discussion about quality criteria for transdisciplinary research projects, or the constitution of groups for young academics.

The second peculiarity of the German science system is the high responsibility of the federal states in the field of education and research. Change agents therefore have to navigate this shared responsibility between the national government and the federal states. At the same time, some of these federal states (for example Nordrhein-West-falen and Baden-Württemberg) form the avant-garde, with the creation of a society-oriented and transformative science system in their territory. Nordrhein-Westfalen patronizes real-world-laboratories and Baden-Württemberg forces the development of sustainable profiles for its universities.

To support the transformation of the German science system (i.e., at the level of the 'regime' in accordance with the DRIFT transition model), networks have formed between advanced universities and sustainability institutes. Ecornet, the ecological research network is one of these networks, bringing together advanced institutes; NaWis-Runde, the group for sustainability science is a network of universities *and* independent research institutes. The Wuppertal Institute participates in both networks; the IASS is a core member of the NaWis network. Both explore common paths for sustainable innovations within the science system. In 2012 the networks collaboratively organized a campaign called "Creating transformative knowledge." During the course of several events, we discussed with more than 1500 participants the institutional potential for the transition of the German science system, such as the funding of new initiatives by foundations, or the potential for engaging with civil society. In May 2013, the corganization Plattform Forschungswende published, for the first time, demands for transparency and the participation of civil society.

Transformative Individuals, Institutions, and Infrastructures as Catalysts for a Science System Shift

A glance at the ongoing processes of change within the German science system reveals three important motors for transitioning towards production of more transformative knowledge:

1. *Transformative individuals/personalities.* Science is ultimately driven by scientists and scientific minds. Without having researchers that take societally relevant challenges as the starting point for their own work, and who are willing to interact with other disciplines and field practitioners, transformative science will not emerge. 'Context partisans' are of crucial importance, meaning people that have developed an understanding of change within different societal environments and a deep empathy for different scientific, political, societal, and cultural contexts. That explains the specific importance of individuals like Klaus Töpfer, who have bridged different environments: Coming from the science system, entering the political sphere on a national and later global level, before returning to the science system to lead a new innovative sustainable think-tank in the German science system—always motivated to address the same challenge in different contexts: a more sustainable world at all levels, from local to global.

2. ***Transformative institutions.*** A critical mass of transformative individuals will only develop if institutional environments exist that support the growth of such personalities. There must be opportunities to develop theoretical and methodological skills as well as career pathways for scientists working in transdisciplinary contexts. The science system still has a long way to go in developing sufficient transdisciplinary environments. Transdisciplinary research institutes like the IASS in Potsdam or the Wuppertal Institute are important hubs practicing and advocating the need for this development. However, much stronger links are needed to similar developments in universities, where disciplinary training and career pathways are formed. Networks such as NaWis offer an approach to bring together pioneering institutions from the spheres of research institutes and universities.

3. ***Transformative infrastructures.*** A transformative science needs 'laboratories for transition processes,' i.e., real-world laboratories to initiate and better understand socio-technological change processes. Cities, specific regions, 'transition towns,' or a regional mobility system can be 'real-world labs'. In such contexts, scientific knowledge production and reflection are deeply embedded in concrete transformation processes. They can be understood as new forms of scientific infrastructure that are urgently needed to create transformative knowledge. For instance, the German 'Energiewende' actually constitutes one large 'real-world lab' on a national scale, with significant impact also on global developments. The process of creating a deeper and more comprehensive interlinkage of this transition experiment with the science system is still under way. The IASS and Klaus Töpfer—as one of the 'fathers' of the German Energiewende who headed the Ethics Commission that initiated and prepared the Energiewende—are playing a central role in establishing this new science–society link.

Conclusion

There is an urgent need for a transition in the science system as a whole. This transition must encompass not only a greening of campuses but a more fundamental and paradigmatical transformation of the way in which science institutions carry out their principal tasks of conducting research and providing education. This also implies a structural transformation among the organizations funding research and in the typical career pathways of scientists, that should not focus exclusively on mono-disciplinary excellence. According to the transformation-perspective adopted by the WBGU this 'turn' includes a deep transformation of scientific infrastructures (universities and research institutes), political decision making, the ways in which way scientific knowledge is produced, and the quality assurance processes in place that tend to reproduce current structures (e.g., the peer-review processes) as well as the self-conception of scientists in terms of their values and basic understanding of the role of science in society. The social contract that the WBGU is calling for builds the unwritten but basic foundation of this process. It enables a new awareness of the relationship and interlinkages between different societal systems—and it may eventually release the scientific system from its ivory tower.

LITERATURE CITED

Beck, U. (1998): World Risk Society. Cambridge: Polity Press.

Beck, U., Giddens, A., Lash, S. (1994): Reflexive Modernization – Politics, Tradition and Aesthetics in the Modern Social Order. Cambridge: Polity Press.

Brundiers, K., Wiek, A., Redman, C. (2010): Real-world learning opportunities in sustainability – concept, competencies, and implementation. In: International Journal of Sustainability in Higher Education 11/4: 308–324.

Dewey, J. (1925): Experience and Nature. Mineola / New York: Dover Publications.

Lang, D.J., Wiek, A., Bergmann, M., Stauffacher, M, Martens, P., Moll, P., Swilling, M., Thomas, C.J. (2012): Transdisciplinary research in sustainability science – practice, principles, and challenges. In: Sustainability Science 7 (Supplement 1), pp. 25–43.

Lave, J., Wenger, E. (1994): Situated learning: legitimate peripheral participation. Cambridge: Cambridge University Press.

Luhmann, N. (1997): Gesellschaft der Gesellschaft. Frankfurt am Main: Suhrkamp.

Michelsen, G., Barth, M. (2012): Learning for change: an educational contribution to sustainability science. In: Sustainability Science 8/1: 103–119.

Miller, T.R., Munoz-Erickson, T., Redman, C.L. (2011): Transforming knowledge for sustainability: towards adaptive academic institutions. In: International Journal of Sustainability in Higher Education 12/2: 177–192.

Nordmann, A., Radder, H., Schiemann, G. (2011): Science After the End of Science. An Introduction to the "Epochal Break Thesis". In: Nordmann, A., Radder, H., Schiemann, G. (Eds.). Science transformed? Debating Claims of an Epochal Break. Pittsburgh: University of Pittsburgh Press.

Nowotny, H., Scott, P., Gibbons, M. (2001): Re-Thinking Science. Knowledge and the Public in an Age of Uncertainty. Oxford: Polity Press.

Nowotny, H. (2008): Insatiable Curiosity: Innovation in a Fragile Future. trans. Mitch Cohen. Cambridge, MA: MIT Press.

Rockström, J. et al. (2009): A safe operating space for humanity. In: Nature 461: 461–472.

Schneidewind, U., Augenstein, K. (2012): Analyzing a transition to a sustainability-oriented science system in Germany. In: Environmental Innovation and Societal Transitions 3, pp. 16–28.

Schneidewind, U., Singer-Brodowski, M. (2013): Transformative Wissenschaft. Klimawandel im deutschen Wissenschafts- und Hochschulsystem. Marburg: Metropolis.

Sterling, S. (2004): Higher Education, Sustainability, and the Role of Systemic Learning. In: Wals, A.E.J., Corcoran, P.B. (Eds.). Learning for Sustainability in Times of Accelerating Change, Wageningen: Wageningen Academic Publishers.

in 't Veld, R.J., Töpfer, K., Meuleman, L., Bachmann, G., Jungcurt, S., Napolitano, J., Perez-Carmona, A., Schmidt, F. (2011): Project Report. Science for Sustainable TRANSformations: Towards Effective GOVernance. IASS Institute for Advanced Sustainability Studies, Potsdam [http://www.iass-potsdam.de/de/forschungscluster/globaler-gesellschaftsvertrag-fur-nachhaltigkeit/transformation-processes/archiv-0; 25 September 2013].

WBGU (2011): World in Transition – A Social Contract for Sustainability. Flagship Report 2011. Berlin: German Advisory Council on Global Change.

Günther Bachmann

Steam Engines, Renewable Energies & Co.

Why Transformation is About Society, Not Techniques

Executive Summary

Our school textbooks present the Industrial Revolution just as confidently as they do the Gallic Wars, which, according to them, Julius Caesar supposedly won. This appearance is deceptive: Caesar was not alone; and the Industrial Revolution is not just a story about steam engines. The history of transformation teaches us that technology can be crucial but is not a condition *sine qua non*. There are even examples for transformation that are driven by social and political frameworks exclusively. However, the contemporary notion of a Third Ecological Industrial Revolution implies a strong technological foundation, mostly associated with renewable energies and green technology. Scientifically, this raises some doubts. The historical mechanism of complex transformations might inform today's conversation about the next major move onto a pathway to sustainable development. Today's political strategies, however, are far from drawing conclusions from the historical evidence of grand transformations. It is fair to say that 'historical science' and 'sustainability' have not yet established any substantive link. This should be changed on the basis of well-advanced historical research and the best practice of today's leading initiatives towards sustainable development.

The German Council for Sustainable Development (RNE) and the Institute for Advanced Sustainability Studies (IASS) invited historians along with experts from business, government, and civil society to take part in a first workshop on the conclusions that can be drawn from historical knowledge of the Industrial Revolution regarding the contemporary challenges of sustainable development. Those conclusions comprise the governance of transformation, the concept of knowledge and society, and the interrelationship of hard-wired regulation and soft policies encouraging voluntary action. It is suggested to further advance the workshop's first exploration into more profound research.

This essay builds on that first exploration and adds further aspects related to transformations and sustainability management today. The contents of this essay are the sole responsibility of the author.

Transformations

The term 'transformation' in itself is vague and attractive in discourses at the same time. It qualifies as metanarrative as does, for example, sustainability. Polanyi (1944: here 1978) originally coined the term 'The Great Transformation' to describe social conflicts between the market and society. There were manifold political transformations in the pre-industrial era, such as the transition from monarchy to constitutional state; in the enforcement of human and civil rights; in the emergence of commercial power without territorial power; and the changing forms of ownership, the commons, and the concept of inheritance, especially those of the Church.

Raskin (2003), Landes (1998), Hawken et al. (1999) as well as Diamond (2005) and Beattle (2010) use the term directly or in a textual context. Historical research identifies several change processes that are not related to war or disruptive conflicts, as characterizing thresholds where a society as a whole changes, such as: demographic change, the social change from a feudal to a civil society, or changes in mindset, culture, and consumption, and not least the energy supply. Deep cultural roots and practices provide valuable insights and can inform today's decisions. The case of Carl von Carlowitz and the sustainable forestry in Saxony in the 18th century (Sächsische Carlowitz Gesellschaft 2013; Mauch 2013; Haber 2010) underpins this assumption, as does the transformation of the world that Osterhammel (2010) attributes to the Industrial Revolution. History saw transformations that were driven and run by societal forces exclusively, and with no causally-determined technological dimension. Prussian history sets an example.

Historians repeatedly designate various parts of the history of Prussia as a 'transformation.' Christopher Clark (2007) speaks of a transformation under the Prussian Great Elector Friedrich Wilhelm, which was set in motion by the social, economic, and moral devastation of the Thirty Years War, and which are known as 'Repeuplierung' (re-population, the migration of people to Prussia). The Edict of October 1807 instigated by Prussian reformers Karl Freiherr vom Stein and Karl August Fürst von Hardenberg is seen as another stimulus for transformation, because it greatly changed the judicial system, markets, and society. Known as the Stein–Hardenberg Reforms, they comprised a series of constitutional, administrative, social, and economic innovations in reaction to the Prussian defeat by Napoleon in 1806 and the weakness of the old absolutist model of statehood.

Similar reforms can be found throughout Europe, but the Prussian way clearly stands out. None of them were based on a specific technology. Based on enlightenment ideas, Prussia transformed government and administration, abolished serfdom, and allowed peasants to become landowners. In industry, competition was encouraged and the monopoly of guilds was suppressed. The nobility lost its decentralized power and strongholds. Parallel to this the military and the educational system were reformed. Looking back, all this may be seen as a great transformation. However, beyond the obvious reaction to a 'failed state' (as we would call similar dysfunctional and disabled states today), there was a larger momentum this change could build upon. This époque produced an impressive line-up of German philosophers, literates, and scientists that Watson (2010) terms a 'Third Renaissance' (after those of the 12th and 15th centuries). As part of our larger question referring to the cause and drivers of transformations, we have to say there is not yet a satisfactory explanation for this. Watson hints to the 17th- and 18th-century religious revival, but this cannot fully explain the cause/effect relationship. Of interest is the emphasis that the Prussian reforms gave to the role of universities. Combining teaching with research in both humanities and science required a new type of expert and created a new type of excellent knowledge. Nevertheless, it still allowed subsequent mindsets to unfortunately choose mystical wholeness and totalitarian politics over humanitarian views and democratic politics, which again underlines that transformation, in this historical example, is not a clear and strictly directed development, but always subject to politics, the mindset of the people, and social development.

There are no obvious general criteria by which a change process may be qualified as transformation, yet there are many conceptual terms that attempt to characterize profound changes. One example is 'saddle time,' coined by Koselleck (1979) (Sattelzeit, as a synonym: threshold time, Übergangszeit), which distinguishes a time when change is imminent, but has not yet occurred. Koselleck referred to the beginning of the Industrial Revolution and to the changes in key concepts such as citizen, state, and family. Such emerging concepts prepared for a new understanding of time/change/progress as overall tools of political thought at that time, and eventually provided the basis for further political changes. Any of the change processes that are termed a transformation might raise some doubts about whether or not this category applies. As of today we may judge whether or not we find ourselves at the beginning of a transformation or within—or maybe even missing our chance to hit the 'go-button.' But this self-assessment is not all that important. The saddle-time concept, however, is more apt to describe the open and ambivalent character of our times where, absurdly enough, we see increasing dispute over the (yet only) theoretical insight into the necessity of change, and also the emergence of problems stemming from environmental damage and social inequity.

Undisputed, however, is that the steam engine—the icon of the Industrial Revolution—is seen as a central driver of this transformation. This leads to the question of whether at all—and if so, to what extent—technology drives change; or to what extent transformation is a result of a governance that allows change without foreseeing it.

The Industrial Revolution
and What it tells us About Transformation

The steam engine epitomizes the Industrial Revolution. Its legendary triumph initiated fossil economies and consumption. The economic model based on the burning of coal, oil, and gas still generates today the utopian idea of infinite growth—just as it also demonstrates the immensity of the destruction of the environment and the disorder of the human mindset in understanding ecology. At the same time, this model also reveals its ability to change and set boundaries when under strain. What still predominates, however, is the idea that, in a finite world, material growth can continue unbounded.

That is, however, only the most obvious 'take-away-message' the Industrial Revolution holds for us, and there are more hidden messages as well. The first lesson is well discussed. Over quite some years, among people, politicians, and entrepreneurs the realization is growing that the promise of unlimited growth is fragile; and that, at any rate, a further Great Transformation has to be accomplished: a Third, this time 'Ecological,' Industrial Revolution, encompassing a green economy—be it green growth, be it smart growth, or be it even a concept of prosperity without growth—but with a fundamental efficiency revolution (Schellnhuber 2007; Jänicke & Jacob 2008; Raskin 2003; Weizsäcker 2010; BMU 2008; Jaeger 2011). The German Advisory Council on Global Change chose the term 'Great Transformation,' previously coined by Polanyi's publication of the same name (1944, 1978) as the title of its 2011 report (WBGU 2011). The German Council for Sustainable Development, a multi-stakeholder body reporting to the Federal Government, advocates the notion of a sustainable development that frames fundamental changes throughout society. What is expected of such a change is that it combines the preservation of the environment with the creation of wealth and justice bearing in mind the global nature of climate change and resource constraints. National sustainability strategies (where they exist) as well as global multilateral environmental agreements are making this point. The corporate global business community, with its think-piece 'Vision 2050' (WBCSD 2010), underlines that the business case of tomorrow lies not just in the continuation of what is produced and consumed today. The UN has recently set up an intergovernmental Working Group on universally applicable Sustainable Development Goals.

The more obscured messages are about timing and governance. Assuming that the historical lesson holds true for our contemporary times, thus, one cannot determine a clear moment for the beginning and timing of the transformation. A flickering of action, differentiated over time and space the transformation resembles an oscillation that, over time, succeeds in revolutionizing almost everything. But no-one ever gave a starting signal or perceived contemporary actions as epoch-making. People lived through the Industrial Revolution without perceiving it as such. Thus, the exponents of contemporary historical analysis—Ricardo, Adam Smith, and John Stuart Mill—did not write with an awareness of living in an industrial revolution; even Karl Marx was rather pessimistic about industrialization.

In some pre-industrial core areas, including Saxony, the consumptive use of the environment at that point led to sensitive crises in the supply of wood (Mauch 2013). Shortly after the 'invention' of sustainability by mining administrator Carl von Carlowitz (Sächsische Carlowitz Gesellschaft 2013), the steam engine decided the problem of resources in favor of coal. Industrialism has since been connected with the idea of bigger, powerfully expansive, uniform, and centralized solutions. According to Osterhammel (2010) it was the multitude of small and medium steps towards industrialization that produced a history of change. Taken together, in an ex-post view, they can be characterized as a transformation of the world. The relationship between man and nature, between people among themselves and technology was subject to profound change, and the steam engine relates a significant part of that history. The introduction of steam ends the previous energy system, which was predominantly based on the combustion of wood—in this respect a solar or wood-based energy system—and thus anticipates a possible collapse of the ecological foundations for the resource of timber.

Transferring those circumstances to today, it is hard to envision a big-bang-type of start with a formalized consensus such as, e.g., the release of some new generation's treaty or some international agreement. We should instead assume more diverse and 'viral' processes that rely on people's engagement, curiosity, and spontaneity; markets' and innovators' inventiveness; and reflexive and inclusive governance.

The Legacy of the Steam Engine

Like steamrollers that level the roads and carry out civil engineering work, so the steam engine literally rolled through society. By combusting coal, steam machines heat water in a boiler and force the resulting steam under pressure to power crankshafts, drive-belts, or turbines. Huge productivity gains were thus achieved in the generation of energy, mechanical engineering, textile manufacturing, railway infrastructure, and car manufacturing. As opposed to machinery run by water energy, steam machines could technically be installed anywhere, and this universal access multiplied the expansive force of industrialization.

The history of the steam engine is particularly impressive in the delayed industrialization of Prussia. According to Matschoss (1901), Prussia had only 419 steam engines in 1837, but by 1898 there were already 84,648; and while these engines combined produced 3,000 horsepower at the beginning of the century, by the end of it they produced a thousand times more, namely more than three million, which corresponded to a labor force of 78 million people. This progress is symbolic of the then completely undisputed "subjugation of the forces of nature" for the good of the people, and was "the prince who woke the Sleeping Beauty of industry from its slumber" (Matschoss 1901, p. 16 ff., whose book Radkau (2008, p. 29) referred to as the founding work of the German history of technology). No wonder, then, that the steam engine is regarded as an icon of the Industrial Revolution, at best rivaled by Henry Ford's car, known colloquially as the Tin Lizzie.

The original steam engine appeared as a driving force, then matured, and was quietly and unobtrusively replaced. In the collective memory, however, it survived until today and casts a shadow that even coins future thinking, of no avail.

Is There a TransGov Engine?

Recently, momentum has been gained in the search for governance approaches that would implement, support, and strengthen sustainability reforms (in 't Veld 2011; Meuleman 2012). Emphasis is being laid on how to better involve non-state organizations and civil society in political decision-making. The notion of transformative governance, TransGov (as in in 't Veld 2011) invites people, organized civil society, and the private sector to think beyond dichotomy and beyond the TINA ideology (There-Is-No-Alternative). Contributions to this debate stem from the fields of social science and from those disciplines that investigate the impact of knowledge on decision-making processes.

Taking historical lessons into account, however, one might also ask if we can assume the emergence of a technology that would serve the Third Industrial Revolution as a techno-driver equivalent to what the steam machine stands for in the past? As an answer, the metanarrative about the great transformation often considers renewable energies a key technology. There might also be other clean technologies, but that is not the point here. The transition towards sustainable development needs specific technology and it needs innovative technical solutions. But neither must it be seen as a question of technology alone, nor does it make sense to emphasis the social and political dimension alone. Again, the dichotomy of 'either/or' cannot adequately explain what is at stake, and it is debatable whether up-to-date governance will benefit from those concepts.

Technologies themselves are subject to change and, provided regulatory frameworks are supportive, they may form part of the social transformation and the transformative governance. The steam machine and the evolution of valves exemplify this. Initially, the operation of a steam machine tended to lead to the boiler exploding; "bursting boiler" was the technical term. Dramatic accidents, many deaths, the destruction of material goods, and high risk for the workers and the operational processes were the result. Polluters were prompted to a previously unknown step: They gave joint interests more weight than the temptation to profit from the misfortune of the competitor. They established associations that monitored their boilers, and were tasked with preventing accidents and making the equipment safer. The success of the steam boiler inspection agencies (Dampfkessel-Überwachungs-Vereine, DÜV) was huge. In 1900, the DÜV gained the monopoly on monitoring boilers and later, in 1909, cars too. The steam boiler monitoring and auditing associations became what we know today as the TÜV inspectorate (Technischer Überwachungsverein, Technical Inspection Association). Thus, the evolution triggered by bursting boilers was both technical and social; most interesting is the interdependency of both. As to what this means in terms of a Grand Transformation is a question that needs further thought.

Brüggemeier (1996) adds the governance dimension when he regards industrialization as the cause of the emergence of modern environmental policy. According to Radkau (2008, p. 231), this self-monitoring was, however, a "questionable learning process that had led to the perception that security is solely an issue for experts and is best guaranteed by the collective self-regulation of the industry." This approach is said to result in a lack of safety standards and of legislation on technical security as a uniformly structured field. Consequently, even at the beginning of modern environmental protection in the 1970s, there was criticism that the state's environmental policy tended to adopt the easy route of "peripheral intervention" (Hinz & Mayer-Tasch 1974) and thus enjoyed short-term successes (e.g., in line with the dictum 'the solution to pollution is dilution'), but ignored the full context of ecology, local economy, and the long term. What was 'feasible' in the short term then postponed the structural solution to any ecological damage. For example, the high chimney policy shifted the burden of air quality to that of investment in the wider environment of rural areas; the spreading of sewage sludge on soils distributes pollutants across the countryside. These were very simple cases, and the even coarser example of dumping acid waste on the high seas has long since been impermissible. However, these cases clearly demonstrate that environmental problems that have been pushed aside force politicians to resubmit the measures—provided they were only of a peripheral and not a transformative nature.

Gradual technical improvements and safety engineering accompanied the emerging practice of inspection, monitoring, and surveillance. Every explosion enabled and enforced new learning. The probability of damage occurring and the extent of any loss are significant parameters for the technical design of a system. The industry of deliberative risk arises and with it the mathematics of risk, consisting of the probability and extent of damage. Such considerations could improve aircraft and car engines, kitchen equipment—and shape the definition of risk far beyond the realm of mechanical engineering. The latter is not always advantageous: risks are subdivided and fragmented. Ultimately, each risk can gradually be controlled, according to certain pre-set assumptions. Risks that cannot be calculated properly—quite often those relating to the environment and social interaction—are structurally neglected. The end result is the 'turkey syndrome' (Gigerenzer 2013), which describes the systematic usefulness of this definition of risk: The turkeys are concerned about the risk associated with the intrusion of a keeper into their sphere of life. With this ever repetitive (feeding) event, they determine their risk on the basis of the positive outcome of previous events. This is ostensibly rational, and is oriented to knowledge and to learning processes. Thus, from the perspective of the turkeys, the risk apparently shrinks—up to the day before Thanksgiving.

In its report on the phasing-out of nuclear technology in Germany, the so-called Ethics Commission for a Safe Energy Supply (2011) described this phenomenon without referencing the turkey metaphor: As the Commission stated, "The risks of nuclear energy have not changed since Fukushima, but the perception of the risks has. More people have become aware that the risks of a major accident are not merely hypothetical but that such a major accident can actually happen. As a consequence, the perception among a significant section of society has been reoriented to the reality of the risks. Significant factors for the change in the perception of risk are:

♦ Firstly, the fact that the reactor disaster occurred in a high-tech country like Japan. This has caused people to lose faith that such an event could not happen in Germany. This applies to both the accident itself and the long period of helplessness in the subsequent attempts to get it under control;

♦ Secondly, the sustained inability for weeks after the accident to see an end to the catastrophe, to come to a final estimate of the damage, or to specify a definitive geographical boundary for the affected area. The widespread view that the extent of damage even for accidents on a larger scale is limited and can be sufficiently ascertained, which enables this damage to be compared with the disadvantages of other energy sources in a scientifically-based assessment process, has lost a considerable amount of its persuasive power.

◆ Thirdly, the fact that the disaster was triggered by a process that the nuclear reactors were not 'designed' to withstand. These circumstances shed light on the limitations of the technical risk assessments. The events in Fukushima have made it apparent that such assessments are based on specific assumptions, for example on seismic safety or the maximum height of a tsunami, and that reality can disprove these assumptions."

This notion is in contrast to the classic risk management that we are accustomed to since the Industrial Revolution. This classic assumption is that no (major) industrial installation enjoys zero risk; and that the risks of diverse technologies are comparable and manageable thanks to ever-growing knowledge and experience. As a consequence, no single risk would be so great that it would challenge the whole society or region of production. Still today, this is seen as a baseline for plant safety and material science, toxicology and medical technology. Here, risks that can be assessed will continue to be weighed-up carefully, taking into account the state of the science. At the same time, the systemic limitations of this approach are becoming apparent, namely when the potential damage (e.g., being eaten on Thanksgiving) is outside what has been scheduled or calculated (outside the systemic framing).

Between the turkey's perspective and their reality there is a fundamental difference. We can see a similar difference between the steam machine-type of risk and the additional type of risks in the second modernity and in societies. Ulrich Beck (1998) termed the 'second modernity': Industrial safety concepts involving relativistic risk assessment lose their verifiable rationality once the worst case becomes increasingly bigger and more complex. The topos of exploding steam machines belongs to the world of the known possibilities, or known unknowns. But with accumulated and complex risks stemming from the use of nuclear energies and from climate change, the risk grows into the sphere of the unknown unknowns. Those cannot be reliably forecast, and are beyond limits of national jurisdiction or corporate responsibility, and definitely beyond any reasonable framing. And they demand methods of precautionary prevention and governance that create chances and transformational trajectories whereas traditional (virtually all we are familiar with) policies seek to control damages, try to manage risks within the limits of jurisdiction, and create a culture of avoidance.

Transformative Technology Agents?

The improved safety of steam boilers required optimized materials and combustion techniques, while the decisive contribution came from the ability of valves (from ventus, the Latin for wind) to regulate the flow of steam and thereby prevent the boiler bursting. The valve represents, in our context, technologies of a modulating and potentially transformative nature. It is used in a variety of different machines, and can be found in the fossil age as well as in the age of renewable energy technology. Valves meter the flow of materials in a tube and isolate these substances from the environment; they make it possible to control and modulate pressure conditions and thereby utilize them. Valve control is common practice in many drive systems, irrespective of the power source. Other applications include medical technology, the chemical industry, water treatment, and sorting systems. Valves modulate and control devices such as the steam engine, the solar panel, and the internal combustion engine, which presently represent evolutionary end-points as mature technologies. Consequently, the Industrial Revolution also produced transformative technologies used in the transition from an (old) end-product to another (new) end-product. They moderate and control the transformational bridge between what has become and what will yet be.

The question is how such technological bridges can be made operational and made subject to measuring, reporting, and verification. They cannot simply be apprehended as another sector or industry like chemicals, steel, food, or renewable energy. Regarding traditional categories, they are in-between and designing new integrative approaches. The talk of a 'sustainable economy' should probably be geared more towards processes, checks, and balances, modulation of existing procedures, participation, and target systems. There can hardly be any question of a general de-materialization of economic activity; often, the opposite is the case. In the sustainable circulation economy the use of energy, raw materials, global public goods, the mining of goods from closed landfills, and consumer goods as well will fundamentally increase in significance. Rather, de-materialization is to be understood as moving away from fossil fuels and the high turnover of materials. Efficiency strategies (Weizsäcker 1997; 2010) are essential components of transformations that would mitigate climate change, over-fishing in the world's oceans, the use of harmful substances in the food chain, and problems associated with resources such as phosphorus or palm oil.

The Virtue of the Plural

Interestingly, the start- and end-points of the Industrial Revolution cannot be neatly dated. This observation might be of some worth for future strategies, assuming that this process of emerging rather than being overtly announced and started is a general feature of transformative times. From today's perspective of practical sustainability policy, the category 'transformation' usefully interprets the many small events and happenings ex post as part of a process that has a multitude of facets, time frames, regional specifications, winners and losers. Taken literally, a 'transformation' does not specify whether it occurs intentionally or unintentionally. In the case of the Industrial Revolution, one can probably not speak of a volonté générale, and can hardly infer a conscious converging of all actors. In this respect, industrialization is the result of a multitude of individual actions and processes that were by no means 'coordinated,' were not even similarly oriented, and were in part even contradictory. The meaning of these historical properties for great transformations is an issue that is interesting not only from a scientific perspective but also from a practical one.

The common linguistic usage presents us the concept of transformation in the singular, sometimes even singling it out as the (one) 'great transformation.' However, opposed to this, transformations were not exactly planned monolithically or at least logically foreseen, and there is no present indication that this might differ in the future. Historically, transformations were slow, isolated, and partly even illogical, or they repeated themselves at different locations. They also were nontechnical and societal in the sense of opening broad opportunities for people to share and contribute. In the First Industrialization there was alternation between the 'pioneers' and 'imitators' of technologies and business concepts. Intellectual property rights did not stand in their way initially, but were themselves a field of unlimited and even unfair competition. Projects such as the first steam locomotive did not seem to pay off at first, and were opposed by anti-railway lobbies. The use of steam engines was quickly halted again at individual locations or remained isolated and without any lasting effect. The erratic ups-and-downs can also, from time to time, be well described as 'flaring up.' The Industrial Revolution is not to be compared with a burning torch that, once ignited, irresistibly begins its triumphal procession; in its formative stages, it is more like a will-o'-the-wisp. The technologies of the Industrial Revolution were largely perceived as fanciful pastimes: good for spending money on; bad for making money; they appeared to be too discontinuous and fragmentary, as well as too diverse, too differently anchored. Few could be described as continuously increasing, aiming at a holistic style of development, based on a steady inflow of knowledge and, at the same time, promoting innovation in the knowledge system — in other words, transformations were 'great' only in the historically retrospective singular, not in the contemporary experience. Seen from this observation it is at least debatable whether using the attribute 'great' or using the concept of Grand Design is building credibility and confidence in public communication.

With regard to the dissemination of the 'Third' industrial transformation, the word 'revolution' misdirects the ideas and images of changes. With regard to the historical development of industrial production, abrupt upheaval and disruptive innovations into new frontiers stand next to piecemeal engineering and slow step-by-step evolution.

The Industrial Revolution primarily took place in the European — and later in the American 'West' — or to put it more precisely, in the English and Rhenish West as well as in some regions with coal reserves and cheap transport routes for coal and ore. Even to date, this Industrial Revolution has not taken place everywhere in Europe.

All types of expansion of industrial society produce asymmetries in regional development, since they are based on different living and working conditions, and the creation and distribution of knowledge; however, these asymmetries differ. One can simplistically differentiate between the following types (listed here without any evaluative ranking): the so-called extractivism relating to primary commodities; expansion via armaments and structures based on the economy of war; growth through domestic consumption; export-based growth of consumer goods or of industrial capital goods; and finally the type geared towards global financial services. A domestic-oriented economy is most likely able to contribute to fighting poverty and creating regional prosperity, although such outcomes are not assured even in this context. The history of the Industrial Revolution in the key European centers allows a simplistically clear assignment to a certain category, as is the case with the Chinese growth type or extractivism. What remains to be debated is what basic type, what blend of types, or which new models appear most suitable for a green economy or sustainable business practices. The lack of such an analysis—either as a historical comparison or as the benchmark of today's economic strategies—must be identified as a serious deficit of the current sustainable- and green economy debate. No answers can be expected from the current discussions, ranging from regional currencies to economic growth strategies such as EU 2020.

Planning Exercises

The discontinuity of the First and Second Industrial Revolutions created the dominant infrastructure for fossil fuels. In the process, the rather small—and at first inconspicuous—decisions combine to form development paths. There were no master plans, roadmaps, models, or scenarios. The beginning of the Industrial Revolution is characterized by slowness and asymmetries in markets and knowledge. The breakthrough only came with the industrialization of warfare, which turned national wealth into a resource that was used without restraint. The Second Industrial Revolution is typified by the intensification and expansion of existing trends. Fordism characterizes the tip of the organizational form of industrial mass production as well as the emergence of managers as a social group, with top-level responsibility but no genuine stake in the industrial assets of the company.

Modern capitalism—of a post-industrial revolution and pre-transformation nature—developed planning instruments. Although often questioned politically and discredited as being typical of the Soviets or reminiscent of the days of centrally controlled economies, a 'business plan' has long been commonplace, and large companies plan their product life cycles, supply chains, and innovations on a significant scale. The growing importance of infrastructure for logistics, manufacturing, and public services is another indication that old and new forms of planning are part and parcel of the modern state.

For the development of statehood, the introduction of the steam engine and coal-fired electricity generation along with subsequent Fordist mass production and the first World's Fair in 1851 are landmarks alongside the known roles of imperial wars in Europe, the social struggles of the labor movement, and the efforts to enforce democracy. At that time, the role of the state was completely different from present, which—along with aspects of modern public services—becomes evident solely from the fact that the public expenditure quota of 7% of GDP up to the 1880s is eclipsed by modern-day expenditures of around 50%. These days, the state has a steering role as a market participant. This role also encompasses the growing financial expenses for research and education. With regard to the depth of knowledge and the dependence of the product on infrastructure (transport, use and added value in network structures), current production has many more preconditions and is more dependent on science. Scientific policy advice is not comparable to the contemporary state in any way.

Infrastructure plays a significant role because it requires planning exercises. In the 19th century, the railroad was evidence of a transformative character, because its demands on infrastructure and the decision-making ability of society and the public pointed to the prototypical business of the 19th century Industrial Revolution. It forced society and politics to adopt a civil policy towards industrialism that was not originally intended or desired. The same can be observed in the urban development of the early 20th century, as comprehensive sewage networks and supply infrastructures had to be developed, which was largely accomplished via the obligation to get connected in order to make use of them. What does that mean today with regard to the infrastructure of the great transformation? Do we not face similar yes/no questions? Is not today's primacy of economic incentives for non-binding decisions (e.g., in the energy performance of buildings), the use of renewable energies in construction, and the production of renewable energy in accord with historical experience?

Art of Transformation

Soft factors are more important than hard factors in understanding when and why change is happening. A culture of innovation is more important than a single breakthrough. The social environment that allows and encourages people to innovate can sometimes derive from free market exchange, institutional economics, the use of technologies, or land use. It may also stem from politics and society. The day-to-day action was not driven by vision; as a political term, 'vision' did not have a major political career, and remains a rare resource in politics. The period of the Industrial Revolution was rich in visions and utopian views. For example, discussions in Germany regarding homeland conservation (Heimatschutz), on nature conservation, and on a good quality of life, on a different concept of progress, and the end of poverty were still mostly marginal; but at the end of the 19th century, prompted by 'future angst' and a pessimistic attitude towards society, they then laid one of the foundations for the terrible totalitarian fascism of the 20th century.

However, visionary exercises are clearly necessary for any attempt towards a great transformation. Vision may then be most effective when it acknowledges the limits to knowledge. This would be a vision linked with scientific evidence, and maybe even binding itself to rationality. This is an important insight for modern transformation processes. It reflects the experience of the 'arts of the drawing room' from the time of the Industrial Revolution as a distant reminiscence in order to deal much more intensely with contemporary issues, and to allow the polarity of elitist cultural pessimism as well as a scaremongering technological utopia to be left behind.

For transformation processes—assuming they are long-term, protracted, contradictory, exciting, and dynamic—artistic processing and reflection are nourishment. This is generally true and is a special feature of the climate protection or biodiversity issues. Here in particular, this cultural dimension has been rather lacking or neglected. The aesthetic and cultural-political aspects of these factual issues have not been addressed in a way that transcends mere visual aesthetics, such as Arctic glaciers calving. Nevertheless, there is creative and socio-political potential here (Goehler 2013; Welzer 2013) which, on top of everything, has the advantage of going far beyond the social milieu of artists and creative people, and broaches the issue of the form of social—even political and economic—reflection itself in all camps and settings.

Towards 'Extractive' Studies on Historical Science and Transformation

German politics recently initiated transformative policies towards sustainable development, the most recent and significant of which was the Energiewende (Energy transition). We see governance processes evolving, such as strategies and institutional platforms; The private sector is developing corporate codes and standards for reporting and for the sustainable business case; Pure and applied science has long produced significant results. Still missing, though, is research for sustainability that would benefit from the tremendous depth of historical science, particularly from the knowledge of previous times of transformation. Where appropriate, historical evidence can inform future strategies; otherwise, insights into past transformation may sharpen the understanding of priorities and processes in the present context.

The said workshop invited a first, and therefore explorative, conversation between historians and sustainability researchers. This dialogue should be continued and deepened. This paper suggests establishing a scientific program that would review historical research into past transformative processes against the characteristics and challenges of today's knowledge-based transformation strategies. The first explorative approach should be matured or transformed into an extractive approach using advanced study practices.

The relationship between knowledge and change is never easy to interpret. Knowledge may cause transformative change, and is sometimes the actual change that is prompting the scientific system to react and refocus the research agenda. As interpreted by Gigerenzer (2013), the dispute between Sapientia as the goddess of knowledge and Fortuna as the goddess of luck (here: development) sees Sapientia burden Fortuna with an ever-increasing stream of positive knowledge regarding causalities, and ends with Fortuna contaminating the certainty of knowledge by means of statistics and probabilities. In other words, knowledge and ignorance are linked, and knowledge always gives rise to ever more areas where it becomes obvious that data, information, and knowledge are still missing. Where the quality of life and the pursuit of happiness are sought only through causality and the calculation of indicators, this is sure to go wrong. The story of the two goddesses matches the shortcomings and deficiencies of everyday consumer culture, just as it does the everyday life of the political debate regarding new models of prosperity and the quality of life (Bundestag 2013).

The Industrial Revolution had no thinking tools as we use today in the debate concerning strategies for future energy supply: the analysis of path dependencies and non-linear trends, forecasts, and models. These days, we are making ever more money available for research and development. Policies rely on scientific evidence to an extent never known before. Enterprises are seeking to increase their knowledge of their carbon emissions and the external effects of their supply chains. Granted, there is some green-washing involved and not every project lives up to expectations. But the new dimension can rarely be doubted. Young people in Germany today—despite all the justified criticism of the selection mechanism of the secondary and tertiary education system and its structures—have good opportunities for securing jobs, learning languages, learning about the world, and of satisfying their curiosity. All of this stands in contrast to the quality of life during the Industrial Revolution, with the role of a science for sustainability standing out.

The social and economic subsystem of 'science' is one of the drivers of changes in attitude and practice of each individual and of institutions (Rietschel 2013). Science has already widely incorporated the idea of sustainable development and its application (Hacker 2013); however, 'science in the Anthropocene' demands much more extensive participation. New methods and a working mode must act beyond pure observation; this assumes enhanced responsibility for processes and outcomes of knowledge work, and uses ignorance as a regenerative energy for the scientific community. Science would thus effectively play a part in decision-making and leadership issues oriented towards transformations (Meuleman 2013; Rietschel 2013).

At any rate, society's expectations of science will increase the more clearly and consciously sustainable development is sought. This calls for new reflection on the criterion of excellence. Internal assessment by the scientific community is a necessary criterion, but must be regarded as characteristic of 20th century approaches and as no longer adequate. To grasp the scientific dimension of the issues related to sustainable development and transformations, a co-determination rule for the public should be developed, similar to that which exists between a company and its workforce. What has to be considered here is the transparency of information; the self-efficacy of science (not just doing research into sustainability, but also practicing it within a research facility); and agreement on the identification and falsification of research topics and processes, as well as on the adequate measurement of transdisciplinarity and its acknowledgement within the framework of excellence criteria. What science transfers back to society should be viewed as part of the academic benefits and not as an extra-scientific commitment by individuals (Jahn 2013).

However, implementation is weak if there is any at all. The so-called knowledge society is often complacent. Consequently, excellence in sustainability research is emerging too slowly. The relationship between Sapientia and Fortuna emphasizes the transdisciplinary science of sustainable development, which persists and which must yet be intensified.

Tentative Assumptions

In concluding, the article proposes some tentative assumptions. It seems fair to say that, as yet, virtually no substantive links have been established between the history of transformation and contemporary efforts consisting of science for sustainability. This should be changed on the basis of a well advanced historical research and the best practice of today's front-running initiatives towards sustainable development. It is suggested to further advance the IASS workshop's first explorative approach into a full research program.

Democracy in politics, information, and personal data, and in enterprises is of relevance for transition management, and has to be further explored. Although (very) frequently suggested in politics, media, and academia, the absence of democratic procedures does not help to manage transition; or at least the historical and recent examples do not convincingly prove this assumption. New types of knowledge and expertise need to looked at more closely, as the networking character of transformation is not yet fully explored. Rather impressively, historical examples make the point for soft policies being more effective than hard regulation, but here the context and the interrelation between stately-enforced standards and voluntary action in civil society and private sector seems to be crucial, and not easy to understand.

The notion of the end of the nation-state might be a bias stemming from the one-sided architecture of historical narratives in times of imperialism and post-imperialism. In a closer look this might turn out to be an artifact resulting from the dominant mainstream of history science.

There is evidence that the relationship between economic growth and development is complex and does not underscore the often repeated credo 'only growing economies can afford change.' This credo sees growth as a precondition for transition, and any deceleration as bringing transformation to a halt. In view of the present challenges of modern societies this suggests that eradicating poverty is a prerequisite for growth. This paradigm needs to be adjusted to specific conditions of economies and societies, but generally, it challenges the common understanding of growth strategies.

LITERATURE CITED

Beattle, A. (2010): False Economy. A surprising economic history of the world. London: Penguin.

Beck, U. (1996): Das Zeitalter der Nebenfolgen und die Politisierung der Moderne. In: Beck, U., Giddens, A., Lash, S. (Hrsg.). Reflexive Modernisierung. Eine Kontroverse. Frankfurt am Main: Suhrkamp, pp. 19–112.

BMU, Bundesumweltministerium (Ed.) (2008): Die Dritte industrielle Revolution – Aufbruch in ein ökologisches Jahrhundert. Dimensionen und Herausforderungen des industriellen und gesellschaftlichen Berlin: Wandel Verlag. [http://www.boell.de/downloads/oekologie/broschuere_dritte_industr_rev.pdf; 22 July 2013].

Brüggemeier, F-J. (1996): Das unendliche Meer der Lüfte. Luftverschmutzung, Industrialisierung und Risikodebatten im 19. Jahrhundert. Tübingen: Klartext Verlag.

Bundestag (2013) Bericht der Enquete-Kommission. Wachstum, Wohlstand, Lebensqualität – Wege zu nachhaltigem Wirtschaften und gesellschaftlichem Fortschritt in der Sozialen Marktwirtschaft, Drucksache 17/13300.

Clark, C. (2007): Preußen. Aufstieg und Niedergang. 1600–1947. München: Deutsche Verlags-Anstalt.

Diamond, J. (2005) Kollaps: Warum Gesellschaften überleben oder untergehen. Frankfurt am Main: S. Fischer.

Ethics Commission for a Safe Energy Supply (2011): Germany's Energy Transition: A Collective Endeavor for the Future, on behalf of Chancellor Angela Merkel. Berlin, 30 May 2011: [http://www.nachhaltigkeitsrat.de/uploads/media/20110530_German_Ethics_Comm_on_nuclear_phase_out_summary_EN.pdf; 22 July 2013].

Gigerenzer, G. (2013): Risiko. Wie man die richtigen Entscheidungen trifft. München: C. Bertelsmann, 397 S.

Goehler, A. (2013) Konzeptgedanken zur Errichtung eines Fonds für Kunst und Nachhaltigkeit. [http://www.z-n-e.info/PDFfaen/de/Fonds_Aesthetik-deutsch.pdf; 28 July 2013].

Haber, W. (2010): Die unbequemen Wahrheiten der Ökologie, Erste Carl-von-Carlowitz –
Vorlesung 2009 des Rates für Nachhaltige Entwicklung. München: oekom.

Hacker, J. (2013) Nachhaltigkeit in der Wissenschaft. Deutsche Akademie der Naturforscher
Leopoldina – Nationale Akademie der Wissenschaften, Halle (Saale). Stuttgart: Deutsche
Verlagsgesellschaft, 126 S.

Hinz, M.O., Mayer-Tasch, P.C. (1974): Umweltschutz, Politik des peripheren Eingriffs: eine
Einführung in die politische Ökologie. Bd. 24 der Reihe Demokratie und Rechtsstaat. Darmstadt
und Neuwied: Luchterhand, 248 S.

Hawken, P., Lovins, A., Lovins, L.H. (1999): Nature Capitalism: Creating the Next Industrial
Revolution. Boston, New York, London: Little, Brown and Company.

Jaeger, C. (2011): Wachstum – wohin? Eine kurze Geschichte des 21. Jahrhunderts, Carl-von-
Carlowitz-Reihe Band 2. München: oekom. [http://www.nachhaltigkeitsrat.de/aktuell/carl-von-
carlowitz-vorlesungen/archiv/archiv-2-cvc-vorlesung/].

Jänicke, M., Jacob, K. (2008): Eine Dritte Industrielle Revolution? Wege aus der Krise ressourcen-
intensiven Wachstums. Eine Begriffsbestimmung. In: Bundesumweltministerium (Hrsg.) (2008):
Die Dritte industrielle Revolution – Aufbruch in ein ökologisches Jahrhundert. Dimensionen und
Herausforderungen des industriellen und gesellschaftlichen. Berlin: Wandels. [http://www.boell.
de/downloads/oekologie/broschuere_dritte_industr_rev.pdf].

Jahn, T. (2013): Transdisziplinarität – Forschungsmodus für nachhaltiges Forschen. In: Hacker, J.
Nachhaltigkeit in der Wissenschaft. Deutsche Akademie der Naturforscher Leopoldina –
Nationale Akademie der Wissenschaften, Halle (Saale). Stuttgart: Deutsche Verlagsgesellschaft,
pp. 65–75.

Koselleck, R. (Ed.) (1979): Geschichtliche Grundbegriffe, Bd. 1. Stuttgart: Klett Cotta, S. XV.

Landes, D. (1998): The Wealth and Poverty of Nations. Why Some Are So Rich and Some So
Poor. New York: Norton & Company.

Matschoss, C. (1901): Geschichte der Dampfmaschine: ihre kulturelle Bedeutung, technische
Entwicklung und ihre großen Männer. Berlin: Julius Springer, 451 S. [http://ia600300.us.archive.
org/1/items/geschichtederdaoomatsgoog/geschichtederdaoomatsgoog.pdf 19 July 2013].

Mauch, C. (2013): Exkursion in Zeit und Raum – eine historische Perspektive auf die Nachhaltigkeit. 4. Carl-von-Carlowitz-Vorlesung. Bergakademie Universität Freiberg, 19 Juni. [Video-
mitschnitt: http://www.nachhaltigkeitsrat.de/projekte/eigene-projekte/carl-von-carlowitz-
vorlesungen/?subid=7829&cHash=8785f57740] (forthcoming).

Meuleman, L. (Ed.) (2013): Transgovernance. Advancing Sustainability Governance. Heidelberg:
Springer.

Osterhammel, J. (2010): Die Verwandlung der Welt. Eine Geschichte des 19. Jahrhunderts.
München: C.H. Beck.

Osterhammel, J. (2011): Geschichtskolumne: Große Transformationen. In: Merkur. Deutsche
Zeitschrift für europäisches Denken. Heft 746, Stuttgart: Klett-Cotta, pp. 625–631.

Polanyi, K. (1978): The Great Transformation. Politische und ökonomische Ursprünge von
Gesellschaften und Wirtschaftssystemen. englischsprachige Erstausgabe erschien 1944. Frankfurt:
Suhrkamp.

Radkau, J. (2008): Technik in Deutschland. Vom 18. Jahrhundert bis heute. Frankfurt am Main: Campus. 533 S.

Raskin, P. et al. (2003): Great Transition - Umbrüche und Übergänge auf dem Weg zu einer planetarischen Gesellschaft. Herausgegeben von ISOE, HGDÖ, SEI. ISOE-Materialien Soziale Ökologie 20. Frankfurt am Main. 107 S. vgl. [http://www.isoe.de/ftp/gt_deutsch.pdf].

Rietschel, E.T. (2013): Nachhaltigkeit und Wissenschaft, Dinner-Rede zu Ehren der Robert Bosch Juniorprofessur. Berlin, 12 Marz.

Sächsische, Hans-Carl-von-Carlowitz-Gesellschaft (Ed.) (2013): Die Erfindung der Nachhaltigkeit. Leben, Werk und Wirkung des Hans Carl von Carlowitz. München: oekom, 288 S.

Schellnhuber, H.J. et al. (2007): Potsdam Memorandum. Main Conclusions from the Symposium: Global Sustainability. A Nobel Cause. Potsdam, 8–10 October. [http://www.nobel-cause.de/Potsdam%20Memorandum_eng.pdf; 28 July 2013].

Töpfer, K. (2013): Wissenschaft im Anthropozän. In: Hacker, J. (2013) Nachhaltigkeit in der Wissenschaft. Deutsche Akademie der Naturforscher Leopoldina – Nationale Akademie der Wissenschaften, Halle (Saale). Stuttgart: Deutsche Verlagsgesellschaft, pp. 31–40.

in 't Veld, R.J. (2011): Transgovernance. The Quest for Governance of Sustainable Development. Project Report Science for Sustainable TRANSformations: Towards Effective GOVernance. Potsdam: IASS Institute for Advanced Sustainability Studies [http://www.iass-potsdam.de/sites/default/files/transgovernance_-_the_quest_-_nov_2011.pdf; August 2013].

Watson, P. (2010): The German Genius: Europe's Third Renaissance, the Second Scientific Revolution, and the Twentieth Century. New York: Harper Perennial.

WBCSD, World Business Council for Sustainable Development (2010): Vision 2050: The new agenda for business. Geneva. [http://www.wbcsd.org/pages/edocument/edocumentdetails.aspx?id=219&nosearchcontextkey=true; 5 August 2013].

WBGU, Wissenschaftlicher Beirat Globale Umweltveränderungen (2011): Welt im Wandel. Gesellschaftsvertrag für eine Große Transformation. [http://www.wbgu.de/fileadmin/templates/dateien/veroeffentlichungen/hauptgutachten/jg2011/wbgu_jg2011_ZfE.pdf; 28 July 2013].

von Weizsäcker, E.U., Lovins, A., Lovins, L.H. (1997): Faktor Vier. Doppelter Wohlstand – halbierter Naturverbrauch. Droemer: München.

von Weizsäcker, E.U., Hargroves, K., Smith, M. (2010): Faktor Fünf: Die Formel für Nachhaltiges Wachstum. Droemer: München.

Welzer, H. (2013): Selbst denken. Eine Anleitung zum Widerstand. Frankfurt am Main: S. Fischer, 329 S.

Volker Hauff

Governance:
The Deficit on the Way to Sustainability

Today, sustainability faces diverse challenges and many risks: climate change, suitable energy supplies, scarce natural resources, world poverty, the growing gap between the rich and poor, the threat to species diversity, the financial crisis—all these are examples of current critical developments on the way to sustainability.

There is no lack of knowledge about the causes and trends behind these crises. There is also no lack of knowledge about undesired, harmful, or even dangerous risks. Scientific advice to improve understanding about the complexity of the problems remains an ongoing task—despite all the successes that have been achieved. There is no lack of goals that need to be achieved—neither qualitative nor quantitative. However, there is a lack of resolve when it comes to turning knowledge into action. Here, there is a real deficit: namely in the successful implementation of what is recognized as right. This is due to many reasons, not all of which relate to government action. In addition to institutions concerned with the democratic decision-making process, all stakeholders are called upon who can exert influence on the action taken: business, science, and civil society all have an influence on whether the step from knowledge to action is successfully taken or not. This cooperation and conflict between stakeholders relates not only to the question of which goals should be achieved, but also to whether the measures envisaged are appropriate and acceptable. This is a very complex task; however, it makes no sense to turn a blind eye to this complexity. There is a lack of governance on sustainability. "As strongholds of democratic, consensus-oriented, cooperative patterns of governance, specific European countries and the EU as a whole had claimed global eco-political leadership and presented themselves as an example of international sustainability politics. But on many of their promises they have failed to deliver." (Blühdorn 2012, p. 1).

Klaus Töpfer, to whom I feel a close affiliation after ten years of fruitful and friendly collaboration in the German Government's Council for Sustainable Development, comes to a similar conclusion in his prologue to the 'Transgovernance' project report produced by his new Institute for Applied Sustainability Studies (IASS) in Potsdam: "twenty years of sustainability governance ... has not led us very far, to say it politely." (in 't Veld 2011, p. vi). If that is the case—and I believe it to be—then we need to look for the causes. That is what the TransGov research project at the IASS attempted to do, which I had the pleasure to serve as a discussant at the project's presentation event. And, in this article for the anniversary publication on Klaus Töpfer, I would like to make a few comments on the findings of that project.

In this article the authors of the IASS TransGov report present their work under a clear, directional heading: "Change is needed. This is the governance question" (in 't Veld 2011, p. xii). I think it would be helpful and productive to first examine the cultural conditions and prerequisites for a successful transformation before turning our attention to the technical and practical aspects of governance.

Since the United Nations Conference on Environment and Development (UNCED) held in Rio in 1992, sustainability has been defined in terms of environmental, economic, and social aspects. This 'three pillar model' determines the currently standard interpretation of the term, yet does not originate from the Brundtland report of 1987. Perhaps this model was sensible, perhaps even necessary, in order to make the term 'sustainability' manageable—for which there are good reasons. However, this pillar theory is a constriction that makes it difficult to suitably embed the term sustainability within its cultural context.

A glance at the text of the Brundtland report from 1987 puts us on the right track: this refers to the 'cultural determination' of sustainability and the notion that: "Sustainable development requires the promotion of values that encourage consumption standards that are within the bounds of the ecological possible and to which all can reasonably aspire." The cultural determination of sustainability is admittedly not a fourth pillar. Rather, it is the linking architrave above that endows meaning. This cultural determination creates clarity and provides orientation. It helps in dealing with contradictions and conflicts. Returning to such values can help free the concept of sustainability from its arbitrary use and associate it with the right ideals: "Anyone who wants to change something must create meaning" (Lange 2012, p. 15).

The Culture of Alertness

In his preface, Roeland in 't Veld—who headed the IASS research project—writes: "Cultural diversity is one of the majestic treasures of humanity." That is a statement that ties in with the Brundtland report. The IASS research project impressively demonstrates how the cultural determination of sustainability and the growing importance of transdisciplinary science can be linked to the politically normative discussion on sustainability. That is the decisive and trend-setting aspect of this report—ahead of all other important individual aspects: "Today's societal evolution is characterized by the emergence of tense relationships between contradictory phenomena, by 'and' instead of 'or'" (in 't Veld 2011, S. 6). Those wishing to pursue this line of thinking, as elaborated by Ulrich Beck, must not only be open to a 'second glance' for the sake of it but must also, with a certain restraint, concern themselves with the conditions for developing a successful political decision-making process and its implementation. In doing so, one will encounter conflicting interests and controversy, and to some extent opposing views. This is where the conceptual approach adopted by the TransGov research project could be pursued further, namely that sustainable development can only flourish in a 'culture of alertness.'

"Every enemy is a teacher"; these wise words from Confucius can help to identify and correct undesirable developments of our age. You only have to think of 11 September 2001—or 'nine-eleven' as it is popularly known. This criminal attack, this mindless slaughter, was carried out by people who in their blind hostility to America considered all means to be justified that harmed America; their hate was boundless. America responded to this hate with a war against the 'axis of evil'—and was not particularly discriminating in its choice of means. The validity of those wise words from Confucius has been confirmed in an almost demonic way: with US legislation in the form of the Patriot Act, the justification for the Iraq War, and the work of the intelligence agencies at Guantanamo Bay. That represents a loss of alertness. I believe we would be well advised to search for sustainability in the world beyond mere knee-jerk responses. This is suggested by the comment from Peter Sloterdijk: "I believe that in the democratic process you also become more and more responsible for your enemies." (Sloterdijk 2013). The second glance really is necessary.

The IASS report 'Transgovernance—The Quest for Governance of Sustainable Development' includes a raft of valuable recommendations and suggestions for improving the governance of sustainable development. Two recommendations are particularly important and shall be dealt with here in more detail:

- The role of nation-states; and
- New diplomacy for international agreements.

The Role of Nation-States

We are currently in the midst of fundamental changes, but we perceive this to such an extent that we remain too caught in the moment and fail to recognize the larger picture. The proposed energy transition (Energiewende) in Germany is a prime example. At the beginning—almost 60 years ago—all the political parties in Germany were in broad agreement: we want to base our energy system on nuclear power; that was the clear consensus and the great hope of the 1950s. A special federal ministry was founded for this major undertaking. Everyone was in agreement: that is progress. In the end, all the political parties in Germany were in broad agreement: we can and want to phase-out nuclear energy; that was the official position adopted in 2011. Almost everyone agrees: that is progress. Some refer to it as a 'new advance.'

The government has focused on passing several laws and ordinances, setting goals, and taking measures. But when measured against the criteria of the aforementioned report, the governance of the energy transition remains rather modest and testifies to a certain 'agency incapability': neither has a concise strategy been developed to organize the various fields of action in relation to one another, nor have clearly defined roles and responsibilities been determined for the necessary processes; there is still no monitoring of this megaproject and still no sign of a serious public debate. For all the talk of about the 'new advance' in energy policy, it still does not provide any orientation. For me, the 'new advance' reminds me of the sarcastic comments made by Niklas Luhmann in his 'Sociology of Risk,' where he responds to the term 'new social movements' with the question: 'What is actually new? That is a stop-gap term that goes to show that the intended meaning does not fit into any predefined scheme.'

The starting point for any deliberations must be the fact that political capability today should be achieved "increasingly less by just the state but through a diverse range of successful social processes" (Ueberhorst 2012, p. 20). In other words, in addition to representatives of institutions concerned with the democratic decision-making process, stakeholders from business, the media, science, and civil society play a not-to-be-underestimated role in the success or failure. None of them can achieve this goal alone. Not even the representatives of the nation-state. But it plays an important role when it comes to enabling, facilitating, and fostering political capability. The necessary communication processes first of all demand one thing: they need time; and they demand a second thing: they can't be done in haste. "There are namely things that cannot be done immediately. Things that have to mature first" (Han 2013, p. 63). That applies not just to goals but—much more importantly—to measures for achieving the accepted goals. Sustainability can only succeed if the public debate is conducted without any time constraints. The TransGov report leaves no room for doubt: those who want to successfully steer large changes must withstand and accommodate the tensions and conflicts that result in all areas:

- Representative democracy is being challenged by powerful action groups, and needs to respond with new forms of participation;
- Classic media are challenged by social media, and need to respond with new formats;
- Traditional scientific disciplines are being challenged by unconventional research approaches, and need to respond with cooperation.

Adopting this courageous approach is 'knowledge democracy.' As has already been mentioned, that cannot be achieved without debating the appropriate methods. And nobody can be promised an easy ride. All demands for a fundamental change (e.g., regarding climate, finance, energy issues, etc.) mostly originate from society itself. However, not from the center, since this is where the people are found who wish to preserve structures. Instead, the changes tend to come from the margins, which is where the people who wish to preserve values are found. The decisive aspect for a successful change: everyone has to be involved if it is to succeed. This confronts politics with unusual demands. In this context, perhaps it is helpful to recall another quote from Confucius: "Each issue has three sides. The first is my view of things. The second is your view of things. And the third comprises those sides and points of view that we have both overlooked." That is the second glance, which is necessary. The report recommends that nation-states should adopt a new role as 'architects of processes.' That is a broad field—and its importance will grow.

When it comes to actual changes, we constantly encounter the following dilemma:
+ Stakeholders representing the status quo reach their limits with their previously tried-and-tested practices;
+ The stakeholders for change refer, in their arguments, to the possible future successes.

Both are damned to coexistence, which must lead to a joint search for the right way. That demands unusual cooperation. In this context, Reinhard Ueberhorst refers to necessary 'stakeholder alliances' that need to be applied in the long term, and at the same time must also be able to accommodate the status quo in the changes. "Success in maintaining and further building open democratic and culturally diverse systems is not guaranteed" (Klaus Töpfer: in 't Veld 2011, p. viii). Given the recent developments in Greece and Italy, it is difficult to doubt this statement.

New Diplomacy for International Agreements

Following the 1992 Rio Summit, with its euphoric spirit of optimism, successes with international sustainability treaties have become increasingly rare. It cannot be denied that there has been stagnation in recent years. That requires an explanation.

The negotiations in Copenhagen in 2009 for a new global climate change convention not only provide a particularly extreme example of the stagnation but are also particularly instructive in this regard. The EU entered the negotiations with a concept that was rightly accused of establishing—whether intentionally or unintentionally—a postcolonial hegemony of the industrial states. There was little sign of any real preparedness to accommodate the interests and negotiating positions of the non-OECD countries. The TransGov report states in this regard, "The attempt at agreeing on percentages of reduction of emissions must resemble a postcolonial hegemonic gesture for those former colonies which had earlier experienced a delay in economic development and are only now seeing their economic growth percentages increase" (in 't Veld 2011, p. 25). Nor did the EU have a 'Plan-B.' The result was a disaster—and in a double sense: no agreement was reached and the chances of finding solutions in the future had deteriorated.

The interests and perceptions of individual nation-states or groups of nation-states do not provide a reliable foundation for international agreements; from the outset there must be a jointly developed understanding of the further procedure—an agreement on the basic principles. "What is needed is a mutual Declaration of Dependence—an admission from the entire world to the rest of the world that it won't work without one another" (Sloterdijk 2013). With such a Declaration of Dependence an attempt could be made to define underlying principles and procedures for how the climate issue is dealt with in the world of mutual dependencies—divorced of any dogmatism and with a disclosure of national interests. That might sound unrealistic to some people, but I consider such an 'innovation' to be essential for overcoming the stagnation at international negotiations. I am a passionate advocate of the policy of small steps. But I also know that those who want to achieve their goals with small steps also need a clarity of thought that creates orientation, need partners for coalitions and compromises, need to be prepared to participate in joint projects at different speeds, and need the wisdom to link the negotiating levels of local communities, regions, nations, EU and the global community. Those who demand everything—and demand it at once—frequently end up with nothing. However, Erhard Eppler's call for restraint provides hope: it is not the size of the individual steps that matters but the recognizability of the direction.

A recommendation in the TransGov report reads: "Our advice to decision makers in the political, business, science, media and civil society organisations is to work together and create governance arrangements that cross traditional borders, fixations and stereotypes" (in 't Veld 2011, S. xiv). This aspect of governance beyond nation-states recognizes idiosyncrasies that are worthwhile examining in more detail.

Governance Across Borders

In 2009 a group of academics with quite different backgrounds—including sociologists, economists, political scientists and jurists—established an online research blog on 'governance across borders.' Most of the academics were based at the Max Planck Institute for the Study of Societies in Cologne. By the end of 2012 a total of 214 articles were available for discussion. In 2013, 127 of the articles were selected for publication in a blog book that is available online. Each of the articles is linked to an associated online discussion board. The researchers are absolutely delighted with the results of this unconventional academic discussion: "Now, nearly four years later, we see the benefits of maintaining a research blog that we could never have imagined when starting" (Dobusch et al. 2013, p. 21).

The main focus of this research on 'governance across borders' covers a colorful range of themes: the environment, copyright, climate, labor, accounting, and microfinance are the most important examples. In almost all cases considerable uncertainties had to be expected. Mostly there were neither hierarchies for decisions, nor roles and responsibilities, nor procedures for legitimizing the various actors—let alone an integrated concept for the monitoring. For all these reasons, the academics view the 'one model for all' concept as a risk—particularly when it concerns the transfer of models from the Global North to the Global South. However, the academics did not merely qualify the situation but also presented several results that are of general interest (Dobusch et al. 2013, pp. 18–19):

- A sound theoretical basis is not sufficient for the success of a 'governance across borders' model; decisive is the type and means of the implementation;
- "The inclusion and mobilisation of non-experts became more and more important"; and this is irrespective of whether the issues require particular expertise, such as copyright and accounting, or whether the topics are more open to greater participation—such as the environment and labor;
- Several chapters such as forest certification, labor standards, and copyright "point to the power of framing strategies of less well-resourced civil society actors in shaping the directions of transnational governance."

These results merge seamlessly with the underlying principles of the TransGov report; they mostly refer to specific individual projects that were investigated empirically.

The TransGov Report: A Prelude—Not a Recipe Book

The report is not a recipe book, but it does provide an invitation to all responsible actors to equip themselves with the requisite scientific know-how in order to take these findings into account in their decisions. The report therefore sets itself agreeably apart from those alarmist or even appeasing 'appraisals' that are currently being flogged on the market.

In order to turn knowledge into action, the report demands that 'transgovernance concepts' should be developed that bring together separate areas ('AND' instead of 'OR'):

- Knowledge **and** action;
- Responsibility **and** awareness;
- Engagement **and** reasoning.

This is where several fields still await academic treatment. It remains to be seen whether the positive assessment of sustainability governance in cities will be confirmed—or whether further research will require differentiation here. I am also curious as to whether the cautious attitude towards indicators proves to be resilient or whether the opinion of Christian Kroll from the London School of Economics will prevail, who sees here the beginning of a 'culture of justification.' These are important questions; they go into the detail.

The TransGov report arouses curiosity—primarily via its profound suggestions and findings:

- About the volume of material, with contributions from the members of the research team, which will no doubt provide additional insights; I hope that this particularly applies to new forms of participation that are suitable for strengthening representative democracy;
- About the further work of the institute, which will no doubt also focus on individual fields of action; I hope that this applies to monitoring the energy transition in Germany;
- About the political response. Will the relevance of the work be recognized? Those seriously attempting that must also be prepared to modify the political decision-making practice in accordance with governance for sustainability: Will the nation-state adopt the role of the 'process architect'?

The IASS:
A Beacon in the Era of Sustainability

The Institute for Applied Sustainability Studies, with its founding director Klaus Töpfer, differs from other academic institutions in one essential aspect: This institute is also, of course, dependent on appropriate financing; however, to a much greater extent than any other institute its researchers deal with the integration of sustainability theory and practice within a knowledge society: new findings create new knowledge that influences practice; and changed practice gives rise to new findings that lead to new knowledge. For this reason, such an institute requires not only the appropriate funding to support its innovative work but, to an even greater extent, the active understanding that will draw attention to the research findings.

The issue of sustainability has entered into mainstream society. It is concerned with shaping our future—that is: more than optimizing the present. This work on sustainable and realistic blueprints for the future and their implementation still lies ahead of us. We are right at the beginning of a formative discussion: sustainable development will be the overriding issue of the 21st century. The last century was concerned with seeking a balance between social and market norms, which was answered with the social market economy. The regulatory principle has been recognized, but sustainable development still has a long way to go in correcting social inequality.

Our century, the 21st century, will be informed by the question: How do we achieve a balance between globalization and sustainability? We still do not have an answer. This makes it even more important that there are academic institutions that help to avoid unnecessary errors. The IASS is one such leading institution. It provides a beacon in the era of sustainability. I and many other people are now looking forward to its further pioneering work. Who could be more predestined to achieve this than Klaus Töpfer, the founding director of the IASS?

LITERATURE CITED

Blühdorn, I. (2012): Democracy and Sustainability – Opening the discursive arena – Struggling for an innovative debate. Berlin and Bonn: Friedrich Ebert Stiftung.

Dobusch, L., Mader, P., Quack, S. (Eds.) (2013): Governance across borders – Transnational fields and transversal themes. Berlin: epubli GmbH [http://www.mpifg.de/pu/mpifg_books_pdf.asp].

Han, B-C. (2012): Der Eros besiegt die Depression. In: Philosophie Magazin July/August 2012.

Kroll, C. (2012) Wir brauchen neue Indikatoren - und ein 'Glücks-Audit' für die Politik. In: Aus Politik und Zeitgeschichte 27/28: 27–32.

Lange, H. (2012): Positiver Nihilismus – Meine Auseinandersetzung mit Heidegger. Berlin: Matthes and Seitz.

Sloterdijk, P. (2013): Speech at the presentation ceremony for the Ludwig-Börne Awards. 16 June 2013. Paulskirche, Frankfurt, FAZ 19. 06. 2013, p. 28.

Ueberhorst, R. (2012): Brauchen wir einen Neuen Gesellschaftsvertrag für unsere gesellschaftliche Politikfähigkeit? In: Plate, G. (Ed.). Forschung für die Wirtschaft. Göttingen: Cuvillier.

in 't Veld, R.J. (2011): Transgovernance – The Quest for Governance of Sustainable Development. TransGov Project Report. Science for Sustainable TRANSformations: Towards Effective GOVernance. Potsdam: IASS Institute for Advanced Sustainability.

Addressing Diversity

WAN Gang

Professor Klaus Töpfer: Promoter of Scientific Cooperation

Prof. Klaus Töpfer's cooperation with China dates from when he was the Federal Minister for the Environment in Germany during the 1980s. During the past 20 years Prof. Töpfer has made tremendous efforts to promote Sino–German, Sino–African, and Sino–UNEP cooperation. He provided valuable advice to the UNEP–China–Africa Cooperation Program on the Environment, the 2008 Beijing Olympics, the 2012 Shanghai World Expo, the development of Chongming Eco-Island, the Suzhou Creek Pollution Control Project; and the establishment of the Key Laboratory of the Yangtze River Water Environment, introducing new concepts and technologies for water treatment, water resource management, sustainable development, etc.

UNEP–China–Africa Cooperation Program on the Environment

China and African countries have a long and consistent relationship of cooperation on environmental and scientific issues. With Prof. Töpfer's support, the Forum on China–Africa Cooperation Beijing Summit and the first Ministerial Conference were held in Beijing in 2000. Since then, the Ministerial Conference has been held every three years in different countries, and this kind of cooperation has flourished in many crucial environmental areas, including water treatment and climate change. In 2005, Prof. Töpfer attended the Conference on China–Africa Cooperation on the Environment, together with Mr. Zeng Peiyan, the then Vice-Premier of the State Council of China. He also promoted and witnessed the establishment of the UNEP China–Africa Environment Center in 2006. In 2008, UNEP together with the Chinese Ministry of Science and Technology (MOST) established the UNEP–China–Africa Cooperation Program on the Environment, which aims to build the capacity of African countries in the fields of ecosystems management, disaster reduction, climate change adaptation, and renewable energy. Thanks to MOST's strong support, the program has made remarkable progress. It has now entered a new phase under the theme 'One River, One Lake, One Desert,' targeting the Nile River, Lake Tanganyika, and the Sahara Desert. The Chinese team within this program consists of 16 institutes, while more than 10 African countries have participated in the program. In 2013, Tongji University, as one of the participating Chinese institutes, cooperated with UNEP and seven universities in Africa in publishing *Green Hills, Blue Cities: An Ecosystems Approach to Water Resources Management for African Cities* as part of the Global World Water Day celebrations.

The 2008 Beijing Green Olympics

In 1999, under Prof. Töpfer's guidance as Executive Director, UNEP collaborated with the International Olympic Committee (IOC) to adopt the Olympic Movement's Agenda 21 to promote sustainable development. In 2000, when Beijing bid for the 2008 Games, it included Green Olympics as one of the three Olympic themes and pledged to host a Green Olympiad.

In 2005, Prof. Töpfer on behalf of UNEP, and Liu Jingmin as Executive Vice-President of the Beijing Organizing Committee for the Games of the XXIX Olympiad (BOCOG) signed a memorandum of understanding (MoU) marking one step forward in Beijing's endeavor for sustainable development while preparing for the 2008 Games.

The two partners cooperated effectively in collecting and sharing environmental information, as well as in promoting education and publicity on environmental protection. BOCOG used the 2008 Olympics as a platform to improve the quality of the urban environment, explore methods of environmental management in hosting the Games, and enhance public awareness on environmental protection—actively responding to UNEP's call for sustainable and concerted development of global economy, society, and environment; UNEP, meanwhile, used its worldwide information, technical resources, and publicity channels to assist BOCOG in carrying out the Green Olympics concept and furthering its impact.

The 2010 Shanghai World Expo

The 2010 Shanghai World Expo proved to be the greenest and most environmentally-friendly Expo, embodying the theme 'Better City, Better Life' to show the way towards a greener future. Prof. Töpfer, as Advisor to the Shanghai Mayor, provided substantive suggestions to the Shanghai Government. UNEP, as Shanghai's long-standing partner, launched the *'Shanghai Expo Green Report,'* which outlined Shanghai's efforts in these key areas, including: sustainable urban living; providing a sunlight channel to underground walkways; rainwater harvesting and recycling; zero-emission vehicles; and a world-class green transport system comprising a 400-kilometre rapid transit network, which left an indelible impression on 70 million visitors.

The Chongming Eco-Island Project

The Chongming Eco-Island, as Shanghai's most important ecosystem, provides a refuge for millions of birds and diverse marine life. Following the co-hosted *Chongming Eco-Island Forum* in the UN Pavilion of the 2010 Shanghai Expo, which was also attended by Prof. Töpfer, the *'MoU on Chongming Eco-Island Construction and Development'* was signed between UNEP and the Science and Technology Commission of Shanghai Municipality (STCSM) on 24 November 2011.

Suzhou Creek Pollution Control Project

During the long-term project to control pollution in Shanghai's Suzhou Creek, Prof. Töpfer initiated much cooperation between UNEP, the Shanghai Government, and many other international organizations, and closely followed the progress of the project. During the second phase of the project, Mr. Mahesh Pradhan the then Environmental Affairs Officer at UNEP's Regional Office for Asia and the Pacific Region, and Tokiko Kato the UNEP Goodwill Ambassador also paid a field visit to the Suzhou Creek and met with the local scientists and researchers. In 2003, Prof. Töpfer even wrote a letter to Mr. Han Zheng, then Shanghai Mayor, to express his congratulations on the preliminary achievements and expectation of future improvements.

Key Laboratory of the Yangtze River Water Environment

Prof. Töpfer also promoted the establishment of the Key Laboratory of the Yangtze River Water Environment. In cooperation with Tongji University and the Jülich Research Center, together with eight other universities and institutes, this laboratory focuses on the aquatic environment of the Yangtze river basin, and has created an international scientific research and exchange center on water quality and the evolution of ecological environments. The Jülich Research Center also contributed to the Sino–Germany–Africa Summer School, which each year attracts more than

60 students from China, Germany, and African countries to take part in an intensive learning and communication placement at Tongji University Shanghai, and the Jülich Research Center, Germany.

Acknowledgements

In recognition of his great contribution to international collaboration and environmental diplomacy with China, Prof. Töpfer was awarded the Friendship Award of the Chinese Government (2006), the Shanghai Magnolia Award (2007), the Shanghai International Cooperation Award (2008), and the International Science and Technology Cooperation Award (2011). Meanwhile, as a member of the China Council for International Cooperation on Environment and Development (CCICED), Prof. Töpfer has seen the strong determination of China's leadership and contributed to constructive strategies required for the sustainable development of China.

The Way Forward

The profound insight and wise guidance of Prof. Klaus Töpfer have helped UNEP, China, Africa, and both developed and developing countries to establish deeper and stronger cooperation on many scientific issues—especially those related to environment and sustainable development. On this occasion of his 75th birthday, I sincerely wish him happiness and health, and hope that the scientific cooperation that he fostered between UNEP and China will continue to benefit research and practice both in African countries and China.

Fengting Li, Jiang Wu, Dahe Jiang, Dong Li, and Sun Jie

Professor Klaus Töpfer: Leading the Way to a Sustainable Future

UNEP–Tongji Institute of Environment for Sustainable Development, College of Environmental Science and Engineering, Tongji University

Despite his many titles—former Under-Secretary-General of the UN, former Executive Director of UNEP, former Federal Minister for Environment, Nature Conservation and Nuclear Safety, and former Federal Minister for Regional Planning, Building and Urban Development—we would prefer to call him Professor Klaus Töpfer, which in the traditional Chinese culture indicates our respect for his greatness and humbleness. Most important, Prof. Töpfer is as active as ever: as founding Director of the Institute of Advanced Sustainability Studies in Potsdam, Germany, and as Honorary Professor of Tongji University, Shanghai.

As the old saying goes, a great man needn't manage people but lead people. Prof. Klaus Töpfer is known internationally for his commitment and devotion to promoting environment and sustainable development. Throughout his career, millions of people all over the world have been fascinated and awed at how his charisma has touched their lives, leading people via initiatives and inspiring them by his learning, his experience, and his understanding of life.

So today, on the occasion of Prof. Töpfer's 75th birthday, we would like to share with you his *long and lasting love* with Tongji University.

When Tongji Met Prof. Töpfer…

Tongji, as one of the top universities in China, attaches great importance to international cooperation and plays a leading role in environmental issues in China. The core strategy of Tongji has always been to develop into a sustainable university and to strengthen environmental education in the international context. Just as 'Great minds think alike,' Prof. Töpfer greatly appreciated the concept proposed by Tongji, and agreed that education is an essential pillar in promoting the environment and sustainable development. Based on this common understanding and vision, Tongji was honored to appoint Prof. Töpfer as Honorary Professor in 1998. Since then, Prof. Töpfer has forged a profound friendship with Tongji and provided wise guidance during the university's journey to achieving remarkable milestones.

Milestone 1:
The UNEP–Tongji IESD Partnership

With the initiation and promotion of Prof. Töpfer, since the late 1990s, UNEP and Tongji entered into an agreement that led to the establishment of the UNEP–Tongji Institute of Environment for Sustainable Development (IESD) on 9 May 2002. At the ceremony, Prof. Töpfer (by that time Under-Secretary-General of the UN and the Executive Director of UNEP) and Prof. Qidi WU, former President of Tongji University, signed a Letter of Agreement. Mr. Zhenhua XIE, the former Minister of the State Environmental Protection Agency of China, and Mr. Zheng HAN, the Mayor of Shanghai attended the ceremony. Mr. Geping QU, former Chairman of the Environment and Resources Committee, Standing Committee of National People's Congress of China, sent a letter of congratulations to the Institute. The establishment of the Institute received worldwide attention, and it became the first institute in China to enjoy this unique cooperation with UNEP.

As the Chief Professor of IESD, Prof. Töpfer gives lectures to students annually and teaches the graduate student courses 'Global Environmental Issues' and 'Environmental Policies and Diplomacy.' He also acts as a supervisor to graduate students and PhD candidates. Moreover, he helps IESD to connect with international organizations, overseas governments, and international companies. Furthermore, with his help, Tongji University signed a cooperative agreement with Bayer AG to set up the Bayer–Tongji Professorship at IESD in 2007. In addition, with the great support of Prof. Töpfer, the HSBC–Tongji Project, Asia-Pacific Leadership Programme, and Sino-German Cooperation Projects have been successfully launched.

With the profound insight and strategic leadership of Prof. Töpfer, IESD made substantive progress: 2012 marked the 10th anniversary of the UNEP–Tongji partnership since the establishment of IESD in Shanghai. At the IESD Board Meeting in 2012, Prof. Töpfer also delivered a video message of congratulations on the great achievements of IESD, and expressed his willingness to continue to contribute to the development of IESD. In 2013, the year of his 75th birthday, he lectured on energy transitions in the context of the debate on sustainable development goals. He underlined that poverty is largely energy poverty, and engaged in vivid discussions with our

I am convinced that the signing of the cooperation with the UNEP–Tongji University Institute for Environment and Sustainable Development is exactly a concrete step in the direction we need to go. And this is timely: On the one side, knowing that UNEP celebrates this year its thirtieth birthday. Thus, UNEP is a result of the first global conference, at Stockholm in 1972, which was still called the United Nations Conference on the Human Environment. Thirty years later, we'll hold this global conference again on August 10 of this year in Johannesburg, South Africa; and interestingly enough, it is now called the United Nations World Summit on Sustainable Development. This is a huge change in these thirty years: Human Environment then; Sustainable Development today. In between, as you may know, we held the conference in Rio de Janeiro 1992, ten years ago, and this conference also ran as the United Nations Conference on Environment and Development. This gives, on the other side, a good reason why this Institute is named for 'Environment and Sustainable Development.' Because after Rio, as well as after the Stockholm conference, especially the developing countries were convinced that the developed countries cannot make the environment something like a 'limiting factor' for the development of their countries. They remain concerned that the environment is misused as a means of blocking the development needed to fight poverty, and to provide new jobs and new perspective for young people in the developing world…

And more and more it is clear that the environment is absolutely necessary for development. Therefore, we decided in this year, at UNEPs 30th anniversary, that our slogan is: 'Environment for Development,' not just 'Environment and Development.' We want to give a clear signal that, without the environment component, economic development cannot be successful. We need this to integrate, and we need for this scientific research.

Therefore, I am so glad, so honored, that we can come to this common stage. And I will give you just three examples where we need your contribution: the contribution of young people of universities; of the utmost importance are the natural resources we have; and the human aim that is your activities and thinking. That is human capital. Therefore, it is so great to be back to the University…

students. At the same time, he was impressed by the ambition of the Shanghai authorities to set up an emission trading scheme, and proved to be a most valuable dialogue partner for the local authorities to learn and seek advice on that innovative approach.

Over the past decade, IESD has played a key role in capacity-building as well as facilitating China–Africa environmental cooperation. By providing environmental education for more than 200 students from nearly 50 countries, and by building capacity in developing countries through training programs, technology transfer, and research projects, IESD has represented itself as a green platform to promote environmental education not only in China but around the world. In the run-up to Rio+20, IESD supported the launch of the Global Universities Partnership on Environment and Sustainability (GUPES) on 5 June 2012, which was chaired by the Vice-President of Tongji, Prof. Jiang WU.

More recently, the Brown Bag Event to celebrate 10 years of partnership between UNEP and Tongji was successfully held at the UNEP Headquarters in Nairobi. It reviewed the history and achievements of IESD since it was launched by Prof. Töpfer, and also presented the outlook for the next 10 years.

Milestone 2:
The Klaus Töpfer Environmental Scholarship

Although Prof. Töpfer is Chief Professor at IESD, he declined a salary; instead, he used 1 million RMB of his own money to establish the Klaus Töpfer Environmental Scholarship. Since 2007, the fund has awarded scholarships to the 10 most gifted environmental-major students out of hundreds of applicants each year. This was the first scholarship created for environmental-major students in China. Irrespective of the distance involved, Prof. Töpfer would travel to Tongji in order to present the awards to the winners. Meanwhile, he would share his experience and thoughts with students, inspiring them to be the future leaders for the environment. We still remember how on one occasion, despite his busy schedule, he managed to attend the award ceremony and make a speech for students. But even more importantly, he used his precious time to sit down with the group of students, to learn more about each individual project and to start a discussion both on details and the broader vision and how these promising young professionals can best contribute to this. Afterwards, he headed directly to the airport for another commitment. We can see that Prof. Töpfer attaches great importance to the scholarship, as he said: *"Youth are the future of a country. We cannot let them down."* When we gazed at his distant receding figure at the airport, our eyes were blurred but our thinking was clear and full of motivation to tackle common challenges.

Further to the scholarship, Prof. Töpfer also supports the 'Klaus Töpfer Environmental Innovation Student Competition' initiated by the German Consulate General

Shanghai and IESD. The competition is designed to foster environmental creative thinking, raise awareness of environmental-friendliness, and encourage Chinese students to create innovative proposals to contribute to environmental protection. In this context, Professor Fengting LI had the opportunity to spend some time as a Senior Fellow at the IASS in Potsdam in order to continue his work, this time at the home institute of Professor Töpfer.

Milestone 3:
Contribution to the Concept of 'Sustainability-Oriented University'

While universities around the world are still trying to make their campuses 'green,' Tongji University has already taken a step further, and is on the road to building a 'Sustainability-Oriented University.' As Honorary Professor at Tongji, Prof. Töpfer worked with dedicated scholars on how to achieve this. To have a better understanding of Tongji, Prof. Töpfer visited the existing green projects on campus and contributed profound insights and innovative ideas.

Tongji has pioneered the application of energy efficiency and environmental protection, as well as green technologies in every aspect of campus life, such as geo-heat pumps, thermal insulation systems, rainwater collection, and recycling systems. The university has also set up a special energy-saving management committee, and established the Office of Energy Management committee to put our green talk into practice. Our keen students play a key role in developing and promoting various kinds of green systems. The Green Road Association aims to promote awareness of environmental protection and is a positive force among students. In line with its slogan, 'on the green road, for our green dream,' each member is practicing their commitment to a greener world. An article published in the journal *Nature* gave a vivid description of the situation among universities in the United States and around the globe who are dedicated to the mission of reducing the emission of greenhouse gases (GHGs) and increasing energy efficiency. Tongji was the only Chinese university mentioned in this article, which is 'greening' its campus by upgrading projects and constructing energy-saving infrastructure.

Milestone 4:
Promoting International Student Exchange by
Initiating and Supporting Student Events

As a board member of the Jülich Research Center, Prof. Töpfer has promoted the establishment of the Key Laboratory of Yangtze River Water Environment at Tongji University. Meanwhile, the Jülich Research Center also contributed to the Sino–Germany–Africa Summer School. Each year, it attracts more than 60 students from China,

Germany, and African countries to engage in intensive learning and communication at both Tongji and the Jülich Research Center.

University students, as future leaders and decision makers of our society, should be engaged and empowered in different areas of environmental protection and sustainable development. Supported by UNEP and Tongji University, the International Students Conference on Environment and Sustainability (ISCES) was successfully held over the last three years. Around 400 students from more than 40 countries have taken part in the conference, exchanged views and ideas on topics relevant to environment and sustainable development, and adopted the Global Youth Tongji Declaration. Prof. Töpfer strongly supported the event and delivered the keynote speech, which helped to promote the concepts and practices of environment and sustainability amongst university students. As this conference takes place around 5 June—World Environment Day—there is no better way to underline the importance of such an event organized in China.

Now, as Executive Director of the Institute for Advanced Sustainability Studies (IASS), Prof. Töpfer continues to explore new paths with Tongji in terms of education, research, and outreach.

The Way Forward to a Sustainable Future

The United Nations calls for education for sustainable development (ESD) as one of the key strategies to combat environmental pollution and resource deterioration. Given the role of universities in fostering and disseminating knowledge, ESD in higher education (HE) has a critical role in transitioning towards a green economy specifically, and in attaining sustainable development more generally. It is important for universities to position themselves strategically, and to respond to expectations in leading and contributing to the shift towards a green economy, with focus on students—the current and next generation of leadership.

With the profound insight and wise guidance of Prof. Töpfer, Tongji will continue to mainstream environmental education and promote sustainable development across the world; and to facilitate inter-university networking on sustainability issues to advance sustainable development within the broader context of the United Nations Decade of Education for Sustainable Development (UNDESD, 2005–2014).

Juan Mayr Maldonado

Klaus Töpfer: A Visionary Leader, Charismatic, and Humanist

I remember well the first time I met with Klaus Töpfer. It was in February 1999, during the first trip I made to Nairobi to participate in the ministerial segment of the UNEP Governing Council. Colombia was at that time one of its members, and I had taken office as Environment Minister for my country just a few months earlier. There, together with a group of Latin American colleagues, I went to his offices to present a formal greeting. The impression I had was of a kind person, charismatic, with a great sense of humor and open to dialogue. His concerns not only addressed the many challenges that lay ahead for UNEP and global environmental institutions—which then, as today, continue to be a matter of great debate; he was also concerned that his words—simple but with great educational tone—should pose the complexity of the political, social, economic, and environmental challenges before us in seeking to achieve true sustainable development. His extensive experience and knowledge of global realities, but above all his great political sense, enabled him to focus conversation on very specific topics to be discussed in the following days as part of the agenda. I never imagined that this would be just one of many meetings that we would have over the following years.

Cartagena de Indias, Colombia

Our paths crossed again some months later in Colombia, as a result of negotiations that would conclude with the signing of the Protocol on Biosafety during the ExCOP of the Convention on Biological Diversity (CBD), in the city of Cartagena de Indias. The Colombian government had offered to host delegates from nearly two hundred countries and, in my capacity as Environment Minister, I was to formally preside over the meeting. It was a critical moment for the credibility of the CBD, as the Protocol would become its first legally binding development. Because of the difficulty posed by the negotiation on regulating transboundary movement of living modified organisms, better known as GMOs, the negotiations—which had been advanced over the past five years by a working group chaired by an expert in the issue, the lawyer Veit Koester—had not been concluded. Time was scarce and agreement had not yet been reached on a number of controversial points, which, as we would later see, needed further rounds of negotiation. Faced with such difficulties, Veit Koester took the decision to conclude the discrepancies and disagreements by presenting, for consideration by the parties, a final text: the text of the President. This was the sign that his work was completed. While the text sought a balance between the different positions presented and laid the foundation for what later became the Cartagena Protocol on Biosafety, it left no-one happy and therefore, as expected, did not allow for the negotiations to be concluded. However, the ExCOP would schedule a couple of additional days amid strong pressure to reach an agreement as time was fast running out. At the express request of Veit Koester, I took on responsibility for the negotiations. As the host, during the preceding days I had the opportunity to meet and greet all delegations arriving in Cartagena and to hear first-hand their expectations. This first approach was followed by a series of consultations with the different stakeholders for their views, and to adopt new formats for a negotiation that seemed impossible given the complexity of issues and interests.

Fortunately, I found myself again with Klaus Töpfer, who had come to Cartagena. His experience in these types of negotiations was invaluable. There were many conversations on which I requested his opinion and it was he who—once it became clear that it was not going to be possible to conclude the negotiations in a satisfactory way despite the enormous efforts made to bring the parties together on the points of disagreement—suggested at the last minute to "stop the clock," a scheme unknown to me, which allowed the negotiations to stop in time. So it was Klaus' suggestions that saved the negotiations, and with them the Biosafety Protocol. Although in Cartagena a definitive agreement was not reached, the following months of work would allow a redrawing of positions and achieve a more robust Protocol.

Furthermore, discussions with Klaus Töpfer reaffirmed what in Nairobi was just an initial perception: not only was he a kind, charismatic person with a great sense of humor and open to dialogue, but also a great politician and strategist, with a comprehensive view of the complex realities and interests at play in the world, and with sufficient tact and patience to seek consensus.

After Cartagena there would be many occasions when our paths crossed, giving me the opportunity to know the many other facets of his extraordinary personality.

75 Years of Permanent Changes
and Unique Challenges

The life and work of Klaus Töpfer—who seems immortal thanks to his extraordinary vitality—has developed over 75 years in the midst of profound societal and world transformations. Born in 1938 in Waldenburg, now Poland, at a time of enormous political upheaval, he has not only witnessed the events of recent German history, including World War II, the fall of the Berlin Wall, and the reunification of Germany—milestones of contemporary European and world history—but also a number of other events of global impact such as the enormous transformations that our planet and its ecosystems have undergone, and particularly the impact of these realities on the economies and societies of different countries, especially on the most vulnerable social groups. Climate change, pollution of fresh water sources and oceans, deforestation, desertification, and overexploitation of natural resources which have led to an unprecedented loss of species; and the exponential growth of the world population and its increased concentration in mega-cities—to cite just some of the most striking and challenging situations—are part of the experience and the world through which Klaus has lived; along with the globalization and liberalization of markets, with unprecedented progress in science, technology, computing, and communications. Added to these events are the moments of enthusiasm and optimism for change in the new millennium; but also the acute economic crises; and the political tensions and transformations experienced more recently, due to the attacks of 11 September 2001 and the subsequent wars and internal conflicts such as the Arab Spring. These are all part of the realities, each one interdependent, that Klaus has incorporated into his exemplary track-record, seeking answers and solutions for building a better world but—perhaps most importantly, a viable world.

With his training as an economist and his political background as a parliamentarian and minister, not only for the environment and nuclear safety, but also for regional planning and urban development of a First World country, and a little later as director of UNEP with its headquarters in Kenya, Klaus has been at the forefront of one of the major challenges facing humanity: the maintenance of our natural base, in a fast-developing and complex world, as guarantee for quality of life for all inhabitants of this planet, which is in permanent transformation and where uncertainty and challenges prevail.

The End of Complex Negotiations

After many meetings and numerous other approaches—some of them informal such as the parties meeting in Vienna, the birthplace of the 'Vienna Setting,' a new format to facilitate the often tedious international negotiations and to make these processes more agile and effective in their results—various delegations were meeting in Montreal to conclude, on this occasion, the Biosafety Protocol negotiations. With a temperature of minus 30 degrees Celsius (a great ally for keeping delegates concentrated in the negotiating room) and after many tensions and difficulties, the divergent and extreme positions were drawing closer. This time the meeting sought not only the presence of representatives of the press, NGOs, and business as observers, which established a climate of greater transparency, but also the participation of heads of delegation of the highest level. The European Union participated as one bloc, with ministers of the various countries accompanied by the Commissioner for Environment. Others, including the host country, did the same.

There were times of great stress and difficulty, and I remember with gratitude the constant companionship and advice from Klaus Töpfer, who was always there to answer and share concerns, who always offered his analysis and useful comments. Without his support, not only in Montreal but also throughout the process, it would not have been possible to announce the successful completion of this complicated negotiation.

The Coffee Region

The Biosafety Protocol negotiations allowed a bond of trust to be established with Professor Töpfer, which continued growing over the months and years to follow, when we often met for both professional reasons and friendship. Despite his very busy schedule—with work often conducted during flights between different continents—when activities took place in the American continent, we sometimes managed to coordinate visits to Colombia and for him to participate in meetings or events.

In 2000, I was elected Chair of the Commission on Sustainable Development at its eighth session (CSD-8), and the issues to be addressed there would be of particular significance for UNEP, which is why discussion of the agenda expanded and highlighted the spectrum of our relations.

During one of his trips to Colombia, I especially remember our visit to the coffee-growing region, where we held a meeting at CENICAFE—the globally recognized Coffee Research Centre, where as a witness of honor he accompanied us in the signing of an agreement between the main coffee producers for the promotion of biodiversity research in coffee areas. The heads of other biodiversity research centers accompanied us, among them Christian Samper and other environmental authorities, as well as the then Finance Minister, now President of Colombia, Juan Manuel Santos. There we had the opportunity to fly in a helicopter across the region, and with Töpfer an expert on productive landscapes, he was obviously interested in how to give greater international visibility to this good example of integration between production, biodiversity, water management, and good rural quality of life. Thanks to his actions, a few months later the coffee region of Colombia was included among the good examples for the Millennium Ecosystem Assessment, a major initiative in which UNEP was very active. This important contribution would reach greater heights a few years later, with UNESCO designating the region a World Heritage Landscape.

CSD-8 and the Big Apple

New York, site of the negotiations of the Commission on Sustainable Development (CSD), was another of our meeting places. One of the UNEP main offices operated there, and for obvious reasons the environmental and sustainable development agenda within the United Nations system was discussed and negotiated in New York. The agenda of the CBD was no exception, and the CSD-8 would tackle various topics of interest due to their environmental impact, among them financial resources, trade and investment, and economic growth, as well as sustainable agriculture. It would also present the progress of the Intergovernmental Forum on Forests. Because of its importance, UNEP gave special attention to this period of negotiations, as did I as Chair of the CSD-8. Thanks to a friendly gesture by Klaus Töpfer, I could count on the support of the UNEP offices and his entire team over the previous months of preparation, and for holding working meetings with stakeholder representatives of UN observer status who wished to share their positions and opinions with me. There were several working sessions held at the UNEP offices.

Finally, Klaus Töpfer came to New York to participate in the meetings of the high-level segment, which involved ministers of the various countries that formed the CSD, but also senior representatives and experts in various topics on the agenda. After the long work sessions we had the opportunity to escape to friendly New York places to have a beer—that as a good German, he enjoys; or for a plate of delicious pasta and good wine with him and Mechthild, his charming wife, at one of the Italian restaurants in the Big Apple.

This is how I got to know the most human and family side of Klaus, the friend. They were good times, a chance to talk about more informal matters, sharing stories of our lives and of our countries, but also to talk about future events, including possibilities for a country to host the next meeting of the UNEP Governing Council, which alternated each year between Nairobi and another country that volunteered for this event. How about proposing Colombia as a candidate for the next meeting to be held a few months later? We did not hesitate for a moment.

UNEP Governing Council, Cultural Diversity and Biodiversity

In Nairobi, it was approved that Cartagena de Indias would host the XXVII meeting of the UNEP Governing Council. Among other agenda items, and a particularly vital point for UNEP financing, was for a greater financial contribution from member countries in order to increase the limited budget that the Programme had at that time for achieving its objectives. It would also give guidelines on strengthening global environmental management—a critical issue in international policy discussion.

Over time, through the course of many international meetings, a group had formed, comprising fellow ministers from Latin American countries who viewed the extraordinary biodiversity of our countries as a great potential for development and as a great opportunity for political negotiation in the international arena. While Klaus, as Director of UNEP, always maintained careful neutrality, the trust that he generated permitted us to approach him for feedback on our ideas.

The ambiance in Cartagena was conducive to achieving not only agreements and innovations that could benefit the work of UNEP, but also for the protection of biodiversity and improving the negotiating capacity of the megadiverse countries.

The Cartagena meeting then allowed approval of an important modification in countries' financial contributions to UNEP, and gave guidelines for more effective global environmental management—significant achievements for its Director. Moreover, all the ministers of the main biodiversity-rich countries agreed to travel to Cancún at the invitation of the Environment Minister of Mexico, Victor Lichtenberg, for a meeting that would create the group of Like-minded Megadiverse Countries, whose guest of honor was obviously Klaus Töpfer.

As a preamble to this trip, while still in Cartagena, I travelled with Klaus and a group of minister friends to visit the spiritual leaders of the indigenous Kogi of the Sierra Nevada de Santa Marta, a magical isolated mountain range along the Caribbean coast, that reaches 5,775 meters above sea level and harbors a representative sample of the ecosystems, flora, and fauna of tropical America. The Kogi are one of the few ethnic groups in America that have maintained their pre-Hispanic culture and traditions virtually intact after more than 500 years since the arrival of Europeans. Their interaction with the environment and respect for all forms of life is exemplary and is part of 'The Law of the Mother,' a complex set of rules that dates from time immemorial.

Juan Mayr Maldonado

We left very early in the morning on a flight from Cartagena to Santa Marta, where we would board the helicopters that would take us to one of the sacred villages, located next to a river of crystal-clear waters, amidst huge mountains and forests, where the principal *Mamas*, the name given to the Kogi spiritual leaders, awaited us. After the reception by the Kogi political leader (Cabildo Gobernador) and the astonishment of all the visitors faced by this extraordinary and unique world that was opening before their eyes, we were invited to sit on small wooden seats facing the huge temple where ritual dances are held at solstices and equinoxes. A deep conversation started that would last several hours. After explaining who the visitors were, and from what parts of the world they came, including the "head of the environment at the global level" the elder *Mama* intervened, mentioning the importance of the work and the great responsibility that all the visitors had to protect the environment and the balance of the universe. The Cabildo Governor translated the *Mama's* words into Spanish and I then translated into English. The *Mama* explained how the culture of 'younger brother' (the Western world) was affecting the animals, forests, water, air, and earth. For this reason even they—the 'elder brothers'—who are mandated by the Law of Origin to care for all of nature, were beginning to have serious problems because the rains and dry seasons were no longer in balance, affecting their crops, causing diseases, and extreme weather events triggering landslides; these were symptoms of the damage caused by 'younger brother' and his desire to accumulate wealth. The *Mama* asked, "What has become of respect for nature?" Thre were many questions and answers from both sides.

During our return flight to Cartagena, I saw Klaus judiciously writing in his note-book. When I asked about his impressions, he told me that he had been impressed by the clarity with which the *Mama* had described the problems facing humanity today, and how in such simple words and from their local traditional knowledge they had linked the behavior of today's society with the impacts of global climate change.

The visit to the Kogi would open new paths for interactions with Klaus, this time regarding the close relationship between biodiversity and cultural diversity. And some years later there would be another meeting with the elder *Mama*, only this time not in the Sierra Nevada de Santa Marta but in Berlin, more precisely in Potsdam.

Group of Like-minded Megadiverse Countries

On the plane sent by the President of Mexico, Vicente Fox, we said goodbye to Cartagena and headed towards Cancún. The group that travelled along with Klaus Töpfer consisted of Environment Ministers of the megadiverse countries. Victor, as host, had prepared a careful agenda, which after a couple of days of discussion resulted in the signing of a document that created the Group of Like-minded Megadiverse

Countries. The meeting was a success and exceeded expectations. We were all well aware of the political importance of the union of countries that share near to 80% of the planet's biodiversity. The signing of the founding charter of the group was celebrated with visits to Chichén Itzá and other events, such as a live ball game, a show that recreates the demanding pre-Hispanic sport played by Aztecs and Mayans. We also visited one of the Cenotes with deep waters, where Klaus—in a wonderful demonstration of athletic ability and to everyone's surprise, dived head-first from a 10-meter-high springboard into the crystalline waters. It was a similar feat that, many years previously, had made him famous for jumping into waters of the river Rhine.

Preparations for the Johannesburg Summit

After completing the Cartagena and Cancún meetings, preparatory meetings were already underway for the Summit on Sustainable Development to be held in 2002 in Johannesburg. Ten years after the Summit on Environment and Development in Rio, finally the issue of sustainable development would be addressed in a holistic way. In Johannesburg it was Professor Töpfer, together with French President Jacques Chirac, who promoted an important high-level meeting on the issue of cultural diversity as a prelude to what would later be a major effort by UNEP to achieve recognition of the relationship between biodiversity and cultural diversity—a visionary topic of enormous importance, yet only a marginal issue until then.

Nairobi and Cultural Diversity

The Johannesburg Summit was overshadowed by the terrorist attacks of September 11th, and by the change of tack in global politics towards a security agenda and the fight against terrorism. The issue of environment moved into the background. But in the midst of these realities, Klaus Töpfer always maintained his enthusiasm and optimism. He extended a special invitation for me to participate as a consultant within a UNEP team with a specific mission: to promote recognition of the indivisible relationship between biodiversity and cultural diversity. The Colombian Government of which I had been a part had just completed its term of office, and the invitation from Klaus was of particular interest to me. In the following months I would have the opportunity to join the UNEP team in Nairobi and to learn more of his great leadership, not only as a director of a complex and bureaucratic UN organization, but also within the UN system as a whole. It was not difficult to see why Mr. Töpfer—as he was commonly known—always gained the highest respect from his colleagues and collaborators, for his kind yet clear, compelling, educational, and strict conduct of multiple subjects allowed him to achieve the desired results. With his vast experience, he did not miss the opportunity of any moment or situation to argue the importance, the implications, or consequences of an action or intervention at the right time. Besides this, he has always been a person who has understood very well the limitations imposed by complex situations in which the solution is not always in your hands, and he always found a way to transform constraints into new opportunities. His political instinct pointed with startling clarity to the appropriate place, time, and manner for actions to be taken. These are just some of the characteristics of this great leader.

Klaus is also, by definition, a restless soul, a person who is always seeking our — and deepening his own — knowledge on new topics. He is clear about the challenges of the complex reality within which humanity unfolds today, and focuses his efforts on cutting-edge themes. He is a great visionary, with his feet firmly on the ground and with a great anticipatory capacity, which is why a few years after initiating discussion about the importance and respect for cultural diversity this issue is now part of the international agenda.

Germany and Potsdam

A few years would pass before meeting- up again, this time in Potsdam, a center of former Prussia. Through news releases and environmental networks I had followed his path. After completing his work with UNEP he returned to his native Germany, where he was recognized with the most honorable awards for his outstanding work; he maintained his contacts and international relations, participating in major political, environmental, and economic forums; and his name was always among those favored as candidate for the German presidency, an honor conferred by the German Parliament upon its most prominent leaders.

His energy and vitality keep him as active as ever. He is a member of several governing boards of the most prestigious German research groups, and leads major working groups as well as being an advisor to the German Government and the broader political community in Germany on highly topical issues such as transforming the energy matrix, on which he is an expert. As if that were not enough, he accepted to be the founding Director of the Institute for Advanced Sustainability Studies in Potsdam, an institute for transdisciplinary studies at the forefront of research and thinking about the most critical challenges facing humanity today. It was there that we met again, not only to share memories of the past, but also to discuss various topics of common interest in finding ways for cooperation and exchange.

It was also at the IASS where he convened an interesting and unimagined meeting with the elder Kogi *Mama* who was visiting Berlin, and where they deepened the dialogue that began some years previously in the Sierra Nevada de Santa Marta.

After Professor Töpfer's welcoming words, the *Mama* began by saying: "We are not scientific people but I consider myself the son and messenger of nature; a messenger of water, animals, earth, wind, all that is in nature. Nature is sacred and we know how to live with her. I am grateful for allowing us to come to this country. Although we are from different cultures we could draw close because we are brothers. We were all born of nature, so we are brothers […] and that is why we decided to go into the world to fulfill our mission, which is to be messengers of nature. Mother Nature is like a woman, her body is being affected, and she may get sick. 'Younger brother' gives priority to his own interests rather than collective interests, so Mother Nature has become sick."

With these simple yet profound words, the Kogi *Mama* describes one of the main challenges facing humanity—the same challenge that has guided the successful career of this beloved professor and friend—a visionary leader, charismatic, and humanist. I have tremendous gratitude and appreciation for Klaus Töpfer's invaluable and tireless contributions. I wish him much happiness and many more years of life.

Juan Mayr Maldonado

Massoumeh Ebtekar

Klaus Töpfer:
A Pioneer for the Environmental Dimension
of Dialogue among Civilizations

In the Name of Allah, the Compassionate, the Merciful

People in leadership positions are looked upon as mentors and role models. Their positive behavior and attitude can lead to good governance. Their personal influence may be vast and long-lasting. Positive and ethical role models can create favorable images. They inspire friends and colleagues as well as personnel, and in cases of high political office or international posts they inspire the public and may create hope and motivate people. Since the UN has an important leadership role in today's world, officials in this international body are looked upon as global leaders. Their sense of responsibility and commitment can resonate not only in their organization but among the greater public with whom they interact.

I knew Klaus Töpfer before my appointment as the Vice President of Iran and Head of the Department of Environment in 1997. My late father, Dr. Taghi Ebtekar, who had also occupied my post several years before, spoke about Prof. Töpfer with much admiration. He told me: "Töpfer is a *real international figure*," implying that he understands the diversities of cultures and traditions, and has great respect for Iranians and their religious aspirations.

I had the honor of working with Klaus Töpfer in my capacity as Vice President from 1997 to 2005. In 1998, in one of my first attendances at the UNEP Annual Session, during my address to the plenary, I brought up the idea of taking stock of the social mobilization that millions of religious believers throughout the world might create to protect nature and to prevent pollution and degradation of resources. After my speech, Prof. Töpfer asked me to bring up, during the ensuing Ministerial Roundtable, the importance of religious beliefs and how the UN can address this issue in its policies when dealing with the environment. I was surprised at his words of support.

I had dealt with UN leaders at various levels before. Their secular approach and tacit resentment in the face of religious views surfacing in UN negotiations and documents was usually very evident. Yet now, I was facing a UNEP Executive Director who understood—and hoped to promote—the significance of religious values as motivating factors for the general public in protecting the environment.

Other countries supported the idea, and the issue was included in the minutes of the meeting. Religious values on the protection of the environment had to be studied and analyzed, for every religion had its own approach and its specific methods for conveying the message. In Iran, we began a series of seminars on *The Environment in Islam*. We invited both religious seminaries and the universities to perform research on the various dimensions of Islamic teachings and how they relate to the modern concepts of sustainability and environmental protection. The religious seminaries and academia both responded favorably, and even prominent religious thinkers like Ayatollah Javadi Amoli presented a thesis on the interpretations of the numerous verses in which the holy Quran deals with nature, the laws of nature, human responsibility, and recommended lifestyles.

On the basis of Prof. Töpfer's support and with the collaboration of UNEP, Tehran hosted an International Seminar on Religion, Culture, and Environment in May 2001. Religious leaders from ten major monotheistic religions presented their views and discussed the potential ways religion could play an effective role in changing lifestyles and consumption patterns to promote a more sustainable society. The guests met with the Supreme Leader and the President. Prof. Töpfer had a private meeting with President Khatami and expressed his recognition for the proposal of Dialogue Among Civilizations. Since the President knew German they had spoken in German; both were impressed by the meeting and Prof. Töpfer told me how he thought the charisma and rational conduct of President Khatami would serve not only Iran but much of the Islamic world.

The proposal to engage the global community in *A Dialogue Among Civilizations* was offered to the UN by President Khatami and the year 2001 was designated as such. This event, during the same year that the September 11 events occurred and the US launched its invasion against Afghanistan, was highly symbolic and meaningful. The Dialogue opened new vistas for a global interface, underpinning new horizons for proactive international decision making and dialogue-based conflict resolution. As part of this trend, priority was given to the dilemmas that trouble the human race. Dialogue should deal with issues that have preoccupied the global psyche and threaten humanity. Today, environmental degradation is challenging life on Earth, and the roots of this destructive phenomenon lie in the mentality and actions of the human race.

Later that year, on the occasion of the international year of Dialogue Among Civilizations, Prof. Töpfer hosted a seminar on the sidelines of the Environment Ministers Forum in Nairobi, Kenya. Entitled the *'Environmental Dimension of Dialogue Among*

Civilizations,' the session recognized the value attached to the proposal of President Khatami; it emphasized the importance of dialogue as opposed to clash, and the importance of multilateralism in dealing with environmental issues as opposed to the unilateral and militaristic approach that certain powers pursed. Prof. Töpfer arranged for the publication of a small booklet on that event and the session received quite favorable media attention. Since Iran was also the President of the G77 during that year, we made additional efforts to benefit from the synergy of the two occasions and open new horizons for a North–South and East–West dialogue.

In many UNEP sessions and ministerial events, champagne was served as part of the ceremony. In recognition of our religious norms, which require that Muslims refrain from alcoholic beverages and do not sit at tables where alcohol is served, I informed Prof. Töpfer that I would not attend the social events and dinner invitations of UNEP. Prof. Töpfer, however, quickly found a solution that was joined by some of the other Ministers who also refrained from alcohol and thought that it was inappropriate to serve alcohol at an environmental event: In all UNEP receptions and ceremonies, an alcohol-free table was designated for those who wished not to be served with champagne. More interesting was the fact that, even when I was among the guests at the Head Table, he would arrange so that no alcohol was served. Apart from my religious convictions, I once told Prof. Töpfer that I believed we had to promote a healthy lifestyle — i.e., no smoking, no alcohol — starting from such high-level sessions. I think he also believed in this, and led a campaign at the ministerial level to disseminate this message.

Prof. Töpfer was weary of the escalation of war and violence, as well as the ongoing aggression on natural resources in the world; he genuinely believed that dialogue and understanding was the only road map ahead to salvation. The international conference on 'Environment, Peace, and the Dialogue Among Civilizations' was convened in May 2005 in Tehran, with the support of UNEP. Prof. Töpfer attended and spoke very eloquently about the role that UNEP had played in promoting the environmental dimension of Dialogue Among Civilizations.

He noted in his opening speech: "The notion of Dialogue Among Civilizations is not just a philosophical concept. It is indeed a pragmatic, inclusive, and instrumental model in enhancing cooperation, security, and peace even through environmental cooperation. Environmental degradation, inequitable access, and unsustainable use of natural resources are important sources of human insecurity that could trigger conflict and war. Environmental concerns can present opportunities for dialogue, cooperation, and peace-building. Cooperative actions around common environmental concerns can be a powerful tool for preventing conflict and promoting security and peace."

The conference generated vast reactions of support and recognition. Later in Tehran, based on the concept of the interrelatedness of war and environment, we established an NGO entitled 'Center for Peace and Environment' (www.pengoo.ir) and began a campaign of advocacy, awareness raising, and diplomatic efforts to recognize the disastrous effects of regional wars and conflicts on the global environment.

The terms that Prof. Töpfer had emphasized in 2005 still resonate strongly today: "Shared environmental concerns could play a valuable role in catalyzing cooperation, initiating dialogue, and providing alternative dispute resolution mechanisms. It has been observed in many cases that cooperation and dialogue have been catalyzed as a result of pressing common environmental concerns and their transboundary effects. Such shared environmental concerns have even paved the way for political reconciliation between or among neighboring countries." These words are indicative of the profound vision and sublime aspirations that Prof. Töpfer embodied during his tenure as UNEP Executive Director. His astute personality and dynamic activism created a great asset for UNEP and for the global environment. Prof. Töpfer has been an advocate of ethical leadership and policy, and his legacy will remain in the minds and hearts of all.

Today more than ever, we require a serious ethical commitment at the international level. Politicians have broken their promises too many times. They have taken the global environment to the verge of destruction. Leaders of global powers pursue policies that enhance global tensions and may lead to escalation of violence and conflict. Humanity longs for politicians who retain their moral integrity while in power and consider themselves accountable in face of the people and in face of their Creator.

James Gustave Speth

New Economy Transformation: The Eight-fold Way

It was my great pleasure to serve in the United Nations with Klaus Töpfer. We led different agencies, but they were both dedicated to the cause of sustainable development. Töpfer was a remarkable leader of the United Nations Environment Programme, and my already great respect for him was only deepened by the dedication and foresight I saw him bring to his job.

In recent years, many of us concerned about sustainability have begun framing our work around the theme of a new economy. Let us define the 'new economy' that we are seeking as one where the true and actual purpose of economic life is to sustain and to strengthen people, place, and planet, and is no longer primarily to grow profit, product (as in gross domestic), and power (See the accompanying box on a 10-point charter for a new economy).

At least eight forces, working together, can drive transformative change toward this new economy. As I describe them, ask yourself how far along your country is on each. Unfortunately, I can reliably report that in the United States we have a long way to go in most of these areas.

1. Fed up, and seeing the system as the problem. The journey to a new economy begins when enough people have come to two important conclusions. The first is that something is profoundly wrong with the current system of political economy. In the United States and in numerous other places, that system is now routinely generating terrible results—failing socially, economically, environmentally, and politically. When big problems emerge across the entire spectrum of national life, as they surely have in America, it cannot be for small reasons. We have encompassing problems because of fundamental flaws in our economic and political system. The second conclusion follows from the first—it is the imperative of system change, of building a new political economy that routinely delivers good results for people, place, and planet.

2. Crises. Crises—economic, environmental, or other—point to underlying failure, raise difficult questions, and send people searching for answers. They can wake people up and shake them up. If severe enough, they will delegitimize the current order. America's political economy is already stressed by multiple pressures, general over-load, and buffeting events at home and abroad, and the intensity of these stresses will likely increase. Having lost resiliency and coping capacity, the system will be highly vulnerable to crises that will open the door to major potential for change, but only if we are prepared.

3. Progressive fusion. If progressive interests are as fragmented and 'each-in-its-own-silo' as we in the United States are today, they won't be able to take advantage of positive opportunities opened up by rising popular disenchantment and ongoing crises. What's needed, for starters, is a unified progressive identity; concerted efforts to institutionalize coordination; a commitment to creating a powerful, unified move-ment beyond isolated campaigns; and a common infrastructure capable of both for-mulating clear policy objectives and strategic messages, and coordinating joint action. Progressive fusion can be seen as necessary to the transformative forces discussed in the paragraphs that follow.

4. Envisioning an attractive future. A powerful part of the drive for transformation must be a compelling envisioning of the world we would like to leave for our children and grandchildren. When systemic change does come, it does so because the people agitating for change have painted a compelling vision of a better future. As Victor Hugo wrote in *Les Misérables*, "there is nothing like a dream to create the future. Utopia today, flesh and blood tomorrow."

We need an attractive depiction of life in this desirable future, and we need a description of the policies and other measures that can get us there. These are essential to dispel the myth that there is no attractive alternative to the current system.

5. Actually building an attractive future. From the ground up, we need to see the future emerging into the present through a continuing proliferation of real-world (predominantly local) initiatives, new forms of community revitalization, and inno-vative community action; transition towns; new business forms focused on local liv-ing economies, rootedness, and sustaining people and nature (e.g., public–private and profit–nonprofit hybrids, mission-protected corporations) as well as new growth of older models (e.g., worker-owned co-ops and other forms of employee ownership), and new lifestyles and workstyles adopted at the individual, family, and organiza-tional levels. These initiatives are worthy in themselves. They also raise consciousness, change people's opinions, and provide inspirational models that can be replicated as the movement grows.

When we think about these dimensions of envisioning and building a better world, it's clear that such efforts are led by individuals whose social values have moved beyond the materialism, anthropocentrism, individualism, and contempocentrism that today dominate so much of life and culture. A transformation of values and culture is a central facet of the overall transformation. Value-change must move in parallel with other transformative change.

6. *Transformative leadership and narrative.* Wise leaders and social narrative can be powerful forces for transformative change. Harvard's Howard Gardner (2006) stresses the potential leadership in his book *Changing Minds,* "Whether they are heads of a nation or senior officials of the United Nations, leaders of large, disparate populations have enormous potential to change minds … and in the process they can change the course of history. I have suggested one way to capture the attention of a disparate population: by creating a compelling story, embodying that story in one's own life, and presenting the story in many different formats so that it can eventually topple the counterstories in one's culture … The story must be simple, easy to identify with, emotionally resonant, and evocative of positive experiences."

Here in the United States, Bill Moyers (2007) has written that "America needs a different story … So let me say what I think up front: The leaders and thinkers and activists who honestly tell that story and speak passionately of the moral and religious values it puts in play will be the first political generation since the New Deal to win power back for the people."

7. *Building a grassroots movement and pro-democracy reform.* In the United States and no doubt elsewhere, the struggle for deep, systemic change will be met with more determined resistance. It follows that the prospects for systemic change will depend mightily on the health of democracy and the power of the social and political movement that is built. Transformative change, and even many of the proposals for incremental reform, will often not be possible without a new politics. In the United States, pro-democracy reform and building a powerful new grassroots movement in America must be priority number one for all progressives. A vital first step is for progressives to agree on an agenda of political reforms and to agree to work together to get them adopted.

8. *Rebirth of protest and direct action.* In the end, achieving meaningful changes will require a rebirth of marches, protests, demonstrations, nonviolent civil disobedience, and other forms of direct action. Certainly, one major driver of direct action in the years immediately ahead will be the already disastrous impacts of climate change.

To sum up, imagine the following: As conditions continue to decline across a wide front, or at best fester as they are, ever-larger numbers of people lose faith in the current system and its ability to deliver on the values it proclaims. The system steadily loses support, leading to a crisis of legitimacy. Meanwhile, traditional crises, both in the economy and in the environment, grow more numerous and fearsome. In response, progressives of all stripes coalesce, find their voice and their strength, and pioneer the development of a powerful set of new ideas and policy proposals confirming that the path to a better world does indeed exist. Demonstrations and protests multiply, and a powerful movement for prodemocracy reform and transformative change is born. At the local level, people and groups plant the seeds of change through a host of innovative initiatives that provide inspirational models of

---

Ten-point Charter for a New Economy

1. Economic Goals. The reigning priorities of economic life shall be human and ecological well-being, not profits and GDP growth. Public policy shall recognize that economic growth has costs as well as benefits and that, after a certain point, the former can outweigh the latter.

2. Economic Democracy. Investment and other economic decisions shall be guided by democratically determined priorities. All economic institutions, including corporations, shall be governed by—and held accountable to—all those affected by their activities. New patterns of corporate governance, ownership, and operational management involving workers, communities, and stakeholders shall be the norm. Corporate chartering shall be at the level of corporate operations and periodically reviewed in the public interest.

3. Regulation. Democratically determined regulatory initiatives shall guide market activity in socially and environmentally beneficial directions; ensure that prices are honest and reflect all real costs of production; and prevent predation of public assets and the commons, the valuable assets that properly belong to everyone.

4. Subsidiarity. Economic policy and regulation shall foster activity at the most localized level consistent with democracy, equity, and effectiveness. Higher-level national, regional, and global governance shall be exercised where human and ecological well-being will be strengthened by so doing.

5. Environment. The economy shall be managed with the overall objective of preserving and restoring natural capital for future generations, preventing climatic disruption, and preserving the integrity of biotic communities and natural systems.

how things might work in a new political economy devoted to sustaining human and natural communities. Sensing the direction in which things are moving, our wiser and more responsible leaders—political and otherwise—rise to the occasion, support the growing movement for change, and frame a compelling story or narrative that makes sense of it all and provides a positive vision of a better world. It is a moment of democratic possibility.

How likely is this scenario? Most US observers today would say, "not very." But circumstances can change rather swiftly, and the emerging climate crisis is the biggest change agent at work in the world today.

6. Equity. Income and wealth shall be equitably distributed within and among countries, and programs shall be maintained to alleviate poverty, ensure freedom from want, and provide economic security.

7. Work. All individuals shall be guaranteed opportunities for decent work, living wages, and continuing self-improvement. The rights of workers to organize, bargain collectively, and participate in the management of enterprises shall be guaranteed.

8. Consumerism. Public policy, including regulation of advertising, shall move society in the direction of 'work and spend less; create and connect more.' Consumerism, where people search for meaning and acceptance through what they consume, shall give way to the search for abundance in things that truly matter—good health, education, family, friends, the natural world, and meaningful work.

9. Money and finance. The system of money and finance shall be operated as an essential public utility for the benefit of society as a whole. Financial institutions shall channel resources to areas of high social and environmental return even if not justified by financial return. Finance shall shift away from institutions that are driven to excess by the search for profits and personal financial gain and that are remotely owned and managed, to institutions that are small enough not only to fail but also to be held accountable by the communities in which they operate.

10. International Relations. The priority of international affairs shall be to maintain peace, security, and harmony among nations, and to promote global governance and international rules that further these 10 principles.

LITERATURE CITED

Gardner, H. (2006): Changing Minds: The Art and Science of Changing Our Own and Other People's Minds. Boston: Harvard Business School Press. p. 69, 82.

Moyers, B. (2007): The Narrative Imperative. TomPaine.com, 4 January 2007 [http://www.tompaine.com/print/the_narrative_imperative.php].

James Gustave Speth

Timothy E. Wirth

Klaus Töpfer at 75: Remarks of the Honoroble Timothy E. Wirth

Throughout a career of hard work and accomplishment, Klaus Töpfer has helped to define the new era and growing imperative of sustainability. In the process, he has helped position Germany and the world to take on the central challenges facing the 21st century. Realizing sustainable development is now the overarching priority of this era.

Klaus helped reinforce and influence my understanding of the nature and scope of planetary threats when our professional lives intersected at a critical juncture in the history of the world, as the Berlin Wall collapsed. In the wake of the Cold War, we both became deeply immersed in the new realities of a world growing increasingly interdependent—economically, environmentally, and socially. He was a newly minted Minister for the Environment in Germany, and I was a freshman in the United States Senate. Our first interactions occurred as the issue of climate change transitioned from specialized scientific journals to broad domestic policy discussions and international negotiations. We experienced the powerful Rio Earth Summit and witnessed negotiation of promising agreements on the Framework Convention on Climate Change and Convention on Biological Diversity. Later, we worked together through the United Nations, where he led the UN Environment Programme and worked closely with the United Nations Foundation on the Millennium Ecosystem Assessment and other initiatives. Over the course of thirty years, we have become close friends and prioritized in our own lives the centrality of sustainable development. Together, we have come to understand that our planet and its life-support systems are at a tipping point. In our professional lifetimes, it has become clear that there are simply too many human beings using too many resources and generating too many waste products. The trends are not sustainable.

For some, the concept of sustainability is amorphous, opaque, elusive. In truth, it is an elegantly simple idea, conceived under the leadership of one of the UN

Foundation's esteemed Board Members, Gro Harlem Brundtland. In the late 1980s, Dr. Brundtland, then Prime Minister of Norway, chaired the groundbreaking work of the World Commission on Environment and Development. The Brundtland Commission's report 'Our Common Future' defined sustainable development as prosperity and progress that "meets the needs of present generations without compromising the ability of future generations to meet their own needs."

This timeless, universal statement of values perfectly captures the interdependence that characterizes the human experience today. People, problems, and opportunities are connected as never before. We see this new reality in world financial markets, in transportation and trade patterns, and in such areas as health and migration. Perhaps most striking of all is the degree to which the health of the Earth's life-support systems links us together. Facing catastrophic climate change, as we do, it matters little whether greenhouse gases emanate from Frankfurt, Germany; Fortaleza, Brazil; or Fort Collins, Colorado ... we all get warm together.

The reality of such interdependence is entirely new in human history. Never before have the fates and responsibilities of the world's people been as intertwined. Never before have we borne such heavy moral responsibilities toward our children and grandchildren. Unhappily, we are not living up to those responsibilities. In fact, we are failing badly as stewards of the natural systems that make human life and planetary productivity possible.

- The oceans, which supply protein for 2.6 billion people, are being hammered by overfishing, pollution, and neglect. Eighty percent of the world's fisheries are over-exploited and verging on collapse. A mass of plastic particles twice the size of Texas has accumulated in what is known as the North Pacific Ocean Gyre. Dead zones and algal blooms are growing more common in the Pacific Northwest, off the Gulf of Mexico, and elsewhere as a result of accumulating fertilizers, sewage, the disintegration of natural gas products, and other polluted runoff.
- Freshwater resources are declining globally as aquifers are drawn down faster than they can be replenished, and existing supplies are polluted. Stream flows in 60 percent of the world's large rivers have been modified by dams and yet 1.2 billion people live with water scarcity and 500 million more are threatened by it. Major river basins (e.g., the Nile, Yangtze, Colorado, and Euphrates) are experiencing reduced flows, while major lakes and inland seas are also shrinking. In the next 20 years, two-thirds of the world's people will live in areas facing moderate to severe water stress.
- We are failing to protect critical land-based resources—soils, forests, wetlands— that are relied upon for food, fiber, and naturally filtering our air and water. One-third of the Earth's arable land and its valuable topsoil have been degraded or destroyed. More than 35 percent of the Earth's surface lands have been transformed

for agriculture, human settlements, and other purposes. Deforestation has been occurring at the rate of 30,000 square kilometers per year for more than a decade.

- Biological diversity—including the globe's rich storehouses of coral reefs and tropical forests—is being lost at a rate 80 times that found in the fossil record. Human activity has spawned one of a half-dozen spasms of extinction we know of. Unchecked, we will lose half the world's biological inheritance during this century—the greatest mass extinction since the age of the dinosaurs.
- And we are using the atmosphere as a vast garbage dump for local and global pollutants. The global climate is changing even faster than many scientists anticipated only a few years ago. Unless we significantly alter emissions, chaotic climatic changes are all but certain in this century.

The facts are indisputable. They have been rigorously documented by the world's best scientists, peer reviewed, and widely popularized. It is dismaying, then, that tangible progress toward sustainable development in the 1970s, 1980s, and early 1990s has stalled, and the international community has become so utterly ineffective, so seemingly indifferent in the face of the overwhelming scientific data and the clear implications for the next generations. The world's future—our future and that of our children and grandchildren—is being mortgaged away because we refuse to acknowledge how much our long-term economic and national security is linked to the health of the planet's life-support systems.

The fundamental obstacle to the pursuit of sustainable development around the world is the misguided belief that protecting the environment is somehow antithetical to economic interests. Too many of today's leaders will say: "I'm for protecting the environment ... as long as it doesn't cost jobs or hurt the economy." This terribly mistaken analysis epitomizes the fundamental intellectual challenge to sustainable development. Over the long term, living off our ecological capital is a bankrupt economic strategy.

Stated in the jargon of the business world, the economy is a wholly-owned subsidiary of the environment. Virtually all economic activity is dependent in some way on the environment and its underlying resource base. This includes everything from food and fuel to water and fiber. These underpin the vast majority of all economic activity and most jobs. When the environment is finally forced to file for bankruptcy under Chapter 11 because its resource base has been polluted, degraded, and irretrievably compromised, then the economy goes down with it.

If you want an example of a country on the brink of ecological and economic Chapter 11, look no further than North America's own backyard. In Haiti, dwindling resources are central to the economic, political, and social collapse that has gripped an island nation that was once the crown jewel of the French Empire. Almost totally deforested, its poor croplands are repeatedly divided into smaller and less-productive parcels as the population grows. That same population growth and the devastation of Haiti's natural resource base have coincided with the erosion of the nation's job base, agriculture, and tourism industry. This same pattern is evident in other impoverished parts of the world, where more than 3 billion people try to eke out a living in squalid cities and marginal lands on less than $2.50 a day. In Asia, Africa, and some parts of Latin America, rapid population growth compounds the daily struggle of the poor for fuel, food, and shelter, turning the world's poorest into unwitting but powerful agents of destruction.

But poverty is not the only—or even the most potent—force at work on the global environment. The appetite of the affluent for timber products is just as much of a menace to forests in Malaysia, Indonesia, the Philippines, Brazil, and the United States. The bulk of the underground water being drained from our future flows into the shining cities of the 'haves,' not the shanty towns of the 'have-nots.' Those same cities, and we who live in them, are responsible for the vast majority of the cars and power-plants that are the furnaces of global warming. These trends demonstrate that rapid population growth and runaway consumption are the twin engines of climate change and the driving forces for our unsustainable ways.

Human population, which took 200,000 years to reach 2 billion around the time Klaus and I were born, has more than tripled in our lifetimes and recently surpassed the 7 billion mark. Every year, the world gains another 75 million inhabitants—the equivalent of another Chicago every two weeks, another Egypt every year, another China every 20 years. Ninety-five percent of that growth takes place in the impoverished countries of the developing world, most of which are already struggling to provide jobs, stability, and sustenance for their people. In fact, rapid population growth in the developing world is less an immediate threat to the global environment than it is to local conditions, life prospects, and the stability of the people and countries experiencing it.

Population and consumption work in reverse in the Northern, developed countries. Despite their stagnating populations, industrialized countries have developed the capacity to consume resources and produce waste at rates unprecedented in human history. Comprising only one-fifth of the world's population, the industrialized countries use two-thirds of all resources consumed and generate more than two-thirds of all pollutants and wastes. Therefore, even relatively modest population increases in developed countries, as is happening in Northern Europe, have major implications for sustainability.

So we're getting ourselves into a terrible fix—the globe's population is growing at a rate that is matched or exceeded only by our capacity to consume resources and produce wastes. The security of our world hinges on whether we can strike a sustainable, equitable balance between human numbers and the planet's capacity to support life. That is why the world's political leaders must make political, economic, energy, and demographic transformations the centerpiece of the global agenda for sustainable development in the 21st century.

Demographic transformation must be at the top of the list; we can't achieve sustainable development unless we know how many of us we are trying to sustain. The UN population scenarios present three very different futures:

- In one of those futures, global population grows by another 50–60 percent to between 10 and 11 billion people.
- In the second demographic scenario we continue to invest in development as we have been, and the world's population eclipses 9 billion people in 2050 before stabilizing.
- Finally and most optimistically, we step up to the challenge of sustainability, and meet human needs and stabilize population at just over 8 billion in the next 30 years.

This third scenario is both feasible and wise. Whether we are talking about prospects for climate change, security, poverty alleviation, equity, or any other aspect of human development, population stabilization at close to 8 billion will significantly improve humanity's prospects for peace, stability, progress, and some semblance of environmental integrity.

Reaching the goal of population stabilization will require concerted efforts to help people receive the information and services they need to determine—freely and responsibly—the number and spacing of their children. The international community has agreed on a sensible, comprehensive framework that includes:

- Making basic health services—including reproductive and maternal health services—universally available. In today's world, more than 200 million women and families want family planning services, but cannot get them. This is our first imperative.
- The second is the empowerment of women, including closing the gender gap in education and ensuring that every child—girls as well as boys—receive primary and secondary education;
- Reducing maternal mortality by ensuring that every birth occurs with a skilled birth-attendant and that every woman has access to emergency obstetric care;
- Slowing population momentum by ensuring that women and girls have educational and economic opportunities and that no child is married at an unsafe age;
- Increasing child survival so that families have confidence that their children will live.

Stabilizing the population at close to 8 billion will also make it much easier for the world to achieve our second major goal for the 21st century: stopping global warming at no more than 2 degrees Celsius. The world's best scientific minds have indicated that warming beyond 2 degrees will likely have catastrophic consequences for the poor, for coastal regions, for agriculture, health, and political and economic stability.

To prevent this kind of a future, the science tells us that we need to stabilize carbon dioxide emissions immediately and begin rolling them back until an 80 percent reduction from 1990 levels is achieved by 2050.

Stabilizing emissions will be a good deal easier if we stabilize population. But we can't stabilize the atmosphere without changing our consumption patterns. And that is why we need to reinvent the worldwide energy system. The requirements are clear:

- Using energy more efficiently is the 'low-hanging fruit' in the world's bid to harvest a low-carbon future. Massive efficiency opportunities exist in the transportation, buildings, and industrial sectors. The McKinsey Global Institute (2008) found that a $170 billion annual investment between 2009 and 2020 would halve projected global energy demand and get us halfway to solving the climate crisis.

  The payoff would be valued at $900 billion a year by 2020, and none of the energy efficiency measures would require compromising the consumer's comfort or convenience. This estimate is based only on existing energy efficiency technology—not on solutions that have yet to emerge.

- Second, we need to rapidly facilitate fuel-switching, so that we can move from the most carbon-intensive fuels, like coal and oil, to cleaner-burning fuels like natural gas. Trends in new generating capacity are encouraging. As of today, renewable energy sources account for 20 percent of global energy supply, and solar and wind markets are growing 15–20 percent annually on a compound annual growth basis. In three of the last four years, gas and renewables have accounted for more than 80 percent of the new generating capacity added in the United States. In the EU, 70 percent of new generating capacity was renewable in 2012.

- For the long term, we need to continue researching and deploying the clean energy technologies and jobs that are emerging in the solar, wind, and biomass industries. And we have to set the right incentives for soil, wetland, and forest preservation—so that farmers can make money through sustainable practices and carbon sequestration.

Reforming and transforming our economic systems is a third priority for the future. We can't continue forsaking all our long-term interests in order to achieve short-term economic growth as our overriding national and international priority. 'Growth' is not the sole indicator of progress, nor is it a true measure of human well-being as it relates to health, satisfaction, social justice, or environmental integrity. In too many places, growth has failed to deliver on promises for reducing income equality or generating the resources needed to protect the environment. Moreover, current economic accounting fails completely to internalize the social costs such as those associated with pollution.

Transforming the world's economic systems will be challenging, but the agenda for reform is becoming clear:

- First, we need to develop new systems of national economic accounting that are capable of capturing concepts such as degradation of environmental resources, the economic contributions of women, and social justice.
- Closing the rich–poor gap is a second priority at the national and international levels. In 'Divided We Stand: Why Inequality Keeps Rising,' the OECD (2011) documents the reasons for—and impacts of—the growing inequality of income within the world's leading industrialized nations. Even among these countries, inequality has reached its highest levels in 50 years. Addressing income inequality is essential not only for global equity, but for social cohesion and long-term sustainability. Expanding educational and economic opportunities for the poor is therefore a top priority for long-term sustainable development.
- Finally, environmental economics must be expanded so that externalities are integrated in the costs of goods and services sold in the marketplace. In this way, we can harness market forces in service of environmental protection and accelerate the pace toward truly sustainable development.

Political reform stands as the fourth and perhaps most fundamental and challenging transformation to be initiated. In too many places, money and its influence determine the direction of local, national, and international policy. Whether through campaign contributions, lobbying efforts, slick public relations campaigns, or corrupt practices, entrenched interests with enormous financial resources are having a disproportionate impact on policies that might move us toward sustainable development. And it is occurring in rich and poor nations alike. At the national level, the political reform agenda includes stamping out corruption and getting money out of politics.

But there is also an international political reform agenda. Simply put, we cannot achieve sustainable development without a strong, effective United Nations and a thoroughly updated international system. The foundations of international cooperation today were created in the aftermath of World War II, in a totally different era. The World Bank, the IMF, the United Nations and its subsidiary bodies are all a little frayed today, and are due for a significant upgrade to ensure 21st century transparency, efficiency, and accountability. Key UN institutions—from established organizations like the UN Population Fund to new ones like the 'Sustainable Energy For All' initiative—are ripe for strengthening. There is much to do, and the leaders of these institutions are eager to work with governments, nongovernmental institutions, and the private sector. But reformed international institutions have to be given authority to do their jobs. Their governance has to be modernized as well—new global powers must be given the opportunity to play roles of leadership and responsibility. Expansion of the Security Council is a good place to start, taking account of the development and influence of such key emerging countries as India, Brazil, and South Africa. In a globalized world, governance designed 60 years ago is neither possible nor wise.

Just as economic, social, and environmental causes must be integrated if we are to achieve sustainable development, so too must the peoples of the world. We need a new global compact that asks all the world's citizens to come together behind a larger sense of purpose—preservation of the Earth's life-support systems. To succeed, this compact must be cross-cultural and inter-generational. It will require the talents and perspectives of all nations; the wisdom of those in the middle or at the end of their professional lives; and will especially require the energy of today's youth.

None of the reforms we need—in energy and economics, health and governance—will occur without the energy and engagement of today's young people. Youth have long powered the great movements for reform around the world—from the civil rights movement in the United States to the Arab Spring in the Middle East. And so it will be in the struggle for sustainable development.

I expect the *Klaus Töpfer Fellows* and other young people in Germany and the United States to play a special role in these efforts. Klaus Töpfer's life work has been all about transforming systems, institutions, and the way we think about national and global challenges.

Throughout his career, Klaus has exercised vision, persistence, and creativity to encourage transformative change. He served the German Government during the historic reunification of East and West. As Minister for Regional Planning, Civil Engineering, and Urban Development, he helped oversee the transformation of Berlin and its emergence as one of the world's most dynamic urban centers. He reinvented UNEP as a world-class agency, and oversaw negotiation of a worldwide Biosafety Protocol and major agreement to curtail the use of persistent organic pollutants. And he helped transform the world's development agenda by putting the environment at the center of the world's global priorities.

At the dawn of the 21st century, we find ourselves at a pivotal moment in the history of the world—one that requires the same kind of innovation, engagement, and political will that Klaus Töpfer has demonstrated. His accomplishments and demeanor demonstrate that if we look at great challenges as compelling opportunities, there are no limits to what we can do. Living up to his legacy is the opportunity of the next generation and the responsibility we all have to the future.

LITERATURE CITED

McKinsey Global Institute (2008): The Case for Investing in Energy Productivity. February 2008, p. 7. [http://www.mckinsey.com/insights/energy_resources_materials/the_case_for_investing_in_energy_productivity].

OECD (2011): Divided We Stand: Why Inequality Keeps Rising. Organization for Economic Cooperation and Development, 5 December 2011. [http://www.oecd.org/social/soc/49170768.pdf].

Timothy E. Wirth

Ralf Fücks

End or Beginning?

The 1990s was a time of historic optimism. The Berlin Wall had come down and the Cold War was over. Democracy was on a victory march. The digital revolution was opening-up seemingly unlimited opportunities. The mood, however, has now changed. The world has become more crisis-ridden. Europe is mired in debt. Public confidence has given way to self-doubt. The majority of Germans no longer believe that life will be better for their children. The rise of China and the shift of economic power to the Pacific Rim have strengthened the feeling that Europe has passed its zenith.

A sense of despondency has also set in when it comes to ecological issues: climate change diplomacy is stuck in a cul-de-sac, greenhouse gas emissions are rising, and biodiversity is declining. Just as billions of people find themselves on the way to a modern industrial life, a sense of fatalism is gaining ground: resources are running low; the party seems to be over. Radical belt-tightening is called for, or we will face a series of catastrophes that will reduce civilization to a size that nature can support. Even the success story of renewable energies in Germany has been reinterpreted as a specter that threatens economic competiveness and that will increase costs beyond all measure. However, the opposite is in fact true: the energy transition is the lever that will make our society fit for the future. It is triggering innovations and investments that will give the depressed European economy new impetus.

So why aren't we actively calling for a 'Green New Deal' that will trigger a long wave of sustainable growth? Since Dennis Meadows and his academic team published 'Limits to Growth' in 1972, economic growth has fallen out of favor among environmentalists. What was long seen as a vehicle for social progress is now equated with greed, environmental destruction, and social inequality. The current criticism of growth, however, is acutely schizophrenic: simultaneously there is a call for growth throughout Europe in order to break the vicious circle of debt and unemployment. Even the Greens have castigated the European austerity policy because it does not open up any prospects for sustainable growth.

Faced with a growing global population with its attendant needs, wishes, and ambitions, the dream of a 'post-growth economy' is bordering on fantasy. The decisive question for the coming decades is not *whether* but *how* the global economy will grow. It may seem an attractive option for 'old' Europe to retire to a state of frugal tranquility, but in the eyes of the rest of the world this would be seen as a retreat into oblivion. Greece and Spain are currently experiencing what it means to have a shrinking economy. One would not like to think that this would become the model for Europe's future.

What is true is that we cannot return to the sort of resource consumption and energy-intensive growth of the last century. Climate change, extensive loss of productive agricultural land, and water shortages in highly populated regions are warning signs that our current economic model is destroying the basic elements on which it relies. If continuing with 'business as usual' harms the opportunities for future generations, and simple calls for less consumption are ignored, what then is the alternative?

The current crisis is neither the end of capitalism nor the swansong of scientific/technological progress. Rather, it marks the transition from an industrial age based on fossil fuels to an ecologically-based means of production whose contours are already visible. This new system will derive energy from solar, wind, geothermal, and wave power. To this list of familiar renewables we can add artificial photosynthesis: the transformation of water and carbon dioxide into chemical energy. Bio-reactors will transform waste and algae into fuel and chemicals. Electromobility and electricity generation will form part of a coordinated network. Buildings will become power-plants that will produce more energy than they require. Miniaturization will reduce the consumption of materials: computers, machines, and engines will become smaller, lighter, and more powerful. Biological and industrial waste will be processed back into the system. Permanent innovation will drive increased efficiency in the use of energy and resources. Advanced filtration plants will transform sewage into drinking water. Food production will return to cities. Old factories, roof gardens, and energy-independent tower blocks will produce fruit and vegetables throughout the year. Re-cultivating depleted land, crop rotation, and modern plant-breeding technology will enable agricultural yields to grow sustainably. Biotechnology—the technical utilization of biological processes and resources—will become the new leading science. The Earth is not a tightly constrained place to live but a dynamic system full of undiscovered possibilities. Intelligent growth means advancing in synergy with nature.

Expressing confidence that the crisis in the developed world can be overcome by creative solutions quickly attracts accusations of a naïve belief in technology. However, a realistic look at the dynamics of global growth shows that any call for reduced consumption will be useless unless supported by the flanking measure of a new industrial revolution. It is right and proper to eat less meat, cycle more, and not buy products for which people have been oppressed or rainforests cut down; but without a revolution in production efficiency and a swift move to renewable energy, we will not win the climate change battle.

In the coming 20–25 years, the gross world product will *double* as billions of people now on the threshold of modern industrial development pursue the aim of improving their living standards. While 'old' Europe becomes filled with self-doubt, these societies will strive to acquire the attributes of modern life that we have long taken for granted. We should do everything possible to help them leapfrog the fossil-fuel age. This requires the transfer of technology and expertise. At the same time, the old industrial countries need to steer themselves towards environmentally-friendly production methods. We need to demonstrate that the consumption of natural resources can be dramatically reduced in practice without loss of prosperity. Poor countries need to find new ways to grow in economic terms without increasing their environmental footprint; rich countries need to reduce their footprint drastically without putting their level of social security and personal well-being at risk. It was Klaus Töpfer who once and again pointed out that poverty reduction and protecting the environment have to go hand in hand. We should not preach abandonment for the sake of nature, but demonstrate that social and environmental progress are in fact two sides of one coin.

The great transformation has actually already begun. Millions of people are participating, including researchers, engineers, architects, and town planners; business people and investors; environmental activists and critical consumers; as well as journalists and artists. The major question is whether we can progress quickly enough to win the race against environmental destruction. To achieve this, we need effective environmental policy at the national and international levels. This policy needs to define goals and rules for markets that will successfully decouple economic wealth creation from the consumption of natural resources. This will enable Europe to become a trailblazer for a new industrial revolution.

(This article is based on the author's book 'Intelligent wachsen. Die grüne Revolution,' which was published at the beginning of 2013)

Angelika Zahrnt

On the Recapturing of Alternatives

"If there is a sense of reality, there must also be a sense of possibility. [...]
Whoever has it does not say, for instance: Here this or that has happened,
will happen, must happen; but rather, he envisions:
This or that might, could, or ought to happen.
If he is told that something is the way it is, he will think:
Well, it could probably just as well be otherwise."

Klaus Töpfer might start a speech with this quote from Robert Musil. Criticizing the politics of 'no alternatives' and demanding more of a sense of possibility would be fitting for him. We should not fear the Iron Lady's purse, or her slogan, "there is no alternative." Rather, we should dare to tread new pathways—in our thoughts, in limited experiments, and ultimately throughout the entire breadth of society. On such a journey, Klaus Töpfer would take along a map (as a symbol for scientific precision), plenty of supplies (for political implementation will require some stamina), and also a few works of literature and of the history of ideas, in order to help us see things completely differently. Here too, Musil fits with Töpfer: as a literary source of surprise and inspiration between current IPCC studies and public opinion polls.

Klaus Töpfer thus not only challenges us to develop more political alternatives; his way of thinking, writing, and speaking indeed invites us to do so. These remarks are only incidentally a laudation; their actual core, however, is a cognitive interest: In which soil might this sense of possibility thrive?

One attribute of 'Töpfer texts' is certainly the connection between natural science, social science, liberal arts, political practice, personal everyday experience, and his treasure of quotes—the gems of a well-read man. Also notable is the connection between great concepts—the 'Anthropocene,' the *'Nebenfolgengesellschaft'* [society of ancillary impacts], or the second modernity era—and the small, the concrete, the practical. And finally his style: his presentations become conversations—one does not rush toward a single solution, but rather casts views forward in many directions, but also backward; circles around an issue; and ultimately realizes that one has arrived at a new viewpoint.

In this paper, I would like to trace the search for alternatives in a variety of environmental policy areas, asking myself: where do these dogmas come from, upon which the 'no alternative' assertion is based? Where do they draw their power from, and how can they be broken apart?

The Struggle for Environmental Policy Alternatives

I met Klaus Töpfer in Bonn in 1989 at a panel discussion on the external costs that impact upon the environment, and on the possibilities of internalizing them by means of ecological tax reform. That was new in those days—the idea of burdening polluters with responsibility for the ancillary effects of their individual behavior by means of government measures, and particularly by means of taxation. Although the concept of externalities had already been proposed by the economist Pigou in 1912, it had not really been developed until the beginning of the 1980s. Then, Professor Hans-Christoph Binswanger conceived the idea of an ecological tax reform in view of the massive environmental damage being caused by the largely no-cost use of the environment. Environmental damage was to be included in the price structure by way of taxation, and hence to provide an incentive for more careful management of this scarce asset. At the same time, and by way of compensation, the increased revenue derived from this taxation was to be used to reduce the social security contributions of workers, thus creating jobs. This concept of ecological tax reform emerged within the academic community and was brought onto the political stage through connections that Professor Binswanger and several of his colleagues had with the environmental organization BUND (Friends of the Earth Germany).

As an economist, Klaus Töpfer supported this market-based instrument during the early 1990s and helped its adoption by his Christian Democratic Union (CDU) Party. However, this did not keep the party from engaging, in alliance with the auto lobby, in populist diatribes against ecological tax reform. Not until 1998 did the ecological tax reform become law—under the new SPD/Green-led federal government—in the teeth of resistance from the lawyers who dominated the administrative structure, and who were infatuated with regulatory law. Today, many countries have seized upon this market-based concept, while in Germany, which previously blazed a trail for it, massive protests on the part of the coal and auto lobbies have so intimidated politicians that ecological tax reform has become a taboo.

Other alternatives, too, emerged from NGO- and citizen-led initiatives. The key point of change was often the resistance to political measures that were presented to people as 'necessities without alternatives.' Thereafter, 'alternative' scientists and institutes would underpin the resistance with arguments and studies, for example, on such issues as waste or energy policy, the transportation system, or the rivers.

With the large quantities of wastes and the resulting increase in the number of waste dumps, odors, and incidents of groundwater pollution, resistance among local residents also grew during the 1980s. The simple and elegant solution seemed to be waste incineration, and planners covered the country with such facilities, which in turn rapidly sparked citizens' movements. These groups pointed to the dangers of toxic air pollution, and were able to mobilize very large segments of the population. At the same time, environmental associations and citizens' initiatives developed new ideas and sought other solutions to the waste problem via waste avoidance and waste sepa- ration. They underscored this idea by promoting jute handbags instead of plastic bags; holding no-waste festivals; and organizing the separate collection of paper, cork, and other materials. It was an idea which, in view of the political pressure to act—for neither dumps nor waste incinerators were any longer politically viable—was seized upon by policy makers and ultimately turned into legislation in the form of the Circu- lar Flow Economy Law introduced by Environmental Minister Töpfer. Klaus Töpfer was able to balance this interaction between civil resistance, public pressure, new concepts, and political implementation. He perceived the different groups and their different roles, and had respect for those who criticized his policies. He remained a member of the BUND even when the public attacks upon him became very fierce, to the point where, at one annual Delegates' Assembly of the organization, its youth group introduced a resolution to expel him from membership. It was rejected by a large majority.

A similar pattern for how alternatives can be developed, despite firmly established structures and 'inherent necessities,' can be seen in the area of energy policy, with the resistance against nuclear power, public pressure, early alternative concepts such as the Eco-Institute's energy-turnaround study, experiments with practical approaches to solving a problem, and the first wind turbines and solar collectors at eco-trade fairs. These developments fostered the emergence of the renewable energy industry, which was supported politically by the Renewable Energies Law. That provided the basis upon which the withdrawal from nuclear power was able to succeed. The shock of Fukushima and the intensive struggle in the Ethics Commission, headed by Klaus Töpfer and Matthias Kleiner, turned one of the most controversial issues into a 'com- munity project'—even if there is still plenty of controversy with regard to its imple- mentation.

In the area of transport, the bicyclists' movement has successfully campaigned for improved infrastructure, local residents have succeeded in implementing reduced- traffic zones, 30 km/hr speed limits are the general rule in many places, and some roads are even being dismantled. Also being dismantled, albeit only sporadically, are river engineering works, so that channelized runoffs are restored to living rivers by means of 'soft engineering' methods. Every time there is a flood, the limits of dikes and sheet-pile walls as flood protection become obvious; so too does the necessity to give the rivers more space, the soil a greater capacity to absorb the water, and to limit soil-sealing beneath housing developments and infrastructure. The result should be more floodplains and less soil compacted by intensive agriculture and concrete.

Alternatives are gaining in popularity the more it becomes obvious that the existing solutions will not, or will no longer, have the desired effects. All too often, however, there is a tendency to maintain existing approaches and to insist upon their effectiveness. That is the point where conviction turns into ideology. Economic growth is increasingly becoming an ideology, for it is obvious and widely confirmed that, first of all, economic growth will run up against ecological limits; second, that it cannot, or can no longer, keep its promises in the highly developed industrial countries; and third, that it has run its course, regardless of how one may try to force it forward again.[1]

Economic Growth Causes Ecological Problems

The economic growth of past decades has led to the overuse of ecological systems and of many resource components. Resource use needs to be greatly reduced, not simply stabilized. However, to date, development has been moving in the other direction. Very ambitious environmental and sustainability goals have often failed due to the priority given to economic growth.

Many investigations have confirmed that we have not achieved the aspiration whereby increased domestic product could, by means of efficiency strategies, be absolutely decoupled from increasing resource use and environmental pollution. Although relative decoupling (less use of resources per unit of GDP) has indeed taken place in some countries and with respect to certain environmental problems, these gains have largely been outweighed by growth and so-called rebound effects. A direct rebound effect is defined as a situation where increased energy and/or resource efficiency causes the same product or service to enjoy greater demand, so that the potential savings end up being realized only partially or not at all.

The recent economic and financial crisis has caused a new type of growth—so-called green growth, the Green New Deal, and green innovation policy—to become the new hope of policy makers and economists, especially in environmentally conscious circles. In this way, the increasingly ephemeral promises of economic growth— jobs, incomes, revenues from taxes and rates, and also economic competitive advan-

---

1 Part of the text on the critique of growth is taken from the book *Postwachstumsgesellschaft* [Post-growth society] by Irmi Seidl and Angelika Zahrnt.

tages, which are also useful for exports—are to be achieved after all in the green sector. However, it is questionable whether these strategies can lead to an absolute decoupling over the medium and long term, because the rebound effects are considerable. For this reason, it is too risky to depend on growth and technological progress alone.

The Report of the World Commission on Environment and Development (WCED 1987) stated with regard to this problem that, "… sustainable development clearly requires economic growth in places where [basic] needs are not being met. Elsewhere, it can be consistent with economic growth, provided the content of growth reflects the broad principles of sustainability and non-exploitation of others." Today's level of economic output and our mode of production do not meet these conditions. The desperate striving to increase economic output in industrial countries is aggravating non-sustainability. We cannot: confine impacts within ecological limits, use resources equitably, and preserve similar opportunities for future generations; while simultaneously pursuing: economic growth (as currently defined) including equalizing industrialized living standards across emerging markets and developing countries. For that reason, the demand of then-Environmental Minister Klaus Töpfer at Rio in 1992 was that the production and consumption patterns of the industrialized countries change—and change in such a way as to be transferable on a global scale.

The challenge of Rio to restructure our own economy and society according to the principles of sustainability is one which, in Germany, the NGOs BUND (Friends of the Earth) and the Catholic development aid organization MISEREOR took seriously by commissioning the Wuppertal Institute (Zukunftsfähiges Deutschland; Sustainable Germany 1996) to outline visions, models, quantified targets, and policy measures. They thus organized a broad societal discussion on this transformation process for sustainability, and influenced policy makers from the local to the national levels. The study succeeded in introducing long-term perspectives and thinking into the debate; making sustainability public as a concept of values of generational and global justice; and decisively placing its mark on the outline of the environmental space and the ecological guidelines that show the limits of ecological resilience within which economic and societal development can best unfold. These guidelines were consciously selected as a limiting model of a 'harmless array' of three pillars of equal importance.

But in practice, priorities are different. Climate protection is subject to the prioritization of growth—as former Economics Minister Wolfgang Clement clearly stated; and all other economics ministers and federal governments have proclaimed the same, in different words. While the goals formulated have indeed been ambitious (e.g., in the National Sustainability Strategy), their implementation all too often fails due to the absolute priority of the one goal that is also present within that sustainability strategy: economic growth.

Economic Growth Has Not Kept Its Promise

Economic growth and prosperity: It was long assumed that prosperity, well-being, satisfaction, and happiness would increase with economic growth. This linkage does indeed exist up to a certain threshold, which can be quantified as being roughly half the per capita income of today's rich industrial countries. Beyond that, economic growth increases the satisfaction of life little or not at all, as numerous studies of welfare indicators and economic happiness research have shown. Wilkinson and Pickett (2009) have demonstrated that in the industrial countries, it is primarily fairness of distribution that affects quality of life. Other authors recommend the promotion of such qualities as leisure time and control over one's time, social relationships, health, etc. as the elements contributing to a further increase in well-being.

Economic growth and employment: Economic growth hardly contributes at all to increased employment any more. Since the two oil crises of the 1970s, unemployment has shown sporadic increases in most industrial countries, despite economic growth rates which have in some cases been quite respectable. Thus, relatively high economic growth rates would be necessary simply to maintain our existing levels of employment, because increasing labor productivity, especially which connected with technological progress, actually eliminates jobs.

Social compromise: Economic growth has been tied to the hope for a conflict-free reduction in social inequalities: 'if the pie gets bigger, those with too little will see the sizes of their slices grow without having to take anything away from anybody else.' However, economic growth no longer reduces social inequalities of income and wealth. Rather, these inequalities have increased since the 1990s. Poverty and unequal educational opportunities are still a problem—and a growing one.

Reduction in public debt: for decades, and especially in the current crisis, economic growth is being propagated as the goal that will generate higher tax revenues in order to handle growing public debt. These expectations have long since become unrealistic; now, in view of the great increase in public debt due to the financial and economic crisis, they are clearly completely illusory.

Economic Growth Can No Longer Be Maintained

Saturation tendencies: Active growth policies run up against saturated markets, as has been shown by continually declining growth rates since the 1960s. Even in the early 1940s, Keynes foresaw the phase of saturation of the need for investments and of demand. Today, growth potential exists almost entirely in the emerging markets and the developing countries. But even in these countries, saturation will set-in over the medium and long term. In the course of economic development, these countries will increasingly compete with the global export markets of industrialized countries, and thus ultimately take some of their market shares.

Dependence on the growth-based system of government incentives: In the current economic and financial crisis, hard-hit industries such as automobiles and construction will, in order to achieve growth, have to be supported by special economic policy measures and government-sponsored export initiatives. These measures are questionable over the long term, both in terms of regulatory policy and of national economics. They show the incapacity of policy makers to avoid crises by dealing rationally—and with long-term foresight—with major drops in economic output.

Demographic development: The demographic development in European industrial countries must be taken into account when planning economic development. Even with immigration, longer working careers, and shorter training periods, many Western countries will, over the long term, experience a reduction in their labor power potentials. An increase in labor productivity to an extent that will, nonetheless, allow for an increase in economic output is not very probable. In this respect, too, policy makers will therefore be unable to avoid addressing the task of designing a model of stagnation, reduction of the volume of economic activity, and dealing with its effects.

An Alternative: A Post-growth Society

This raises the question of why policy makers and business leaders continue to cling to the 'permanent growth' model, even though it is contradicted not only by the fundamentally limited nature of the Earth and by its own visible and palpable negative social and ecological effects, but also by the fact that the hopes for decoupling growth from environmental impacts have remained unfulfilled.

There seem to be more deep-seated systemic necessities for why government and economic policy remain tied to the hope of permanent economic growth. Our social systems, such as old-age security, the health system, or the organization of the labor market, all of which are closely tied to economic growth, were created in times of such growth; on the one hand they drive economic growth, and on the other they depend on it. These systems constitute structural resistance to any deviation from the growth course. It is therefore important to address them in order to free ourselves from the constraints they impose upon us, because while societal systems may be difficult to change, the laws of nature are impossible to change.

We are overdue to start thinking about alternatives to a post-growth society, and to develop concepts and take the first concrete steps along a new path—one that is not the path of growth—and to explore its possibilities. One important area is consumption, which is, after all, called the growth engine of the economy. Suppose, for example, we were to get serious about a 100% circular-flow economy. What if we were to make long-lasting, repairable products, and introduce liability regulations that made it more difficult to make products designed to wear out, or with built-in defects? Or if omnipresent advertising—any place from TV to metro stops to downtown building façades—did not constantly urge us to buy more? What if all the skills of the advertising psychologists were applied to helping us recognize our own desires, rather than drowning them in the desire to buy?

How much autonomy would we gain if we not only bought products, but also made and repaired them ourselves? And what would an educational system look like, that would enable us to arrive at this self-realization? What infrastructure would we need—from land for gardening to handicraft centers? How could we change our life-planning and work orientation away from careers and toward a work–life relationship based on a new balance of material and immaterial values?

What effect would it have if ever-more pioneers with modest footprints were to discover such attractive paths and tell others about them; if ever-more people were to follow such patterns? What would mass individual sufficiency mean for consumption and for growth?

These questions are many, but not enough. For what is at stake is not only the goal, but also the path towards it. Which experimental fields do we need for sustainable lifestyles? What might we learn from other countries, especially those of the South? How might we not only re-naturalize industrial brownfields, but also psychological brownfields—and turn them into colorful landscapes of the soul?

How might economics liberate itself from the constrictions of its theoretical model—or does it not need to *be* liberated? How can it be brought to withdraw to a more modest role, and to provide support for the organization and implementation of various societal goals, rather than trying to force the increased economization of various areas of life in order to maximize the monetary production of goods and services? What would a science of economics be like which no longer saw the *Homo oeconomicus* as an anthropological constant, but which also recognized, in its image of the individual, the *Homo socialis* or the *Homo ludens*?

These are questions that are hardly being raised at all in the current debate over growth. On the one side are those who consider them to be as redundant as the entire growth debate itself, because they believe in the ability of the engine of growth to restart. The growth-critics, for their part, concentrate their fire on the growth-believers. Then there are the practitioners, who are busy with their projects: with their urban gardens, their transition towns, their exchange markets, and their shared economies. And finally, there is a fourth group: those engaged in a theoretical debate about a change of values and the ethics of sufficiency.

What is needed, however, is the connection between all these aspects—the critique of growth, the discourse on values, and the experience with alternatives, together with a pragmatic-policy dimension, and the question: what conditions does the wide array of local experiments need in order to prosper and spread? How can a policy of sufficiency at the local level promote that? Which legislative frameworks and what kind of federal budget will be necessary for that purpose?

That means that we need research for a post-growth society, and research on the necessary changes in economic and social institutions, in education and in culture. And also research that investigates transformation processes toward a post-growth society, including within an international context.

With this view of the future, I would like to return to my initial thought and guiding theme, for it is precisely here—with this complex and completely undogmatic question which does not fit into any particular discipline—that Klaus Töpfer and his institute IASS are already engaged in research: how can we move from a culture of economy to a culture of sustainability? I wish him and his staff much success and joy with their sense of possibility.

LITERATURE CITED

BUND/MISERIOR (Hrsg.) (1996): Zukunftsfähiges Deutschland. Ein Beitrag zu einer global nachhaltigen Entwicklung. Studie des Wuppertal-Instituts für Klima, Umwelt, Energie GmbH. Basel, Boston, Berlin: Birkhäuser Verlag. ISBN 3-7643-5278-7; 4. überarbeitete und erweiterte Auflage ebd. 1997, ISBN 3-7643-5711-8 [Published in English as: Sachs, W., Loske, R., Linz, M. (Eds.) (1998): Greening the North: A Post-industrial Blueprint for Ecology and Equity. London: Zed Books].

Musil, R. (1930–43): Der Mann ohne Eigenschaften (The Man Without Qualities). Berlin: Rohwolt Verlag.

Wilkinson, R., Pickett, K. (2009): The Spirit Level. Why More Equal Societies Almost Always Do Better. London: Allen Lane.

Claus Leggewie

Transnational Citizenship.
Ideals and European Realities

Citizenship:
Legal and Cultural Dimensions

Klaus Töpfer is well-known for his national and international contributions to sustainability issues. He has often called for an extension of our thinking and acting in order to capture the far-reaching, often global consequences of human activities. Globalization comes together with a renewed understanding of being a citizen of the world while regional and cultural differences maintain or even increase. Climate change, the loss of biodiversity, and the consequences of the Anthropocene (a newly invented chronological term that serves to mark the evidence and extent of human activities that have had a significant global impact on the Earth's ecosystems) altogether are drivers of cosmopolitanism, whereas the prerequisites for a cosmopolitan democracy have not been established. Within this context, the article modestly addresses one issue that needs to be worked on if people are to become active proponents of transformations towards sustainability: transnational citizenship.

Citizenship Can Mean a Lot of Things:

1. A *formal legal status* that links individuals to a state or another established polity (such as the European Union or a federal province); 2. A *bundle of legal rights and duties* associated with this status, including civil liberties, rights to democratic representation, and *social rights* to education, health care, and protection from poverty risks; 3. A *set of responsibilities, virtues, and practices* that support democratic self-government; 4. A *collective identity* that can be shared across distinctions of class, race, gender, religion, ethnic origin, or way of life (Bauböck 2008, p. 3).

Bauböck connects legal and political aspects of status and participation with cultural and identitarian phenomena that have always intermingled within the framework of modern nation-states (Bader 1997; Fox 2005). Indeed, various efforts were made to resolve the constant tension between the legal and the political features of citizenship, and their identitarian and cultural underpinnings via nation-building: some states were based on linking political status to ethnic descent, whereas most republics pretended to be 'culture-blind.' However, immigration and transnational cultural interconnections have relativized these typologies; and economic and cultural globalization has definitely transcended the legal and political boundaries of sovereign nation-states.

Even before the formation of the modern nation-state, cosmopolitan aspirations were already emerging: *"Me velle civis totius mundi non civis oppidi"* was the answer of Erasmus of Rotterdam in the 16th century, when Swiss Reformation leader Ulrich Zwingli offered him citizenship in Zurich. The humanist philosopher is said to have replied that he did not want to become a citizen of a single city, but of the 'entire world.' World citizenship in this sense was always one of humanity's dreams, one considered as honorable as it was unfulfillable. Now globalization has not only razed the fortress of the nation-state (as progress in ballistics did the fortified walls of medieval city-states), it has also created the opportunity for what is called *transnational citizenship*. Historically, nations provided the framework of modern community and society; they defined (and limited) the space of communication within which political parties and interest groups of all kinds operated, thus creating the prerequisites for equal representation and civic participation. In the welfare state, too, who should be included in and who excluded from the system of mutual support was defined within this national framework. But the universalistic principle of inclusion itself helped migrants gain a highly valued status as residents, without being formal citizens. A person's national citizenship was thus uncoupled from his or her right to have rights, insofar as international laws, for example to protect migrant labor, and human rights conventions became plausible as independent sources of individual and collective rights. The question at hand is: Between local patriotism and global markets, where is *Homo politicus* located?

Emigration and immigration have been the main causes of a growing incongruence between cultural and political collective identities: emigrants from country-A turned their back to their former homeland and forged new affinities in country-B even if many of them retained some emotional ties to their country of origin (A) and tended to assimilate to their country of choice (B) via compatriot communities from country-A. The same is true for immigrants: while they centered their lives on a new location (B), they retained more or less strong loyalties to their 'Heimat' (A), sending money home and keeping up-to-date on what was going on there while continuing to speak their mother tongue (van Bochove et al. 2010; Kaya 2012).

Claus Leggewie

Cheap air-fares, mass-produced communication devices with a global reach, and personal contacts via social media have further relativized the dichotomy between country-A and -B; real-life transnational communities have emerged. Thus, expatriates may want to participate in the political life of their former homeland and may even be inclined to vote in their former constituencies or as a particular voting bloc of non-resident citizens from abroad; and immigrants may stipulate voting and other participatory rights to overcome their status as non-citizen residents (Bauböck 2005; Lopez-Guerra 2005; Rubio-Marín 2006; Owen 2011). As expatriates there (A) are immigrants here (B), they might even have the idea of being a part of two demoi and contributing to the political agenda of two states. It was exactly this prospect that conjured up the evil of "… yalty" in the minds of the administrative agencies in the Westphalian system of distinct and incongruous nation-states (Benhabib 2006; Schmidtke & Ozcurumez 2007).

Nevertheless, nation-states and political elites have allowed not only for the electoral inclusion of citizens living abroad (which is supported by ethnic conceptions of nationhood beyond a territorial state) but also for electoral rights of non-citizen residents. One reason is the desirability of the political integration of immigrants, underpinned by civil and social rights; other explanations can be drawn from historical links (e.g., a common, immemorial past, the Commonwealth etc.), cultural affinities, and linguistic community. Bauböck (2005) has sketched four ideal-typical positions speaking for or against this undermining of traditional concepts of national citizenship:

1. Civic republicans would argue that "only citizens who are present in the polity can govern themselves by participating in making laws" (López-Guerra 2005, p. 685); a republic may be open to newcomers but those should apply for full citizen rights by naturalization and giving up former citizenship(s).

2. Ethnic nationalists would "support the inclusion of expatriates but reject political rights for non-citizen residents" because they conceive the nation as a community of culture.

3. Liberal democrats would, on the contrary, hold that voting rights for expatriates might undermine "the integrity of the democratic process since those who live permanently abroad should not be able to influence the making of laws to which only internal residents will be subjected"; however, they would favor voting rights for non-citizens just because long-term residents are effectively subjected to the local political authority and its laws, so non-citizens should therefore have "equal rights to representation and participation in the making of these laws."

4. Cosmopolitans would claim for voting rights and participation on the grounds of an 'all-affected' principle: quod omnes tangit ab omnibus approbetur. In this case, the demos is not a given entity of people but is constructed by way of those decisions that have a "profound impact on the interests of another country's population" (Ibid., p. 686).

As one can object to all four concepts, Bauböck (2008) introduces a fifth principle he calls 'stakeholder citizenship.' This involves a mixture of republican and liberal-cosmopolitan principles. With regard to the former, it retains the idea that citizenship guarantees the status of full membership in a self-governing polity and that voting rights should generally be attached to such status. In accordance with liberal-cosmopolitan principles, stakeholder citizenship would give stakeholders a subjective claim to membership and electoral rights.

Bauböck provides a balanced conclusion: "Stakeholdership should ... be less vague and overinclusive than affected interests. [...] [It] would require the political inclusion of immigrants, but—different from inclusion derived from mere territorial subjection—it could justify the condition of long-term residence and the common requirement that immigrants have to apply for naturalization instead of being automatically turned into citizens. Stakeholdership would also permit (although probably not require) extending the vote to expatriates, but it would exclude those who have never lived in the country and would not give access to citizenship to persons whose interests lie in economic investment or tax evasion but who do not take up permanent residence" (Bauböck 2005, p. 686).

Transnationalization of Citizenship via Stakeholdership and Participation

Emigration and immigration have given rise to a revision of common understandings of how a people is constituted and what democracy as rule of the people means. The literature distinguishes two principles—the 'all-subjected' principle, where the guiding idea is "that those subject to a rule also should be its authors"; and the aforementioned 'all-affected' principle, "that all those affected by a political decision ought, directly or indirectly, to have a say in its making" (Näsström 2011, p. 120 & 117). The first rule starts from a given people, be it the (very exclusive) demos of the Greek polis or the (more inclusive) demos of a modern republic. The second rule shifts the focus from a given people within polis and nation-state boundaries to (the justifying of) people-making within a democracy whose political agenda becomes transnational as well as transcultural. This means not only that "the demos needs to extend to everyone in a particular territory" (Gould 2006, p. 49), but also enlarges the citizenry beyond the city walls and state borders. The 'all-affected' principle negotiates and politicizes the boundaries of decision making.

With regard to the watering-down of national sovereignties, all citizenship regulations tend to be conservative and exclusive: the naturalization processes within most states continue to be rigid and dismissive. As already shown, mass immigration has put the accepted status of national citizenship in doubt, and the number of people with multiple citizenships in Europe has seen considerable growth. This growth in the possession of one or more nationalities is, however, viewed with suspicion by many states, as they still believe it to promote conflicts of loyalty. The children of immigrants are therefore often forced, as adults, to decide between their cultural and geographical origins. For example, second-generation Turkish settlers in Germany will be made to decide between becoming Turkish or German; a decision that (at present) might ultimately lead to the loss of their EU citizenship—something which, of course, does not happen in families of mixed European citizenship where, should the offspring decide to become French, Dutch, German, or British, they would nonetheless retain their EU citizenship. Nevertheless, the national monopoly on citizenship is gradually beginning to weaken. A great many practical and normative arguments exist for the granting of transnational citizenships and the development of voting rights for foreign nationals. The economic and cultural impacts of globalization are, for example, gradually creating scenarios, where, within many areas, long-term foreigners are able to claim a greater say in what goes on around them. Meanwhile, in legal scholarship and within the social sciences, the term 'global rights' is gaining in influence. Global rights are rights granted to people independent of their locations, and are supported by wide ranging human rights standards. Some of these standards themselves contradict national laws, and yet their impacts can, as in the case of the German Asylum Reform of 1992, often only be reduced through procedural limitations.

Such international developments suggest that reforms of the state citizenship regime are overdue and that these reforms should lead to more inclusive and flexible judicial statuses for people worldwide. Bauböck (2009a) has has repeatedly proposed the 'stakeholder principle' as a broader successor concept to the idea of citizenship: "Stakeholders […] are those who have a stake in the polity's future because of the circumstances of their lives." The so-called 'all-affected principle' goes a step further. It suggests that we can all be affected by global catastrophes and that, therefore, we are indeed 'all-affected.' And if the role of nature as protagonist can be recognized in this sense, then why not also consider the proposal, that not only humans but also non-human sentients and other objects or phenomena should be formed into a "parliament of things" (Latour 2001)? Furthermore, where the rights of future generations play a role in contemporary decision making, there has been debate regarding the consideration of specific voting rights for children, to be exercised *in absentia* by their parents (Goerres & Tiemann 2009).

One note on spatial inclusion: Suppose we take the term 'global society' as being not just a metaphor (as do the majority of sociologists), but a reality forged by communications, transport, and free exchange within a globalized social sphere. It can then be argued that the space within which to exclude someone consequently ceases to exist and that societal exclusions become completely unjustifiable (Stichweh 1997). Stichweh came to the conclusion that exclusions nowadays are only internal and temporary, and that a dynamic exists, within which an act of inclusion occurs with every (attempted) act of exclusion. This is best displayed in total institutions. For example, in a jail, criminals are taken out of the society within which they would normally exist, yet in most circumstances this occurs with the explicit aim of then ensuring their ultimate reintegration into the society from which they have temporarily been removed.

Another note on generational inclusion: The potential heteronomy of future generations will ultimately be determined by their own future circumstances. People today simply cannot judge what coming generations will do, and are equally unable to preordain what they themselves should do or allow to be done to them. The concept of sustainability (and indeed that of budget balancing as recently framed within the fiscal pact in many OEEC states) has, however, inaugurated an important proviso. Namely, it is advisable for people living within a dynamic, growing, global society to refrain from using more of their resources than can then be realistically regenerated, but also to abstain from impinging so much upon future generations that dangerous, existence-threatening tipping points are both reached and surpassed.

A graphic example of unacceptable levels of heteronomy for future peer groups is the program for the 'temporary' storage of atomic waste, which is an issue for most EU member states. As part of this program, waste is temporarily placed in a location while its final resting place is discussed. These discussions, however, tend to last at least two generations, despite the fact that the radioactive outfall from this temporary placement can have a lasting impact upon an area for thousands of years. In this example, the temporal and spatial elements of concern are therefore united, because the risks of atomic energy hardly allow themselves to be confined to either national territories or to specific periods of time. Right now, numerous atomic waste shipments are travelling across national boundaries throughout Europe. An international supervisory commission, however, only exists in the most rudimentary of forms and this despite the fact that a recent EU Commission report stated that the majority of European reactors are insufficiently secure. This example illustrates how political stakeholders can be on the receiving end of international decisions, regardless of state and/or cultural boundaries (Mason 2009; Bauböck 2009b; Owen 2011).

It would, however, likely be difficult to reconcile stakeholder citizenship with the present system of state citizenship. 'Cultural' grounds will doubtless be raised. By which I mean the ethnic and religious differences between nations, which, from a traditionalist perspective, often preclude supranational integration. It is said, for example, that supranational bodies pay too little attention to the respective particularities of individual groups (such reasoning is presently being used by various groups in Spain, Belgium, and Scotland to demand greater (or total) regional independence from the central governments in these countries). Naturally, such objections tend to ignore the binding relationships between various peoples across national borders. Historically, these cross-border affinities have, in fact, been strongly emphasized, and never more so than in post-war societies where long-standing enmities are gradually reconciled through transcultural exchanges and political cooperation. An exemplary model for this can be seen in the case of Germany and France, while moves are also being made in this direction in, for example, the ethnic and religious communities of the countries of the former Yugoslavia.

Prospects for Supranational Citizenship: The Case of the European Union

The challenge, then, is to develop a concept of citizenship that is wide enough to address the ways in which national citizens are affected by global problems of all kinds (e.g., climate change) and concrete enough to represent the identitarian and communitarian bases of being a citizen in the context of a particular *Lebenswelt*. The European Union, until now, provides only a rather embryonic form of citizenship, limited to a formal legal status. The existence or even possibility of a European demos is disputed and contested. 'European Union citizenship' per se does not yet exist, as the individual EU states continue to defend their right to grant and revoke citizenship as a national privilege. Behind this fiercely defended national right lurk the ancient, never-fully-applied, and increasingly undermined myths of the national union of land, culture, and ethnology. Whether Germn, Polish, or French, citizenship is determined either through birth or a demanding process of naturalization. In the case of official national identity, it would appear that there is, as yet, no third way.

For the success of such supranational ventures, high levels of empathy and well thought out routines for cooperation are prerequisite, as well as the ability and desire to understand your counterparts. What is, however, uncertain, is whether a transnational citizenship then subsequently develops out of such a process, bestowing the citizens concerned with institutionally secured and enforceable rights and duties. In other words, rights which are not just morally demanded, but are also successfully exercised. A citizen of the European Union is, according to Article 20 of the Treaty on the Functioning of the European Union, an individual who possesses the nationality of an EU member state. Citizenship of the European Union is therefore an extension, rather than a replacement, of national citizenship. European citizenship rights include the right to appeal to EU representatives, to instigate new legal proposals, and to participate, both actively and passively, in elections relating to the various European institutions. Additional rights bestowed upon European citizens include the freedom of movement within and between EU territories, and certain residential rights for both them and their dependents. These residential rights have also been streamlined in order to minimize the administrative effort involved in establishing one's entitlement to them. Limitations have also been placed on the circumstances within which these rights can be refused. In fact, every citizen of a European Union nation has the right to permanent residency within any other EU state so long as they have spent five or more years uninterrupted within the said state's territory without committing any offences for which action has had to be taken against him or her. This right comes without further requirements and also applies to any familial dependents of the individual concerned—regardless of their own nationality—so far as they themselves have also spent five years uninterrupted within a member state. Both EU citizens and their dependents also have a right to the diplomatic and consular services of all EU member states when in a country not of the European Union.

How, then, would the application of a regional 'all-affected' principle build upon the status quo? As regards a statement of transnational citizenship, the participational rights of residents within European Union states could be improved upon by adopting the proposals suggested at the Arhus Convention: for example, enabling citizens to participate in national votes, citizen initiatives, or class actions (Wallrabenstein 2012).

The following European programs are already in place to promote similar initiatives and should lead to changes in this direction:

- Council Decision 2010/37/EC of 27 November 2009 on the European Year of Voluntary Activities Promoting Active Citizenship (2011), which aims to create conditions that enhance the *participation of civil society in voluntary activities*, as well as increasing the visibility of volunteering.
- Council Decision 2007/252/EC of 19 April 2007 has established for the period 2007–13 the program 'Fundamental rights and Citizenship' as part of the General program 'Fundamental Rights and Justice'; it aims to promote the *development of a European society based on respect for fundamental rights*, to strengthen civil society and encourage an open and transparent dialogue, to fight racism and xenophobia, and to improve mutual understanding between the judicial and administrative authorities and the legal professions.
- Decision No 1904/2006/EC of the European Parliament and of the Council of 12 December 2006 established for the period 2007–13 the program 'Europe for Citizens' to promote active European citizenship; it may create the *preconditions for a European demos by developing a European identity among European citizens* based on recognized common values, history, and culture; and by fostering a sense of ownership of the European Union (EU) among its citizens.

The Charter of Fundamental Rights is more concrete still. It recognizes a range of personal, civil, political, economic, and social rights of EU citizens and residents, enshrining them into EU law. It is grouped into six major fields which I would like to quote extensively because they are almost unknown to the common European citizen:

Chapter I: **Dignity** (Human dignity; the right to life; the right to the integrity of the person; prohibition of torture and inhuman or degrading treatment or punishment; prohibition of slavery and forced labor);

Chapter II: **Freedoms** (The right to liberty and security; respect for private and family life; protection of personal data; the right to marry and found a family; freedom of thought, conscience, and religion; freedom of expression and information; freedom of assembly and association; freedom of the arts and sciences; the right to education; freedom to choose an occupation and the right to engage in work; freedom to conduct a business; the right to property; the right to asylum; protection in the event of removal, expulsion, or extradition);

Chapter III: **Equality** (Equality before the law; non-discrimination; cultural, religious, and linguistic diversity; equality between men and women; the rights of the child; the rights of the elderly; integration of persons with disabilities);

Chapter IV: **Solidarity** (Workers' right to information and consultation within the undertaking; the right of collective bargaining and action; the right of access to placement services; protection in the event of unjustified dismissal; fair and just working conditions; prohibition of child labor and protection of young people at work; family and professional life; social security and social assistance; health care; access to services of general economic interest; environmental protection; consumer protection);

Chapter V: **Citizens' Rights** (The right to vote and stand as a candidate at elections to the European Parliament and at municipal elections; the right to good administration; the right of access to documents; European Ombudsman; the right to petition; freedom of movement and residence; diplomatic and consular protection);

Chapter VI: **Justice** (The right to an effective remedy and a fair trial; presumption of innocence and the right of defense; principles of legality and proportionality of criminal offences and penalties; the right not to be tried or punished twice in criminal proceedings for the same criminal offence).

Since 1995, the European Ombudsman, on behalf of Europe's citizens, has been investigating cases of alleged maladministration by European Union institutions or bodies, that is, the European Commission, the Council of the European Union, the European Parliament, etc. The EU citizenship report of 27 October 2010 'Dismantling the Obstacles to EU Citizens' Rights' (European Commission 2010) has identified the main obstacles that EU citizens may still confront in their private, academic, or professional life when consuming goods and services, or in their role as political actors.

Conclusions and Recommendations

1. There is a continuous tension between (inclusionary) citizenship and (exclusionary) cultural identity. By means of exclusion, ethno-nationalism wishes to resolve this tension in a destructive and often militant fashion. As a result of its cultural blindness, republicanism dispels the tension by ignoring it. In most cases, state authorities can trust transmigrants who have created truly transcultural spaces. They predominantly identify with the local community of their compatriots and with the wider urban community as well as with families and relatives at home — to whom they pay visits, make phone-calls, and eventually send remittances. However, they rarely maintain strong political loyalties relating to their country of origin. Localism and transnationalism challenge the perceptions of the established domestic populations only insofar as their ethnic and/or religious identities are concerned.

2. Global communication and cultural industries, transnational migration and international market relations have led to the relativization of state borders, rendering purely national affiliations a fiction and paving the way for a significant number of instances of dual or multiple nationality. Awarding dual and multiple citizenships irrespective of cultural, ethnic, and religious background should therefore be seen as a more effective integration tool than assimilationist policies that operate on a legal level.

3. Global problems such as climate change or other environmental risks, the crisis of financial markets, and the abuse of human rights have led to the political demands of participation extending beyond nation-state borders and the opening up of a cosmopolitan arena beyond the nation-state and the United Nations system. Being 'all-affected' is not sufficient, in and of itself, to guarantee effective participation; the stakeholder principle must be supported by effective citizenship rights (voting, access to the public sphere, recognition of NGOs, etc.).

4. The European Union serves as an advanced example of an institution that provides a basis for supranational citizenship. Even though the EU is the result of

national citizenship, it is 'over-determined' by numerous cosmopolitan elements. Through supranational legal title, rights of participation of a moral nature are secure and can be effectively exercised. The EU thus provides a replicable model of a regional union that supports supranational citizenship.

A longer online version of this article has previously been published in Eurozine http:// www.eurozine.com/articles/2013-02-19-leggewie-en.html

LITERATURE CITED

Bader, V. (1997): The cultural conditions of transnational citizenship. On the interpenetration of political and ethnic cultures. In: Political Theory 25/6: 771–813.

Bauböck, R. (1994): Transnational Citizenship. Membership and Rights in International Migration. Aldershot: Edward Elgar.

Bauböck, R. (2005): Expansive citizenship: Voting beyond territory and membership. In: Political Science and Politics 38/4: 683–687.

Bauböck, R. (2008): Stakeholder Citizenship: An Idea Whose Time has Come? Migration Policy Institute.

Bauböck, R. (2009a): The rights and duties of external citizenship. In: Citizenship Studies 13/5: 475–499.

Bauböck, R. (2009b): Global justice, freedom of movement and democratic citizenship. In: European Journal of Sociology 50/1: 1–31.

Benhabib, S. (2006): Another Cosmopolitanism. Oxford: Oxford University Press.

van Bochove, M., Rusinovic, K., Engbersen, G. (2010): The multiplicity of citizenship: Transnational and local practices and identifications of middle-class migrants. In: Global Networks 10/3: 344–364.

European Commission (2010): EU Citizenship Report 2010: Dismantling the Obstacles to EU Citizens' Rights. COM(2010) 603 final. 27 Oct. 2010. Brussels: European Commission.

Fox, J. (2005): Unpacking transnational citizenship. In: Annual Review of Political Science 8: 171–201.

Kaya, A. (2012): Transnational citizenship: German-Turks and liberalizing citizenship regimes. In: Citizenship Studies 16/2: 153–172.

Latour, B. (2001): Das Parlament der Dinge: Naturpolitik. Frankfurt am Main: Suhrkamp.

Lopez-Guerra, C. (2005): Should expatriates vote? In: Journal of Political Philosophy 13/2: 216–234.

Mason, A. (2009): Environmental obligations and the limits of transnational citizenship. In: Political Studies 57: 280–297.

Näsström, S. (2011): The Challenge of the all-affected principle. In: Political Studies 59: 116–134.

Owen, D. (2011): Transnational citizenship and rights of political participation. In: Normative Orders Working Paper 06/2011.

Rubio-Marín, R. (2006): Transnational politics and the democratic nation-state: Normative challenges of expatriate voting and nationality retention of emigrants. In: New York University Law Review 81/1: 117–147.

Schmidtke, O., Ozcurumez, S. (Eds.) (2007): Of States, Rights, and Social Closure: Governing Migration and Citizenship. New York: Palgrave.

Stichweh, R. (1997): Inklusion/Exklusion, funktionale Differenzierung und die Theorie der Weltgesellschaft. In: Soziale Systeme 3: 123–136.

Goerres, A., Tiemann, G. (2009): Kinder an die Macht? Mögliche Folgen eines Treuhänderwahlrechts für Eltern. In: Politische Vierteljahresschrift 50: 50–74.

Wallrabenstein, A. (2012): Zum Verfassungsrecht der Unionsbürgerschaft. In: Bäuerle, M., Dann, P., Wallrabenstein, A. (Eds.). Demokratie: Perspektiven. Festschrift für Brun-Otto Bryde zum 70. Tübingen: Mohr Siebeck, pp. 741–763.

Ulrich Beck

Transformations of the Social and Political: Beyond Methodological Nationalism

In honor of Klaus Töpfer

Klaus Töpfer is no ordinary man. Nor is he an ordinary politician, nor an ordinary intellectual. His political and intellectual legacy comes from the way he combines political vision and a cosmopolitan outlook with the art of doing politics. Climate pessimism seems to have become the dominant mood. One of the deep sources of climate pessimism is the disconnection between the need for 'big politics,' and the confrontation with the impotence of politics.

Klaus Töpfer, the pioneer of environmental politics in Germany and the United Nations, does not accept this. Looking at the scientific evidence, he addresses climate change both at the level of local and world politics. Therefore, his question is: how does climate change become a force for momentum in the re-emergence of the historicity of politics, locally and globally? This is one of the many reasons why I am a 'Töpferianer'!

Global climate change is widely seen as being human induced. The mitigation of climate change calls for a global social and political transformation (Töpfer & Yogeshwar 2011). In order to accomplish this, the integration of the social and the natural is as much a first-order necessity as is the need for transdisciplinarity between the natural and social sciences (Hulme 2010; Reid et al. 2010). Climate change is not limited by national boundaries, and so national views and mitigation attempts are not sufficient; the global challenge demands a cosmopolitan outlook and perspective (Beck 2006; 2009). The research and understanding of global risks and global social change presupposes a paradigm shift from dominant 'methodological nationalism'—operating with an unquestioned assumption of a neat correspondence between nation, territory, society, and culture—towards 'methodological cosmopolitanism.' The change from a national to a cosmopolitan perspective enables new questions to be asked and new insights to be gained from the interface of risks and social-cultural, economic, and political realities. One of these realities is the formation of 'cosmopolitan communities of risk' as a way to deal with a 'world at risk,' both locally and globally.

By entailing new forms of power, inequality, and insecurity—as well as new forms of cooperation and solidarity—climate change alters society in fundamental ways. The main research question is: how are new 'cosmopolitan communities of risk' being imagined and realized? Building on knowledge of the natural sciences, I employ the following sociological definition of climate change: climate change is a scientifically determined anticipation of threats to humankind, integrating social and natural aspects, thereby transforming social institutions, cultural understandings of weather, and making the world more cosmopolitan. By 'cosmopolitan communities of risk' (Beck 2011), I understand new transnational constellations of social actors, arising from common experiences of medialized and mediated climatic threats, organized around a pragmatic reasoning of causal relations and responsibilities, thereby potentially enabling collective action, cosmopolitical decision-making, and international norm generation.

With climate change, new trans-boundary cosmopolitan communities are arising: global cities link up to form sustainability networks; low-lying island states join together due to common vulnerabilities; scientists, policy makers, innovators, journalists, and citizens cooperate across geographical borders (Mieg & Töpfer 2013). The more the world is torn apart by dangerous climatic disturbances, the more the world may also be brought together in response to climate change. The social and political future of climate change is open-ended: we may face a world of intensified resource conflicts (the 'Carl Schmitt' scenario), but the option also exists for more enlightened, long-term cooperation (the 'Hegel' scenario). In the first, the Carl Schmitt scenario is highly ambivalent. The expectation of catastrophe sets the political landscape in motion, opening up a power-play (Beck 2005). New options appear on the table; global risks can be exploited in order to gain power. This is the meeting point of the theory of (world) risk society (Beck 1992, 1999, 2009) and Carl Schmitt's reflections on states of emergency. "The exception is more interesting than the rule," Schmitt (1985) says, "The rule proves nothing; the exception proves everything: it confirms not only the rule but also its existence, which derives only from the exception. In the exception, the power of real life breaks through the crust of a mechanism that has become torpid by repetition." In the exceptional situation, i.e., 'the case of extreme need,' of 'a threat to the existence of the state or something of the sort,' the existing order of things may legitimately be suspended in order to defend the common good: "He is sovereign who definitely decides whether this abnormal situation actually exists." (Schmitt 1985). It must be pointed out that, whereas Schmitt focuses on the logic of the threat of war, the theory of the risk society focuses on the logic of global risk.

Ulrich Beck

298

In the Hegelian scenario, national egoisms continue to proclaim solutions to the crisis until the front wheels of the political carriage called Europe are actually hanging over the cliff edge. In that situation the glimpse of the abyss may well bring salutary forces into being if, at the last moment, the actors are able to recognize that to continue further on their own will inevitably lead to disaster. We might say that the cosmopolitan imperative 'cooperate or fail' might well assert itself behind the backs of politicians acting egoistically on behalf of their own country. In this sense, Hegel's 'irony of reason' might well have a historical opportunity here.

Two questions stand at the center of this scenario. In the age of world risk society, how can nationally organized politics recover its ability to act? And how can transnational cooperation and solidarity be achieved by democratic means? Here we have basically and essentially to redefine the concept of imagined communities, in relation to imagined cosmopolitan communities of global risks.

This rationale is evident within climate change dynamics and the concept of imagined communities in the European, South American, and East Asian contexts (Beck & Grande 2010; Chang 2010; Han & Shim 2010; Turner & Khondker 2010). The comparative outlook on Europe, South America, and East Asia is particularly fruitful because it enables us to analyze the emergence of cosmopolitan communities of climate change in developing and developed countries.

The concept of cosmopolitan risk communities is extended from Benedict Anderson's (1991) work on the rise of nation-states as 'imagined communities.' As Anderson showed, nationalism is not the product of face-to-face encounters as much as a conscious awareness that one is affected by and living through similar experiences and events with others. Anderson coined the term 'imagined communities' to refer to how we construct our sense of national identity. At this point I want to extend the concept and address the following question: how can we turn the concept of 'imagined cosmopolitan risk communities' into a strong explanatory tool for the social, economic, and political consequences of climate change and more generally of global risks?

Global risks (such as climate change, economic crisis, terrorist threats) put on the world map the attempt to redefine cosmopolitanism for the globalized world of the 21st century. For me, cosmopolitanism is an idea and a reality—of universalism that contains a particularistic dimension of meaning; of globality that includes nationalism; and of transnationalism that does not exclude a plurality of ethnicities and cultures. This conception includes two steps that set my theory of the 'cosmopolitan outlook' apart from other theories:

First, the sociological turn—the question that arises is: What is cosmopolitanism? and lesser the question: What should cosmopolitanism be? Second, the turn at the level of content from 'either/or' to 'both/and': cosmopolitanism is not the universal antithesis to various forms of particularism (nationalism, localism, culturalism, relativism, etc.); cosmopolitanism must instead be conceived, deciphered, or reconceptualized as a synthesis of other theories. Cosmopolitanism transcends the dialectic of universalism and particularism, of internationalism and nationalism, and of globalization and localization.

In this sense, I propose to distinguish between cosmopolitanism as a norm and cosmopolitization as a fact (Beck 2006; Beck & Grande 2010; Beck & Sznaider 2006; Calhoun 2010; Chang 2010; Maharaj 2010). Cosmopolitanism refers to normative philosophical theories; cosmopolitization to a research program in social and cultural thought that goes beyond 'methodological nationalism.' In brief, methodological nationalism assumes that the nation, state, and society are the 'natural' social and political forms of the modern world. Where social actors subscribe to this belief, I talk of a 'national outlook'; where it determines the perspective of the social scientific observer, I talk of 'methodological nationalism' (Beck 2000, 2006; Beck & Grande 2010; Weiß 2010; Wimmer & Glick Schiller 2002). The current phase of globalization uncovers the core unseen, unwanted consequence of the global interconnectivity: the end of the 'global other.' The global other is here in our midst.

It must be noted here that the dynamics of climate change and global risks are Janus-faced: With climate change, the very notion of 'community' is no longer solely based on shared values. New global interconnections are established via causal interpretations of threats and responsibilities, which transform rather than replace local and national communities. Dynamics of cooperation and conflict continue to intermingle. Climate change remaps global political power and social inequality (Milanovic 2011). It is still an open question as to how European, South American, and East Asian climate actors acknowledge global (as opposed to national) social inequalities. Although nation-states remain important, there is a growing antagonism between national closure versus cosmopolitan opening to the world. But the ways in which climate change and global risks lead to new cosmopolitan communities and how they initiate or promote re-nationalization remains to be explored. Furthermore, arguably for the first time in history, cosmopolitan commitments exert real-world significance in responding to global challenges. The 'Hegelian' scenario promises the emergence of a collaborative cosmopolitan socio-cultural force. However, the radically unequal distribution of climate change impacts, separating the 'rich producers' (the 'global North') from the 'poor receivers' (the 'global South') of (climatic) risks, suggests a possible sinister alternative, embodied by the 'Carl Schmitt' scenario. Yet little is known about how these two opposite tendencies intermingle and what social consequences they carry.

As long ago as 1927, John Dewey (1927, p. 147) was already asking "for conditions under which the Great Society may become the great community." Dewey distinguished between collectively binding decisions on the one hand and their consequences on the other. He linked this to the theory that a public sphere only ever emerges at the focal point of public communication: not out of any general interest in binding decisions but, rather, as a result of their consequences. People remain indifferent to decisions as such. It is not until they begin to communicate with one another about the problematic consequences of decisions that they wake up. It is communication that shakes them out of their complacency and makes them worry. It shakes them out of their indifference, creating a public sphere and a potential community of action. I would put it this way: The staging and the perception of global risks create imagined communities across all kinds of boundaries. It is the reflexivity of world risk society that produces the reciprocal relationship between the public sphere and globality.

Over and above the public sphere and the world public sphere enforces the potential reflexivity. Imagined communities of global risks can then arise when the mass media (Internet, mobile phones) not only constitute a forum for the exchange of information but also produce an awareness that this exchange is taking place. As Benedict Anderson (1991) has shown so brilliantly, it was this conscious recognition of the fact that one is following the development of the same events simultaneously with others and is affected in common with them, that was an original basis of nationalism. But at this point there follows the question: What will be the effect when global risks like the catastrophic effects of climate change (the financial crises, but also or the threat presented by nuclear weapons) are followed as part of an audience that transcends nation-state boundaries? And from there follows the next question: What is the relationship between national and cosmopolitan imagined communities? Anderson reserved the concept of 'imagined communities' for national constructs, and there is good reason to suppose that he, like many others, considers imagined communities to apply mainly or only to nations. But then we are concerned with the question: Is the concept of imagined cosmopolitan communities suitable, in a new, expanded form, for exploring the social and political consequences of global risks?

Social inequalities and global risks are two sides of the same coin. One can no longer conceptualize inequalities without taking the consequences of climate change and global risks into account, and likewise, cannot conceptualize climate change without considering its impacts on social inequalities.

There is no longer any doubt that climate change and global risks globalize and radicalize social inequalities within national contexts and on a global scale; so too, for example, does climate politics: it separates winners from losers, small groups of supporters from large groups of opponents, and it does so across all divides. In order to research them more thoroughly it is necessary to break with the misleadingly narrow framework, restricted to 'gross social product' or 'income per head,' into which the problem of inequality is usually forced. Accordingly, research must concentrate on the fatal conjunction of poverty, social vulnerability, corruption, the accumulation of dangers, and the loss of dignity on a global scale. The region worst affected by all of this (with the exception of island states such as the Maldives, which might disappear beneath the waves) is the Sahel zone south of the Sahara. In the Sahel, the poorest of the poor live on the edge of the abyss, and climate change threatens to push them— who are the least responsible for such changes—over the edge.

The new sociology of social inequality can no longer detach itself from the globalization of social equality. Even if inequalities are not growing, the expectations of equality are increasing and, in the process, are delegitimizing and destabilizing the system of national-global inequalities. 'Developing nations' are becoming more Westernized and reflect the West back to itself, so that the 'equality' of environmental destruction leads to the self-destruction of civilization. There is an overlap—one might also say a collision—between, on the one hand, growing global expectations of equality (human rights) and growing global and national inequalities, and on the other hand the radically unequal consequences of climate change and the consumption of resources; the results could soon sweep away the entire set of premises of a nationally confined inequality, just as Hurricane Katrina swept away the houses of the vulnerable in New Orleans.

In addition, the new sociology of social inequality can no longer rely on the premise that national and international arenas are distinct. To equate social- with national inequality, which methodological nationalism adopts, has become a source of error par excellence.

Furthermore, the founding premise of sociology, namely the distinction between social and natural inequality, has become untenable. Life situations and life chances, previously assessed within the horizon of an inequality confined to the nation-state, are being transformed into survival situations or survival chances in world risk society. The category of vulnerability becomes central here. Some countries or groups are able, to some degree, to absorb the consequences of tornados, floods, and so on, whereas others—the non-privileged on the scale of social vulnerability—experience the collapse of societal order and the escalation of violence (Beck 2009, chapter X).

Anyone who considers these three components in conjunction encounters a paradox: the more that norms of equality are acknowledged globally, the more insoluble the climate problem becomes and the more devastating the social-ecological inequalities. Not a cheerful prospect! But it is precisely this incorruptible realism, open to the world, which is designated by my concept of the 'cosmopolitan vision.' It's not a matter of any official rhetoric of world fraternity, but of sharpening perceptions in everyday life, in politics and in scholarship, for the unbounded explosive force of social inequality in the age of climate change and global risks.

Global risks are a protective barrier, woven of the means of communication, against the particular vulnerability. Global risks link people who otherwise do not (or do not want to) have anything to do with one another. Global risks mean that national peculiarities of culture, language, religion, law must be pushed into the background in order to foster cooperation across borders and differences, even where hostility exists.

The national community becomes an integral part of the cosmopolitan community but must, at the same time, change structurally and open itself up. Nationalism does not imagine and construct otherness according to the principle of above and below, but in accordance with the distinction of inside and outside. Internally, it dissolves distinctions and unifies the sphere of validity of norms. It has this in common with universalism.

It is an internal universalism whose universal claim ends where other nations begin. Hence, in its external relations the nation can oscillate between enlightened tolerance and nationalist excess. Under conditions of the cosmopolitization of the national, that is no longer easily possible. The foe images of nations must be dismantled; other nations can no longer be denied equality. More than that, it is necessary (out of a quite egoistical interest in survival!) to learn not only to see the position of others but to see oneself through the eyes of others. Consequently, to overcome global problems it is necessary to open up a new space of action of causal responsibility (cf. Töpfer 2001).

An essential difference between national and cosmopolitan community, therefore, is this: National empathy is replaced by a causal responsibility as a transnational space of potential obligation to the nationally excluded others.

Global risks, too, are the product of collective decisions. Their consequences can be and are systematically shifted onto others, because—and as long as—national communities draw clear boundaries between those profiting from industrialization processes and those 'recipients of residual risk' whose very existence is threatened.

Unlike national communities, however, cosmopolitan communities are no territorial communities, but non-territorial and overlapping communities with the most diverse affiliations. Nevertheless, these imagined communities, too, have to be created, even where they are 'socially constructed givens,' as (civilizing) communities with a shared destiny. Their creation coincides with the definition and staging of global risks against a background of (changing) global power relations of definition ('meta-power'). The nature of these ties ('acknowledgment') and what follows from them—establishing justice—contradicts the 'life and death' and 'to be or not to be' pathos of the national. The cosmopolitan community is not engaged in establishing bonds between the dead and the unborn, that is, with the mystery of regeneration. Instead, in the thousands of large and small conflict-dynamics of world risk society it is a matter of breaking up and overcoming the container conception of the national. It is, not least, this national relativism (which is in the national interest itself) that could make of imagined cosmopolitan communities something realistic.

That can succeed, however, only under one very demanding and hence fragile condition: All actors and organizations would also have to consider the repercussions of the decisions of others along with the effects of their own actions on others. A degree of consensus has to be found in this active combination ('transnational resonance') because otherwise the global risk that affects all cannot be significantly minimized.

Those who reduce the problematic of risks to that of the 'life chances of individuals' are unable to grasp the conflicting social and political logics of risk and class conflicts. The logic of class conflict is a matter of the antagonisms between labor and capital within the national framework, of the organization of class interests and their representation in parliament and government, and hence of questions of distributing wealth while minimizing risks for specific groups within the national hierarchy of inequality. The conflict logic of global risk, by contrast, is concerned with cross-border cooperation to stave off catastrophes. Class conflicts, by their very logic, spark the us/them conflict—specifically, between labor and capital, and between nations. Living and surviving within the horizon of global risk, by contrast, follows precisely the contrary logic: Here it becomes rational to overcome the us/them conflict and to recognize others as cooperation partners. Risk, therefore, directs our attention to the explosion of a global plurality that the 'class outlook' tends to negate. World risk society opens up a moral space out of which a civic culture of responsibility reaching across borders and antagonisms could (but by no means must) emerge. As the bipolar world fades away, we are moving from a world of enemies to common dangers and risks.

World risk society is distinct from nation-state modernity inter alia in this crucial respect: the 'social compact' or 'risk contract' is increasingly broken down (Ewald 1986). Global risks are now incalculable and beyond the prospect of control, measurement, socialization and compensation; "… it makes no sense to insure oneself against a global recession" (Beck 1999, p. 8).

As regards the state, for example, this implies the following: Confronted with global risks produced by side-effects of the success of capitalistic modernity, the leading patterns of political organization—that since the Peace of Westphalia in 1648 have governed society in terms of its spatial-political and economic configuration—are now being eroded by activities (economic and political) that occur between states and by processes that are not bound to the state. The outcome is the transition from a Westphalian-based system of government to a post-Westphalian system of governance, where the bounds of the state and its capacity to effectively regulate and control all manner of processes, risks, and externalities are fatally compromised (Grande & Zangl 2011).

The crucial question then becomes: Who are the addressees of cosmopolitan social sciences? Who are the constituents of risk governance? "In the age of globalization, methodological nationalism becomes antiquated not only as a conceptual framework but also in its addressee relationship. This is a fundamental reason why highly professionalized social science, on the one hand, loses itself in a nirvana of abstractions and, on the other, breaks down into an esoteric fragmentation of unrelated, highly detailed empirical research projects (Burawoy 2005). In other words, a de-provincialized and re-located post-universalistic social theory, which is re-discovering and reflecting its European roots, finds itself looking for a new, historical 'value relevance'

[Wertbeziehungen; Max Weber]. This new value relevance both possesses cultural (future) validity, and links the historicity of social scientific research problems with new addressees." (Beck & Grande 2010, p. 435).

To put it in nutshell, in methodological nationalism the nation-state categorical frame of research coincides (behind the researcher's back, so to speak) with specifically national actor categories (for example, social classes, civil society movements, national governments, etc.). This definitely does not hold for the addressee relationship of cosmopolitan social science. On the contrary, with reference to the addressee relationship the 'cosmopolitan turn' means: no specific actor categories, that is, neither governments, nor trade unions, employers' associations, social classes, or social movements. Most importantly, a cosmopolitan social science does not follow a false analogy by searching for, and uniting with, new 'transnational classes,' 'multitudes' or 'elites.' Rather, the subjects of cosmopolitan social theory are cosmopolitan coalitions of actors in all their diversity. They are to be found in these heterogeneous, permanently fluctuating coalitions that include governments, national and international 'sub-politics,' international organizations (OECD; WTO), intergovernmental organizations (United Nations), informal gatherings of states (such as the G8 and G20), etc. It is in such coalitions that hegemonic struggles are fought out between conflicting projects, all claiming to represent the universal and to define the symbolic parameters of social life. In forging such coalitions across borders of all kinds, new spheres and spaces of political action open up, under conditions that still remain to be researched. Confronted with a new quality of global dependencies and interdependencies, no single player can expect to win on their own; they are all dependent on coalitions, alliances, and networks (Beck 2005). "This is the way, then, in which the hazy power game of 'global domestic politics' opens up its own immanent alternatives and oppositions, and creates novel collective identities and political subjects." (Beck & Grande 2010, p. 436).

There is to be discovered an 'elective affinity' ('Wahlverwandtschaft') between my theory of world risk society and Ernst Bloch's (1995) 'Principle of Hope' and the anticipating awareness. Risk society comprises the dialectics between 'realistic dystopia' of catastrophe to humanity and 'realistic utopia' of reinventing the political for the 'Global Age' (Albrow 1996). It is, therefore, the opposite of the 'postmodern constellation.' It is a self-critical, highly political society in a new sense (Töpfer & Yogeshwar 2011): the transnational dialogue and cooperation between politics and democracy—and perhaps even sociology—becomes a matter of survival.

In this sense what does '(world) risk society' as a political category mean in the context of research? I argue for the opening-up to democratic scrutiny of previous depoliticized realms of decision-making, and for the need to recognize the ways in which contemporary debates of this sort are constrained by the epistemological and legal systems within which they are conducted. This then is one of the themes that I would like to see explored further, preferably on a comparative transnational, trans-cultural, and potentially global level. It would entail that we reconstruct the social definition of risks and risk management in different cultural framings, that we examine the (negative) power of risk conflicts and definition where people who do not want to communicate with each other are forced together into a 'community' of shared (global) risks, and that we therefore combine these with questions on organized irresponsibility and relations of definition in different cultural-political settings. This, it seems to me, would be a worthwhile new conceptual and political social science (Beck 2000, p. 226).

The routines of the mainstream obscure how breathtakingly exciting sociology could become again. The early sociologists were fascinated by the newly discovered — but yet to be surveyed — continent called 'society.' A reflection of this fascination could reappear if the curiosity of discovering and testing — via highly developed professional methods — the unexplored landscapes, enthusiasms, contradictions, and dilemmas of world risk society and its resources and perspectives for governance and action were to revive the sociological imagination — processes that have already begun.

How can this perspective be realized? I suggest we should distinguish between national realism and cosmopolitical realism. Confronted with global risk, national realism becomes a kind of backward-looking idealism. Cosmopolitical realism calls for neither the sacrifice of one's own interests, nor an exclusive bias towards higher ideas and ideals. In contrast, it accepts that, for the most part, political action is interest-based; but it insists on an approach to the pursuit of one's own interests that is compatible with those of a larger community. Thus, cosmopolitical realism basically means the recognition of the legitimate interests of others and their inclusion in the calculation of one's own interests. In this progress, interests become 'reflexive national interests' through repeated joint strategies of self-limitation; more precisely, empowerment arises from self-limitation. Ideally, individual and collective goals, both national and global, can be achieved simultaneously.

In reality, however, there are often limits and dilemmas of cosmopolitan realpolitik. It is no panacea for all the world's problems and it by no means always works. In particular, whether a problem has a cosmopolitan solution, depends on the normative and institutional framework within which decisions have to be taken. Nevertheless, the basic message of cosmopolitan realpolitik is this: The future is open. It depends on decisions we make. The research we do and the conceptual frameworks we use make a difference. With this in mind, there is a chance to meet climate pessimism as it provides more 'realistic' and hence applicable answers to climate pessimism — a way of fatalism that does not perceive the future as open.

LITERATURE CITED

Albrow, M. (1996): The Global Age: State and Society Beyond Modernity. Cambridge, UK: Polity Press/Blackwell Publishers.

Anderson, B. (1991 [1983]): Imagined Communities: Reflections on the Origin and Spread of Nationalism (revised and enlarged edition). London: Verso.

Beck, U. (1992 [1986]): Risk Society: Towards a New Modernity. London, Newbury Park, and New Delhi: Sage Publications.

Beck, U. (1999): World Risk Society. Cambridge, UK and Malden, MA: Polity Press.

Beck, U. (2000): What Is Globalization? Cambridge, UK and Malden, MA: Polity Press.

Beck, U. (2003): Toward a new critical theory with a cosmopolitan intent. In: Constellations 10/4: 453–468.

Beck, U. (2005): Power in the Global Age: A New Global Political Economy. Cambridge, UK and Malden, MA: Polity Press.

Beck, U. (2006): The Cosmopolitan Vision. Cambridge, UK and Malden, MA: Polity Press.

Beck, U. (2009): World at Risk. Cambridge, UK and Malden, MA: Polity Press.

Beck, U. (2011): Cosmopolitanism as imagined communities of global risk. In: American Behavioral Scientist 55/10: 1346–1361.

Beck, U. (2013): German Europe. Cambridge, UK and Malden, MA: Polity Press.

Beck, U., Grande, E. (2010): Varieties of second modernity: The cosmopolitan turn in social and political theory and research. In: British Journal of Sociology 61/3: 409–443.

Beck, U., Sznaider, N. (2006): Unpacking cosmopolitanism for the social sciences: A research agenda. In: British Journal of Sociology 57/1: 1–23.

Bloch, E. (1995 [1954]): The Principle of Hope. Cambridge, MA: MIT Press.

Burawoy, M. (2005): For public sociology: American Sociological Association Presidential Address. In: British Journal of Sociology 56/2: 259–294.

Calhoun, C. (2010): Beck, Asia and second modernity. In: British Journal of Sociology 61/3: 597–619.

Chang, K-S (2010): The second modern condition? Compressed modernity as internalized reflexive cosmopolitization. In: British Journal of Sociology 61/3: 444–464.

Dewey, J. (1927): The Public and its Problems. New York: Holt.

Ewald, F. (1986): L'Etat Providence. Paris: Grasset and Fasquelle.

Grande, E., Zangl, B. (2011): Varieties of Preventive Governance in World Risk Society. Unpublished manuscript.

Han, S-J., Shim, Y-H. (2010): Redefining second modernity for East Asia: A critical assessment. In: British Journal of Sociology 61/3: 465–488.

Hulme, M. (2010): Cosmopolitan climates: Hybridity, foresight and meaning. In: Theory, Culture and Society 27/2–3: 267–276.

Maharaj, S. (2010): Small change of the universal: Beyond modernity? In: British Journal of Sociology 61/3: 565–578.

Mieg, H.A., Töpfer, K. (2013): Institutional and Social Innovation for Sustainable Urban Development. Oxon, Ox and New York: Routledge.

Milanovic, B. (2011): The Haves and the Have-Nots: A Brief and Idiosyncratic History of Global Inequality. New York: Basic Books.

Reid, W.V., Chen, D., Goldfarb, L., Hackmann, H., Lee, Y.T., Mokhele, K., Ostrom, E., Raivio, K., Rockström, J., Schellnhuber, H.J., Whyte, A. (2010): Earth system science for global sustainability: Grand challenges. In: Science 330/6006: 916–917.

Schmitt, C. (1985 [1934]): Political Theology: Four Chapters on the Concept of Sovereignty. Cambridge, MA and London: MIT Press.

Töpfer, K. (2001): Globalisierung. Konsequenzen für die deutsche Politik in internationalen Organisationen. Stuttgart: Robert Bosch Stiftung.

Töpfer, K., Yogeshwar, R. (2011): Unsere Zukunft. Ein Gespräch über die Welt nach Fukushima. München: C.H. Beck.

Turner, B.S., Khondker, H.H. (2010): Globalization East and West. London, Thousand Oaks, New Delhi, and Singapore: Sage Publications.

Weiß, A. (2010): Vergleiche jenseits des Nationalstaats. Methodologischer Kosmopolitismus in der Forschung über hochqualifizierte Migration. In: Soziale Welt 61/3–4: 295–311.

Wimmer, A., Glick Schiller, N. (2002): Methodological nationalism and beyond: nation-state building, migration and the social sciences. In: Global Networks 2/4: 301–334.

Authors

Günther Bachmann

is the Secretary General of the German Council for Sustainable Development, a multi-stakeholder body advising the Federal Government of Germany, and chair or co-chair of numerous national and international networks or processes for sustainable development. As of 2014, he is an Honorary Professor at the University in Lüneburg, Germany. He has published numerous articles on sustainable development issues, environmental and energy policies.

Christoph Bals

is Policy Director of Germanwatch. He is globally known for his long-standing contributions to climate policy, and is active, amongst others, in klima-allianz Deutschland, on the board of directors of Stiftung Zukunftsfähigkeit, the Renewables Grid Initiative (RGI), or the Munich Climate Insurance Initiative (MCII).

Ulrich Beck

is Professor of Sociology at Ludwig Maximilian University of Munich, and since 2013 Principal Investigator of the European Research Council (ERC) project: "Methodological Cosmopolitanism – In the Laboratory of Climate Change". Since 1997 he has been the British Journal of Sociology Visiting Centennial Professor at the London School of Economics and since 2011 also Professor at the Fondation Maison des Sciences de l'Homme, Paris.

Joachim von Braun

is Director of the Center for Development Research (ZEF) and Professor for Economic and Technological Change at Bonn University. He is Chair of the Bioeconomy Council of the Federal German Government, a member of the German Academy of Science and Engineering, Academy of Science and Arts, North Rhine Westphalia,

Fellow of the American Association for the Advancement of Sciences, and a member of the Pontifical Academy of Sciences of the Vatican. He was Director General of the International Food Policy Research Institute (IFPRI) based in Washington, DC, USA. He also is Vice President of the NGO Deutsche Welthungerhilfe.

Paul Crutzen

was awared the Nobel Prize in 1985 for his pioneering work related to the ozone layer. Between 1980 and 2000, Professor Crutzen was Director at the Max Planck Institute for Chemistry in Mainz, leading the Department of Atmospheric Chemistry. After 2000, his research focus increasingly concentrated on human–nature interactions, a contribution widely known under the term "Anthropocene." Among a multitude of awards and honorary degrees, he became the first senior honorary fellow of the IASS in 2013.

Massoumeh Ebtekar

is currently Associate Professor of Immunology at Tarbiat Modares University in Tehran. Dr. Ebtekar served as Vice President of the Islamic Republic of Iran and Head of the Department of Environment from 1997–2005, a post to which she was reappointed in 2013. In 2006, UNEP designated her as Champion of the Earth in recognition of her efforts. She also served as Councillor from 2006–2013 at the Tehran City Council, where she headed the Environment Committee. She is married and has two sons.

Ralf Fücks

has been President of the Heinrich Böll Foundation, an independent think tank affiliated with the German Green Party, since 1996. The primary focus of his work is on sustainable development, reshaping the welfare state, migration, the future of European integration, and on foreign policy. He is a regular contributor to numerous leading German newspapers, to international political periodicals, and has co-authored numerous books on issues such as ecology and economy, political strategy, and European and international politics. He is the author of the book "Intelligent Wachsen – Die grüne Revolution (Intelligent Growth – The Green Revolution)," which was published in 2013.

Pekka Haavisto

is Minister for International Development at the Ministry for Foreign Affairs and Minister responsible for ownership steering issues at the Prime Minister's Office, Finland. He previously held numerous positions in Finish politics, including presidential candidate in 2012 for the Green League, as well as European and UN affairs. Among many other political and intellectual contributions, he provided input for the work of UNEP and is a member of the international peer review group on Germany's Sustainable Development Strategy.

Volker Hauff

was German Minister for Research and Technology, and German Minister for Transportation. Dr. Hauff was a member of the World Commission on Environment and Development, widely known as the "Brundtland Commission," and was the editor of the German version of the "Brundtland Report." Among numerous other positions, he was the Chair of the German Council for Sustainable Development from 2001 to 2010 and a member of the Ethics Commission on a Safe Energy Supply in 2011.

Reinhard Hüttl

is the Scientific Executive Director and Chairman of the Board at the Helmholtz Centre Potsdam – GFZ German Research Centre for Geosciences, and President of the National Academy of Science and Engineering (acatech). He studied at the Albert-Ludwigs-University (ALU), Freiburg, Germany and at the Oregon State University, Corvallis, USA, and since 1992 has held the Chair of Soil Protection and Recultivation at the Brandenburg University of Technology, Cottbus-Senftenberg. He is a member of a number of national and international Academies and was conferred with the Cross of Merit, First Class of the Federal Republic of Germany in July 2008.

Matthias Kleiner

is President of the Leibniz Association as of 2014. He was Professor at the TU Dortmund, and was awarded the Gottfried Wilhelm Leibniz Prize in 1997. He was also President of the Deutsche Forschungsgemeinschaft (DFG) from 2007 to 2012. He was, together with Klaus Töpfer, Co-Chair of the Ethics Commission on a Safe Energy Supply in 2011. He is a member of numerous national and international academies and boards, and is a jury member for various research programs.

Manfred Konukiewitz

was Deputy Director General at the German Ministry for Development Cooperation. Dr. Konukiewitz has worked with Klaus Töpfer both at the German Ministry for Housing and Construction and at UNEP. He is currently Co-Chair of the Executive Board of the Green Climate Fund, and is a Senior Fellow at the IASS.

Mark Lawrence

is Scientific Director at IASS, where he heads the cluster, Sustainable Interaction with the Atmosphere (SIWA). Before joining the IASS in 2011, he was the head of a Junior Research Group from 2000 to 2005; and a group leader for atmospheric modeling from 2006 to 2012 at the Max Planck Institute for Chemistry in Mainz, where he worked closely with Prof. Paul Crutzen on issues related to the Anthropocene. He completed his habilitation in 2006 at the University of Mainz, where he was a visiting professor for meteorology from 2009 to 2010.

Claus Leggewie

is Professor for Political Science and Director of the Institute for Advanced Studies in the Humanities (KWI), Essen, and Co-Director of the Käte Hamburger-Kollegs / Centre for Global Cooperation Research (GCR21) in Duisburg. Among various other appointments, he is a member of the German Advisory Council on Global Change (WBGU).

LI Fengting

is Professor at Tongji University, Shanghai, and currently serves as Executive Vice Dean of UNEP-Tongji Institute of Environment for Sustainable Development (IESD) and also the Special Coordinator for South-South Cooperation of UNEP. Meanwhile, Prof. Li is Deputy Director of the Water Treatment Chemicals Committee of the China Chemical Industry Standard Council.

Caroline A. Lodemann

studied Modern German Literature and Media, English Philology and Public Law at Christian-Albrechts-Universität, Kiel, Germany. She was awarded her doctorate degree at Georg-August-Universität Göttingen, and has been active since as an academic officer in Universities and Academia. As of 2014, she heads the office of Professor Matthias Kleiner, President the Leibniz Association.

Juan Mayr Maldonado

is founder and first Chariman (1986–1998) of the Pro-Sierra Nevada de Santa Marta Foundation, and a former Environment Minister of Colombia (1998–2002). He was President of the UN Commission on Sustainable Development (CSD) and President of the bio-safety protocol negotiations. The UN Secretary-General appointed him to the Panel of Eminent Persons on United Nations–Civil Society Relations. He is a member of Colombia's National Conciliation Commission, and is an advisor to the UN Resident Coordinator and United Nations Development Program (UNDP). Humanitarian Coordinator in Colombia. During his career, he has received many international distinctions, including the Goldman Environmental Prize, and the Parker-Gentry Award for excellence and innovation in conservation and environmental biology from the Chicago Field Museum of Natural History. Currently, Mr. Mayr serves as the Colombian Ambassador in Germany.

Klaus Milke

has a professional background both in medium-sized enterprise and academia (sociology and political science). Today, he provides professional advice on issues related to development and environment, and has been active since 1979 in development assistant and international solidarity. He is the co-founder and current Chairman of Germanwatch. He is also co-initiator of atmosfair and the Chairman of Stiftung Zukunftsfähigkeit, a foundation operating in close cooperation with Germanwatch.

Veerabhadran Ramanathan

is Distinguished Professor at Scripps Institution of Oceanography, University of California at San Diego, and a UNESCO Professor of Climate and Policy, TERI University, New-Delhi, India. He has received numerous prestigious awards for his original research in climate and atmospheric science, including the Tyler Prize in the US, and "Champion of the Earth" for Science and Innovation of the UN. Among many other issues, in his work on Atmospheric Brown Clouds and Short Lived Climate Pollutants (SLCPs), he has interacted closely with the sustainability agenda of Klaus Töpfer.

Carlo Rubbia

is Scientific Director at the IASS, heading the Earth, Energy and Environment cluster E³. Professor Rubbia was formerly the Director of CERN in Geneva and is one of the world's leading nuclear physicists and energy researchers. He was awarded the Nobel Prize in Physics in 1984. Besides his work at CERN and among other things, he was also Higgins Professor of Physics at Harvard University from 1971 and 1989 and president of the Italian government's National Agency for New Technologies, Energy, and Sustainable Economic Development from 1999 to 2005, as well as the initiator of several international research and development projects in this area.

Maheswar Rupakheti

is team leader of the IASS project, "Sustainable Atmosphere for the Kathmandu Valley." Before joining the IASS in 2012, Dr. Rupakheti was Senior Programme Officer and later the coordinator of the Asia Secretariat of the Atmospheric Brown Cloud project of UNEP.

Andreas Rüdinger

is a research fellow at the energy and climate department of IDDRI. His research focuses on energy transition strategies and energy policy in Germany, France, and at the European level. He studied political sciences in Bordeaux, Stuttgart, and Bogota.

Karsten Sach

is Deputy Director General, European and International Environment Policy at the Ministry for the Environment, Nature Conservation, Building, and Nuclear Safety, Germany. Dr. Sach leads climate negotiations for Germany and, among other duties and activities, was centrally involved in the process of establishing IRENA.

Hans Joachim Schellnhuber

has been Director of the Potsdam Institute for Climate Impact Research (PIK) since he founded the institute in 1992. He is Professor for Theoretical Physics at the University of Potsdam and External Professor at the Santa Fe Institute, USA. Furthermore, he is Co-Chair of the German Advisory Council on Global Change (WBGU).

Uwe Schneidewind

is President of the Wuppertal Institute for Climate, Environment, and Energy. Among other things, he is a member of the Club of Rome and the German Advisory Council on Global Change (WBGU).

Mandy Singer-Brodowski

works as a Scientific Assistant to the management board of the Wuppertal Institute Wuppertal Institute for Climate, Environment and Energy. Furthermore, she is a member of the German National Comittee for the implementation of the UN-Decade "Education for sustainable development" and a lecturer at the University of Lüneburg.

Thomas Spencer

is the Program Director at the energy and climate department of IDDRI. Since 2008 he has worked with a number of European research institutes on European and international climate policy issues. He graduated from the University of Western Australia with a bachelor in English Literature and Philosophy; he has a Master of Science in Carbon Management from the University of Edinburgh, with a focus on energy economics and the public law of climate change.

James Gustave Speth

completed his decade-long tenure as Dean of Yale School of Forestry and Environmental Studies in 2009. In 2010, Professor Speth joined the faculty of the Vermont Law School as Professor of Law. From 1993 to 1999, Gus Speth was Administrator of the United Nations Development Programme and Chair of the UN Development Group. Prior to his service at the UN, he was, among many other high-ranking positions and engagements, founder and President of the World Resources Institute. He holds several prestigious awards and has published extensively, including the award-winning books "The Bridge at the Edge of the World: Capitalism, the Environment, and Crossing from Crisis to Sustainability" and "Red Sky at Morning: America and the Crisis of the Global Environment." His latest book is "America the Possible: Manifesto for a New Economy," published by Yale Press in September 2012.

Mario Tobias

is Secretary General of the IASS and holds doctoral degrees in both biology and political science. Before joining the IASS, he was an appointed member of the executive board of BITKOM, directing the technologies and services division. Based on his broad background and research interests, he developed the interdisciplinary research program "Enabling Technologies for Sustainability" at the IASS.

Laurence Tubiana

is the founder and Director of the Institute for Sustainable Development and International Relations (IDDRI) in Paris, France. She is a Professor at Columbia University and Co-Chair of the Sustainable Development Solutions Network Leadership Council. She was recently appointed as Special Representative for the Climate Summit 2015 in Paris, under the Minister for Foreign Affairs, Laurent Fabius.

Wan Gang

was born August 1952 in Shanghai. Professor Wan was appointed as the Minister of Science and Technology of the People's Republic of China on April 27, 2007. He is also Vice Chairman of the Chinese People's Political Consultative Conference (CPPCC). He is a former President of Tongji University (2000–2007).

Ulrich von Weizsäcker

is Professor in Biology, and was President of the University of Kassel in 1975, Director of the UN Center for Science and Technolgy in 1981, and afterwards Director of the Institute for European Environmental Politics. In 1991, he became the President of the Wuppertal Institute. In 1998, he was elected to the German Parliament where, among other responsibilities, he served as head of its Environment Committee. In 2006, he became the Head of the Bren School on Environmental Science and Management at UCSB, Santa Barbara, California. Today, he is Co-President of the Club of Rome and Co-Chair of the UNEP-initiated International Resource Panel.

Timothy E. Wirth

former U.S. Senator for Colorado, is the Vice Chairman of the Board of the United Nations Foundation and the Better World Fund. He previously served as the UN Foundation's President from its founding in 1997 until his transition to Vice Chair in 2013.

WU Jiang

is Professor at and currently serving as Vice President of Tongji University, Dean of UNEP-Tongji Institute of Environment for Sustainable Development (IESD), and Chairman of the Global Universities Partnership on Environment and Sustainability (GUPES), which has already gathered over 400 universities globally. From February 2003 to October 2008 he served as Deputy Director for the Shanghai Urban Planning Administration Bureau. From January 2008 to February 2009 he held the position of Deputy Director of Shanghai Municipal Planning, Land, and Resources Administration.

Angelika Zahrnt

holds a doctorate in economics from Heidelberg University. From 1998 to 2007, she was Chair of Friends of the Earth Germany (BUND) and was subsequently named honorary Chairwoman. From 2001 to 2013, she was a member of the German Council for Sustainable Development. Prof. Dr. Zahrnt was awarded the Cross of the Order of Merit in 2006, the German Environmental Award in 2009, and the Officer's Cross of the Order of Merit in 2013. She has published extensively on the issues of ecological tax reform, sustainability, and post-growth-society.

* * *

Falk Schmidt

is the Personal Assistant to Klaus Töpfer at the Institute for Advanced Sustainability Studies, IASS, Potsdam. Before that, Dr. Schmidt was Academic Officer at the International Human Dimenions Programme, and for the past decade worked at the interface of science and policy.

Nick Nuttall

was Klaus Toepfer's spokesperson and speechwriter at the UN Environment Programme (2001–2006). Today, he is Director of Communications at the UN Framework Convention on Climate Change in Bonn.